SOCI...   ...LDREN
AND ...

Implications for practice, policy and
research

Edited by ...an and Ralph Catts

Sheffield Hallam University
Learning and Information Services
Withdrawn From Stock

First published in Great Britain in 2012 by

The Policy Press
University of Bristol
Fourth Floor
Beacon House
Queen's Road
Bristol BS8 1QU
UK

t: +44 (0)117 331 4054
f: +44 (0)117 331 4093
tpp-info@bristol.ac.uk
www.policypress.co.uk

North American office:
The Policy Press
c/o The University of Chicago Press
1427 East 60th Street
Chicago, IL 60637, USA
t: +1 773 702 7700
f: +1 773-702-9756
sales@press.uchicago.edu
www.press.uchicago.edu

SHEFFIELD HALLAM UNIVERSITY
WL
302.083
SO
COLLEGIATE LEARNING CENTRE

© The Policy Press 2012

British Library Cataloguing in Publication Data
A catalogue record for this book is available from the British Library.

Library of Congress Cataloging-in-Publication Data
A catalog record for this book has been requested.

ISBN 978 1 84742 927 8 paperback
ISBN 978 1 84742 928 5 hardcover

The right of Julie Allan and Ralph Catts to be identified as editors of this work has been asserted by them in accordance with the Copyright, Designs and Patents Act 1988.

All rights reserved: no part of this publication may be reproduced, stored in a retrieval system, or transmitted in any form or by any means, electronic, mechanical, photocopying, recording, or otherwise without the prior permission of The Policy Press.

The statements and opinions contained within this publication are solely those of the editors and contributors and not of the University of Bristol or The Policy Press. The University of Bristol and The Policy Press disclaim responsibility for any injury to persons or property resulting from any material published in this publication.

The Policy Press works to counter discrimination on grounds of gender, race, disability, age and sexuality.

Cover design by Qube Design Associates, Bristol.
Front cover: image kindly supplied by Billy Alexander.
Printed and bound in Great Britain by Henry Ling, Dorchester.
The Policy Press uses environmentally responsible print partners.

MIX
Paper from
responsible sources
FSC
www.fsc.org   FSC® C013985

Contents

Notes on contributors

Julie Allan is Professor of Education and Deputy Head of the School of Education, University of Stirling. She is also Visiting Professor at the University of Borås, Sweden. Her most recent books are: *Rethinking inclusive education: the philosophers of difference in practice* (Springer, 2008); *Doing inclusive education research* (with Roger Slee, Sense, 2008); and *Social capital, professionalism and diversity* (with Jenny Ozga and Geri Smyth, Sense, 2009).

Marion Allison is employed by South Lanarkshire Council's Youth Learning Services where she has the privilege of working with young people and coordinating youth work activities within two dedicated youth centres and the surrounding communities. As a research fellow with the Applied Educational Research Scheme (AERS) she was part of a team that considered how connections among young people and volunteers affect the operation of a youth club. She is currently reading for the qualification of Doctor of Education (EdD) at the University of Stirling and her main research interests are youth work and social capital.

Rowena Arshad is a senior lecturer at the School of Education, University of Edinburgh. She has had over twenty five years' experience in the field of equality and anti-discriminatory practice working in England and Scotland. Rowena is a qualified community and youth worker. She has worked in the private, public and third sector. She is also a Director of the Centre for Education for Racial Equality in Scotland (CERES) based at the School of Education and was awarded an OBE for services to race equality in 2001. Rowena has also lectured in Germany, the Czech Republic and Canada.

Monica Barry is a senior research fellow at the School of Law, University of Strathclyde. Her main research interests centre on young people, particularly in respect of policy and practice relating to young offenders, youth transitions, social inclusion and risk assessment in social work. She formerly worked with young people in the voluntary sector before becoming a researcher in 1994. She is the criminal justice research adviser to the Association of Directors of Social Work, editor of *Youth policy and social inclusion: critical debates with young people* (2005) and author of *Youth offending in transition: the search for social recognition* (2006), both published by Routledge.

Ralph Catts has recently retired from his role as a senior research fellow in the School of Education, at the University of Stirling and is now an education consultant. His research has embraced two areas. The first addresses access and equity in educational provision for disadvantaged people and deprived communities; and the other strand is concerned with the role of generic skills in higher education with a special focus on the evaluation of information literacy programmes. From 2004 to 2008 he was the AERS Senior Research Fellow for the Schools and Social Capital Network.

Beth Cross has been researching the interface between formal and informal learning contexts for the last ten years and is particularly interested in the insights that dialogic perspectives bring to the issues of learner identities, strategies and trajectories. She has taught in the areas of social policy and children's services in England and Scotland and worked with a number of creative interdisciplinary projects that involve visual and dramatic arts.

Joan Forbes is Director of the Centre for Children's Services Research and Policy Study, University of Aberdeen. She teaches research methodology and her research interests focus on policy, practitioner knowledges and identities, inter-professional social capital, and gender and education. Dr Forbes has recently led two ESRC funded research seminar series that explored *the research and policy discourses surrounding service integration* and *inter/professional social capital*. Her recent book, edited with Cate Watson, is: *Service integration in schools: research and policy discourses, practices and future prospects* (Sense, 2009).

John Horne is Professor of Sport and Sociology and Director of the International Research Institute for Sport Studies (IRiSS) in the School of Sport, Tourism and The Outdoors at the University of Central Lancashire. He is Editor-in-Chief of the journal *Leisure Studies* and a member of the editorial boards of the *International Review for the Sociology of Sport* and *Sport in Society*. His publications include numerous articles in peer-reviewed journals and book chapters, as well as publications as author and co-author, including *Sport in consumer culture* (Palgrave Macmillan, 2006) and *Understanding the Olympics* (Taylor and Francis, 2011).

Bob Lingard works in the School of Education at the University of Queensland, where he teaches and researches in the fields of the sociology of education and of education policy. His research interests are in education policy in relation to globalisation, social justice, gender and school reform. His most recent books include: *Educating boys: beyond structural reform* (Palgrave, 2009), *Globalizing education policy* (Routledge, 2010) and the edited collections *Research by association* (Sense, 2010) and *Changing schools* (Routledge, 2011). He is also editor of the journal *Discourse: Studies in the Cultural Politics of Education*.

George MacBride taught for 37 years in Glasgow secondary schools, for 30 of these in support for learning. George was active in teacher trade unionism, serving as convener of the EIS Education Committee for 14 years. He has been a member of the councils of national curriculum and examinations agencies and has contributed to several government working groups on curriculum, assessment, secondary school qualifications and teacher education. He was a practitioner member of the AERS Social Capital network. Most recently he has been working on educational development projects for the Scottish government and its agencies, directly or through universities.

Susan Maclennan is a primary school teacher with particular interests in early education and parental involvement. As part of her Master's and Chartered Teacher studies she worked collaboratively with Rowena Arshad to explore the nature of social capital within a primary school. She has gained professional recognition in supporting pupil learning and recently completed a postgraduate certificate in supporting bilingual learners. Susan was part of a writing team which produced an emotional literacy curriculum for primary schools. Prior to training as a teacher she worked in the field of management.

Dorothy McDonald was the co-ordinator of the Inclusive Learning Network, a training programme to promote inclusive education in Scotland, which ran from 2003 until 2008. Although she originally trained and worked in a different field altogether (as a chartered surveyor), Dorothy developed a keen interest in inclusion and education following the birth of her disabled daughter. Dorothy currently works part-time as the manager of Achievement Bute, a voluntary organisation that supports families with disabled children on the Isle of Bute. She is also a member of the Additional Support Needs Tribunal for Scotland.

Janine Muldoon is a research fellow in the Child and Adolescent Health Research Unit (CAHRU) at the University of Edinburgh. Her research is mainly educational and psychological in nature, focusing on the views of children and young people and ways of intervening in educational settings to support their development. While at CAHRU, she has taken the lead in a number of projects involving children and young people and is currently coordinating a project funded by DEFRA designed to enhance a sense of responsibility towards animals. Focusing particularly on the move from primary to secondary school, her primary interests are in transitions and relationships and their effects on emotional well-being.

Grace Paton is a retired lecturer of the School of Education at the University of the West of Scotland. She taught on initial teacher education programmes and childhood studies and worked for two years as a research fellow on the Applied Educational Research Scheme. Her research interests focus on issues of social justice and inclusion, particularly the relationship between parents and professionals in integrated children's services in Scotland. Currently she is completing a doctoral study on the early education and care experiences of vulnerable children under two years of age.

Nathalie Sheridan is a PhD candidate at the University of Strathclyde, Glasgow. Her dissertation explores the access refugee children have to creative learning and the impact of social capital on learning processes. She is a member of the executive board of the Scottish Educational Research Association (SERA) and a convener for SERA's New and Emerging Researchers' Network. Her research interests are marginalised children and social aspects of learning processes.

Geri Smyth is Professor of Education at the University of Strathclyde. Her particular research interests relate to the education of bilingual pupils, the diversification of the teaching profession and refugee integration. Geri is co-Editor of the *European Journal of Teacher Education*. She is currently Principal Investigator on an ESRC funded seminar series: *Diverse teachers for diverse learners* and recently edited a special issue of the *Journal of Refugee Studies* on the theme of refugee integration.

Kevin Stelfox started work as a postman and has developed a career in youth and community work, social work and education. He has conducted social science research in academic and professional environments. At present he is a local authority research and development officer and holds an honorary research fellowship at the University of Aberdeen. His research interests are educational opportunities for disadvantaged young people, with a particular focus on achievement and attainment within deprived communities using participatory research methods. From 2005 to 2008 he held a fellowship with the Scottish Applied Educational Research Scheme and undertook research on education and social capital in two case studies.

Gaby Weiner has worked at various universities in the UK and Sweden and is currently Honorary Professor at Edinburgh University and visiting Professorial Research Fellow at Manchester Metropolitan University. She has written and edited a number of publications on gender and social justice in education, and is presently working on a study of women refugees in Britain in the 1930s and 1940s.

Acknowledgements

This publication arises from work undertaken by the Schools and Social Capital Network, which was part of the Scottish Applied Educational Research Scheme funded by the Scottish Government and the Scottish Funding Council. There was a wide circle of contributors to various aspects of the network's activities, and this book reports on one aspect of the output, namely a series of case studies. We warmly acknowledge the contribution of many who attended seminars and forums, the contribution of Principal Investigators, Professor Jenny Ozga and Professor Kay Livingston, and especially the administrative support provided to the network by Sarah Mills and Pam McGibbon.

ONE

Introduction

Julie Allan, Ralph Catts and Kevin Stelfox

This book is about young people and the ways in which their lives and experiences are shaped by social relationships, both those in which their participation is more or less obligatory, such as in families or at school, and those they establish by themselves. These relationships, and the norms and values that shape them, lead to the production of social capital:

> a capability that arises from the prevalence of trust in a society or in certain parts of it ... embodied in the smallest and most basic social group, the family, as well as the largest of all groups, the nation, and in all the other groups in between. (Fukuyama, 1995, p 26)

In this introductory chapter, we explore the interest in, and perceived utility of, social capital. We describe the Schools and Social Capital Network, which was established within the Applied Educational Research Scheme, a major programme of research and research capacity building, then outline each of the chapters.

Social capital: fetish or civilising influence?

The attraction to the concept of social capital by policy makers and researchers alike has been developed and sustained both by politicians as the basis for the new politics of the Third Way to address social policies (Szreter, 1999; Fine and Green, 2000) and by some academics as an important scientific tool. Fine and Green (2000) suggest that social capital has come to be seen as having a use in social discourse as a weapon to deploy in the 'skirmishes' (p 78) between economics and other social sciences. Paterson (2000) argues that social capital is nothing new and in Scotland is no more than the strong sense of Scottish civil society and obligation that was a feature of the eighteenth century enlightenment period. Its popularity, particularly among policy makers, has been subject to resolute criticism (Sturgess, 1997; Portes, 1998;

Woolcock, 1998), yet it remains in place as something that 'provides for (a) civilising flow of ideas' (Fine and Green, 2000, p 91). Here we outline the specific takes of the three main proponents of social capital, identify three 'types' of social capital that are understood to exist and raise our own question about the assumption that social capital can be possessed – or not.

The three major theorists (Bourdieu, 1977, 1986; Coleman, 1988, 1990; and Putnam, 1993, 2000) have developed distinctive standpoints in relation to social capital. Coleman is interested in how social capital, in the form of relationships and networks, helps mediate negative effects of poverty on opportunities throughout schooling. He focused on the mediating and militating role against disadvantage, but in doing so produced a deficit model of poverty based on middle class norms and values. Putnam focused on networks, norms and trust within communities and considered how individuals and groups bonded within and bridged across networks. Bourdieu's theoretical framework placed social capital in relation to other capitals and located it in the practices of everyday life, linking the micro-social and macro-social structures. Incorporating the concept of habitus (Bourdieu, 1986) allows for a more dynamic understanding of how social and other capitals provide a tool for exploring relationships. This use of the concept of social capital can be contrasted with the static and circular models of social capital developed by Coleman and Putnam, which describe social capital as 'a tool or heuristic device for exploring processes and practices that are related to the acquisition of other forms of capital' (Morrow, 1999, p. 749). Although there is commonality between these three approaches, there are significant differences in the assumptions made by them in conceptualising social capital.

Portes (1998) argued that there are two approaches to the application of social capital: one that focuses on it as an attribute of individuals and another that is concerned with collectives. Social capital is clearly relational and exists within networks and the interactions within those networks, but whereas Putman saw the main focus as being on collectives, Bourdieu and Coleman saw it in terms of attributes of individuals:

> Bourdieu and Coleman emphasize the intangible character of social capital relative to other forms. Whereas economic capital is in people's bank accounts and human capital is inside their heads, social capital inheres in the structure of their relationships. To possess social capital, a person must be

related to others, and it is those others, not himself who are
the actual source of his or her advantage. (Portes, 1998, p. 7)

A significant difference between Bourdieu and Coleman is their
philosophical position. Bourdieu emphasises access to institutional
resources, while Coleman emphasises norms (Dika and Singh, 2002).
Gamarnikow and Green (2007) illustrate the different emphases by
looking at the view of networks in relation to inclusion/exclusion:

> Thus, social capital theory constructs networks as forms of
> inclusion and fails, in the main, to recognise their potentially
> and, we would argue, usually, exclusionary and hierarchically
> socially reproductive aspects in competitive and even more
> so in conflict situations. It is vital to keep in mind the
> long history of social analysis of boundary maintenance/
> exclusionary practices as deliberate strategies for competing
> for and/or controlling social, cultural and material assets.
> In this regard, by contrast with the mainstream social
> capital perspectives, Bourdieu's (1986) approach connects
> the social capital of networks as a key mechanism by and
> through which other unequally distributed capitals, cultural,
> symbolic and, of course, economic capital are articulated.
> Here the social capital of networks plays its part in the
> complex constitution of institutionalising social inequalities,
> particularly so in relation to competitive and deeper
> conflicts. (Gamarnikow and Green, 2007, p. 370)

Putman and Colman both emphasised the elements of social good that
social capital produces for society. For Putman the good was in relation
to civic society and for Coleman it was in relation to school attainment,
whereas Bourdieu's approach highlighted the social inequalities of
the distribution of social capital by locating it within a wider social
structure. O'Brien and Fathaigh (2005, p. 73) illustrated this by viewing
educational qualifications as a form of cultural capital that is located
within a wider stratified social structure:

> From a Bourdieuian perspective, an educational qualification
> is in itself a form of cultural capital that is used (consciously
> or otherwise) as a means of vertical stratification. Thus, care
> should be exercised in identifying and applying appropriate
> social capital outcomes from research. This point often goes
> unheeded. There is still a general assumption, for example,

that lower-class parents should simply act more like white middle-class parents for the benefit of their children.

Social capital is recognised as having three different 'types'. Bonding social capital is evident in the connections between individuals with similar characteristics and has value in the promotion of solidarity between people sharing values. Bonding social capital may be seen within families, and sometimes within minority ethnic groups. Bridging social capital occurs when people from different groups come together and may emerge in associations between people of different ethnicities, or between disabled and non-disabled groups. Linking social capital, arguably the most profitable kind (Woolcock, 1998), is established when individuals who have different amounts of power connect. This can be seen in, for example, representations to government by disabled people or student-led initiatives in schools.

Bonding, bridging and linking social capital, together with trust and reciprocity, are the key elements of social capital, but researchers attempting to test the presence of these empirically have had limited success and some have resorted to crude and inappropriate indicators. Schuller et al (2000) have concluded that social capital may be most useful as a heuristic device, provoking questions and reflection rather than providing answers or demonstrating impact. It is possible however, that the lack of success has come from limitations in the ways in which social capital has been understood and operationalised. It tends to be viewed as a possession which people have or can acquire in varying amounts and in the most propitious circumstances. Furthermore, as Putnam (2007) observes critically, the different kinds of social capital have been understood as a zero sum game, with people gaining bonding social capital at the expense of the apparently more valuable bridging or linking social capital. The assumption of the world as hierarchical, with people having to progress upwards in order to access social capital and to achieve the goals of 'embeddedness' and 'autonomy' (Woolcock, 1998, p. 168), adds yet another complicating, and limiting, dimension. It seems to us that normally most people have access to some form of bonding social capital that may either constrain or support their engagement in education and society, including economic activity. However bridging and linking social capital appear to be situated in particular contexts and it is the utility of the information and connections within these networks that determines the extent to which this provides opportunities and advantage. Researchers, working with these understandings, have been constrained in confirming the presence and amount of social capital. However, it seems to be unrewarding to try to quantify the amount, as opposed to the utility, of available social capital for particular purposes.

The Schools and Social Capital Network

The case studies reported in this book were undertaken within the Schools and Social Capital Network, one of three substantive networks established within the Applied Educational Research Scheme, a major programme of research and capacity building in Scotland, funded jointly by the Scottish Government and the Scottish Funding Council between 2004 and 2009. Humes, who has drawn attention to the potential of the AERS acronym for 'unflattering rearrangement' (2009a), reports that the decision to invest in research capacity within Scotland stemmed from concerns about the performance of the Scottish universities in the 2001 Research Assessment Exercise (Humes, 2007). There was also a desire, Humes notes, to invest in research that would directly inform the Scottish National Priorities in education (achievement and attainment; framework for learning; inclusion and equality; values and citizenship; and learning for life) and in particular to undertake research that would affect the lowest achieving 20% of the school population. The consortium of three universities which successfully bid for the AERS grant – Edinburgh, Stirling and Strathclyde – established three substantive networks within which to undertake this work of policy-related research and capacity building. The Schools and Social Capital Network, one part of whose work is being reported here, was one and the other two were concerned with school management and governance and with learners and learning; a fourth network was charged with formal aspects of research capacity building through the development of research training modules.

The Schools and Social Capital Network has been concerned with defining and measuring social capital; exploring its relevance to teachers and other professionals; and building social capital among learners. The network recruited a wide range of 'stakeholders': academics working within higher education (including some without research in their contract), local authority personnel, teachers, students, and members of the Scottish government and Her Majesty's Inspectorate. Participants were able to select an appropriate level of engagement – and work – from being kept informed to working within a group on a particular research activity and writing research papers. The experience of the academics ranged from those who were new to research to highly experienced individuals, and a key feature of the network was that people with different amounts and different types of expertise worked together. This was one of the big ideas of capacity building and demonstrated the potential of linking social capital.

The social capital within the network was an important element in the completion of a large number of activities. Participants developed high levels of trust and commitment to the teams they were working within, and although some people dropped out of activities, a high number sustained their engagement. Social events, occasionally supplemented by Bordeaux rather than Bourdieu, helped to strengthen some of the relationships and an effort was made to flatten any hierarchy that might exist in terms of either expertise or status. The undermining of expertism was not difficult to achieve as it became evident that the insights from individuals who were professionals or who had limited experience of research were extremely important.

Within the network, we set out to 'trouble' and to be playful with the concept of social capital. Participants were encouraged to do this by subjecting the concept itself to critique, examining its use within policy and exploring its utility empirically in a range of contexts (Allan et al, 2009). A number of network meetings were aimed at enabling members to develop and communicate their particular understandings of social capital and preferences for particular theoretical lines, and there was evidence of greater criticality as people became more confident working with, and within, social capital. In the initial phase of the network activity, the meaning given to the term social capital was explored in the context of not only how the construct might be measured, but also how it could be applied to interpret existing policy and research. From these activities, a shared understanding of the construct as including bonding, linking and bridging social capital was developed and described in early publications. Our initial understanding of these concepts was summed up by Catts and Ozga (2005, p. 2), who described social capital as being:

> developed in our relationships, through doing things for one another and in the trust that we develop in one another. It helps in bonding fragmented social life; in the bridging of communities to places and contacts beyond their immediate environment and in the linking of people to formal structures and agencies that they may need for help with opportunities for education or employment.

In the concluding chapter in this book, we draw out a more nuanced view of social capital as practices, with an emphasis on a continuing process rather than the static state implied particularly by Putnam's definition of social capital.

In a previous volume, reporting some of the other activities of the Schools and Social Capital Network, we concluded that social capital did have some powerful potential for 'breathing life into professionalism and enabling teachers to engage their students fully and equitably' (Ozga and Allan, 2009, p. 217). However, we were also cautioned by Humes (2009b, p. 75) about the necessary 'hard discursive work' to be done, involving 'deconstruction of both the orthodoxies of professional discourse and the assumptions of the social capital agenda'. The participants in the case studies arrived at some important insights about the applicability and sustainability of social capital within education.

About this book

This book is in two parts: Part I addresses social capital and inclusion, and contains four case studies which explore aspects of how the social capital of young people, and in one case the adults they interact with, plays a crucial role in determining their inclusion or, indeed, their exclusion. Part II addresses social capital in and out of school, and features a further four case studies in which the role of social capital in fostering engagement within the community (or impeding it) is examined. Each part of the book is followed by a commentary examining the implications of the findings for policy and practice. George McBride provides the commentary to conclude Part I and Rowena Arshad offers the commentary for Part II.

In Chapter Two, Beth Cross, Julie Allan and Dorothy McDonald report on an evaluation of the Inclusive Learning Network, a programme for parents, teachers, other professionals and volunteers supporting the inclusion in schools of young disabled people. The conclusion is that there are lasting returns for teachers from such a network, but only temporary benefits for disabled young people and their parents.

The inclusion of refugee pupils is the focus of Chapter Three by Geri Smyth, George MacBride, Grace Paton and Nathalie Sheridan, who report on how the development of different forms of social capital affect the education of pupils from refugee families in one primary and one secondary school, each of which has a Glasgow Asylum Seekers Support Project unit. The authors conclude that while the schools offered secure environments for such pupils through the conscious development of bonding and bridging social capital within the school, they were less successful at fostering bridging social capital within the local community and also limited in their success in developing linking social capital for young people.

Social capital in the lives of young carers is explored by Monica Barry in Chapter Four. She reports the views and experiences of 20 young carers (10 young men and 10 young women aged 12–23) who were involved in young carers' projects across the Central Belt of Scotland. Barry examines the concept of social capital as it applies to young carers, notably in respect of their interactions with family, peers, teachers and other adults in their lives. Her findings highlight the importance of young carers' projects, including access to social capital, which enabled these young people to obtain support and acknowledgement, but which also allowed them to temporarily detach themselves from their significant caring responsibilities,.

In Chapter Five, Marion Allison and Ralph Catts report on the social capital processes in a council-supported youth club. They discuss how the connections among young people and volunteers in a youth club affect their opportunities to achieve their social, economic and cultural needs. The results indicate that young people rely on the adult volunteers and council staff who attend the youth club for advice and role models and suggest that while the youth club connections were themselves fragile and not enduring, youth aspirations formed through family bonding social capital could be informed and supported by provision of information provided by bridging social capital accessed through the youth club.

In the first of the commentary pieces, George MacBride explores the implications of the case studies for policy and practice, specifically in relation to inclusion. He voices suspicion about social capital being expected to stand in place of state provision for vulnerable groups and is critical of debates that centre on social capital and social mobility and which thereby sidestep the real issues of inequality in society. MacBride also demonstrates vividly how much of the new Scottish curriculum framework, Curriculum for Excellence, encompasses social capital, and outlines the opportunities for developing this among children and young people.

In Chapter Seven, Janine Muldoon and Ralph Catts report on social capital in and out of school. They met young people and the providers of a 'Get Ready for Work' community education programme focused on unemployed early school leavers in East Glasgow. This case study highlights the significant needs of a group of young people at risk of not entering employment and further education after school leaving age. Muldoon and Catts show how significant bonding social capital can have a limiting effect on the young people's aspirations but how affording them access to bridging social capital can alter their perceptions of what is possible and can enhance well-being.

In Chapter Eight, Rowena Arshad and Susan Maclennan report on their case study in an Edinburgh primary school which was seeking to continuously improve its practice in creating an anti-discriminatory and inclusive ethos. The case study provides an evaluation of how social capital operates within the school, and identifies how fostering linking social capital can assist a school to engage positively with diversity and promote good relations as well as countering discrimination. The headteacher's key role in cultivating and maintaining social capital is highlighted and strikingly reinforced by the revelation of the changing ethos and dramatically lower pupil achievement following the departure of this particular individual.

The transition to secondary schooling is the focus of the case study by Kevin Stelfox and Ralph Catts (Chapter Nine), in which pupils in a Scottish Primary 7 class (pupils aged 11–12) were followed until the end of their first year in secondary school when they were aged 12–13. Their experience of the transition was explored within a relational social context. The findings address the role of their social networks in and beyond schools and the potential for pupil alienation in the early years of secondary school.

The final case study, reported in Chapter Ten, provides a striking contrast to other case studies, all of which were located within the public sector. Here Bob Lingard, Joan Forbes, Gaby Weiner and John Horne report on how social and other capitals work together to produce and reproduce advantage in and through independent schools in Scotland. The assumption is that the production of advantage and disadvantage are two sides of the same coin and that therefore an increased understanding of the processes whereby advantage is produced might also illuminate the processes of how disadvantage is produced through schooling. This chapter offers a contrasting perspective which allows a cross-case analysis to illuminate understandings of schooling generally and of the production and reproduction of advantage and disadvantage.

In Chapter Eleven, Rowena Arshad offers a commentary on the roles of social capital in and out of school and considers some of the implications for policy and practice. She highlights the importance of bridging and linking social capital, noting its abundance within the independent schools and bemoaning its relative absence within the state schools studied. Arshad calls for a greater attention to the impact of difference and diversity on social relationships and urges greater attention by schools to the building and sustaining of social networks.

In the final chapter, we review the findings from each of the case studies and reflect upon the roles social capital can play in thinking about learning and the development of young people. We offer some considerations about the utility of social capital for education practice, policy and research.

References

Allan, J., Ozga, J and Smyth, G. (2009) (eds) *Social capital, professionalism and diversity*, Rotterdam: Sense.

Bourdieu, P. (1977) *Outline of a theory of practice*, Cambridge: Cambridge University Press.

Bourdieu, P. (1986). 'The forms of capital', in J. G. Richardson (ed) *Handbook of theory and research for the sociology of education*, New York: Greenwood, pp 241–58.

Catts, R. and Ozga, J. (2005) *What is social capital and how might it be used in Scotland's schools*, Briefing paper No 36, Edinburgh: Centre for Education and Sociology, University of Edinburgh, www.ces.ed.ac.uk/PDF%20Files/Brief036.pdf

Coleman, J. (1990) *Foundations of social theory*, Cambridge, MA: Harvard University Press.

Coleman, J. (1988) 'Social capital in the creation of human capital', *The American Journal of Sociology*, 94, Supplement, pp S95–S120.

Dika, S. and Singh, K. (2002) 'Applications of social capital in educational literature: a critical synthesis', *Review of Educational Research*, vol 72, no 1, pp 31–60.

Fine, B. and Green, F. (2000) 'Economics, social capital and the colonization of the social sciences', in S. Baron, J. Field and T. Schuller (eds) *Social capital: critical perspectives*, Oxford: Oxford University Press, pp 78-93.

Fukuyama, F. (1995) *Trust: the social virtues and the creation of prosperity*, London: Hamish Hamilton.

Gamarnikow, E and Green, A. (2007) 'Social capitalism and educational policy: democracy, professionalism and social justice under New Labour', *International Studies in Sociology of Education*, vol 17, no 4, pp 367–88.

Humes, W. (2007) The infrastructure of educational research in Scotland, *European Educational Research Journal*, vol 6, no 1, www.wwwords.co.uk/pdf/validate.asp?j=eerj&vol=6&issue=1&year=2007&article=7_Humes_EERJ_6_1_web

Humes, W. (2009a) 'Clasped to a warm bosom', *Scottish Review*, 14 April, www.scottishreview.net/WHumes091.html

Humes, W. (2009b) 'The social capital agenda and teacher professionalism', in J. Allan, J. Ozga and G. Smyth (eds) *Social capital, professionalism and diversity*, Rotterdam: Sense, pp 63–76.

Morrow, V. (1999) 'Conceptualising social capital in relation to the well-being of children and young people: a critical review', *The Sociological Review*, vol 47, no 4, pp 744–65.

O'Brien, S. and Fathaigh, M. (2005) 'Bringing in Bourdieu's theory of social capital: renewing learning partnership approaches to social inclusion', *Irish Educational Studies*, vol 24, no 1, pp 65–76.

Ozga, J. and Allan, J. (2009) 'Social capital, professionalism and diversity: prospects and potential', in J. Allan, J. Ozga and G. Smyth (eds) *Social capital, professionalism and diversity*, Rotterdam: Sense.

Paterson, L. (2000) 'Civil society and democratic renewal', in S. Baron, J. Field and T. Schuller (eds) *Social capital: critical perspectives*, Oxford: Oxford University Press, pp 39–55.

Portes, A. (1998) 'Social capital: its origins and applications in modern sociology', *Annual Review of Sociology*, vol 24, pp 1-24.

Putnam, R.D. (1995) 'Bowling alone: America's declining social capital', *Journal of Democracy*, vol 6, no 1, pp 65-78.

Putnam, R.D. (2000) *Bowling alone: the collapse and revival of American community*, New York: Simon and Schuster.

Putnam, R.D. (2007) '*E pluribus unum:* diversity and community in the twenty-first century: the 2006 Johan Skytte prize lecture', *Scandinavian Political Studies*, vol 30 no 2, pp 137–74.

Putman, R.D. with Leonardi, R. and Nanetti, R. (1993) *Making democracy work: civic traditions in modern Italy*, Princeton, NJ: Princeton University Press.

Schuller, T., Baron, S. and Field, J. (2000) 'Social capital: a review and critique', in S. Baron, J. Field and T. Schuller (eds) *Social capital: critical perspectives*, Oxford: Oxford University Press, pp 1–38.

Sturgess, G. (1997) 'Taking social capital seriously', in A. Norton, M. Latham and S.G. Sturgess (eds), *Social capital: the individual, civil society and the State*, Sydney: Centre for Independent Studies, pp 49–83.

Szreter, S. (1999) A new political economy for New Labour: the importance of social capital, *Renewal*, vol 7, no 1, pp 30–44.

Woolcock, M. (1998) 'Social capital and economic development: toward a theoretical synthesis and policy framework', *Theory and Society*, vol 27, no 1, pp 151–208.

Part I
Social capital and inclusion

Evaluating an inclusive education programme: lessons in transient social capital

Beth Cross, Julie Allan and Dorothy McDonald

Introduction

This Inclusive Learning Network (ILN) case study examines how the concepts and theoretical frameworks that are centred upon social capital can be used to understand the dynamics at play in educational projects. The case study focuses on a network of dispersed individuals who came together periodically to undergo training and skills development with a view to improving local authority educational services for pupils with additional support needs. The research team were thus enabled to look at spatiality and social capital, that is, how social capital operates across different spaces and how spaces can be constructed to foster social capital.

The case study also provided the opportunity to examine the role of social capital within processes of transition and the ways in which social capital itself can be said to be transitory. Because the ILN was a time-limited project, the relationships fostered within it could only ever be transient. However, a premise of the learning theory that underpinned its approach, in common with many projects that have the generation of social capital as a goal, is that relations modelled within the course of the project could serve as exemplars that could be transplanted to more permanent contexts. The findings raise important questions about the differing degrees of transferability and durability of social capital for each participant and the way that this depends on the differing factors of each participant's local context and position within that context. A discussion of these interlinked issues concludes with a consideration of the employment of social capital in policy and professional practice and the kinds of investments that it represents.

The ILN as a context for understanding transitional social capital

The Inclusive Learning Network (ILN) was specifically designed to give stakeholders with different levels of engagement in inclusive learning an opportunity to step away from the immediate social structures of their everyday experiences and, within a supported environment, consider the structures, roles, processes and tools that can improve inclusive education. In other words, this gave teachers, parents and a range of support professionals, such as physiotherapists, a chance to interact in a setting other than the often very pressurized context of service review meetings (Slee and Allan, 2001). By stepping back and comparing their experiences with other parents, teachers and professionals in the multi-agency teams, it was envisaged that participants would be able to:

- work more effectively in local contexts;
- facilitate inclusive learning more fully within local contexts;
- change ethos and social relations in those local contexts.

Part of this strategy involved fostering good working relations among participants, in the hope that this would serve as a model for them to replicate in local contexts.

The impetus for the ILN came from Equity in Education, a Scottish organisation for parents of pupils with additional support needs, which had identified a need for better working relations with teachers and support professionals. The ILN was funded by a grant from the Scottish government which also supported the recruitment of participants across a wide range of Scottish local authorities. Participants within the ILN committed to attending five two day residential sessions in its first year. In each session, different course components were combined to meet identified needs. Factual information about changes in legislation, policy implementation, models of good practice and a range of inclusion tools was presented. This information was embedded within activities that encouraged participants to explore the meanings of inclusion and dis/ability and to share their experiences that gave rise to these understandings. Graphic facilitation, the practice of using images and maps to create an engaging visual record of a group's work, was used to record participants' contributions, which worked both to validate their responses and provide an easily accessible record of their progress through the session activities. These activities also developed a sense of team work and personal self-worth. A further important component was the opportunity for participants to compare their own experiences with different approaches to inclusion in other countries. Guest speakers shared struggles, barriers, dilemmas, and their own ways of moving beyond them to innovations and improved relations and outcomes; the course participants heard from teachers, curriculum developers, parents and young people.

In the second year, participants' involvement was focused on working together to conduct pieces of independent research or resource development. Three sessions were convened to provide a framework for participants to support each other through the process, put into practice some of the problem solving and mediation tools learned in the previous year and reflect with each other about the learning and relational outcomes that resulted. The research reports and resources were then published and launched at the Annual General Meeting of the parent group of the project, Equity in Education.

At the end of every session and at the end of each year, the participants completed evaluation questionnaires. An evaluation discussion at the conclusion of each year was also conducted. The notes from this discussion were developed into a report that was then distributed to each participant. The ILN was offered to three successive year groups, hereafter referred to as cohorts 1, 2 and 3. Participants from the first and second cohorts had the option of contributing to successive cohorts either through input at the first-year residential sessions or by acting as a mentor to participants in their second-year research activity.

Study rationale

What is understood by good working relations can be investigated as the dynamics of social capital, specifically the quality of bonding, bridging and linking capital. In translating social capital from a metaphor into a concept with analytical value (McGonigal et al, 2007) the concepts of bonding, bridging and linking capital have been developed to distinguish between different sets of relations and social resources needed to form different kinds of networks with differing uses and value. In these terms, social capital can bond people together who share the same conditions and locality and can help to build bridges between people who share similar conditions within differing or extended circumstances. However, social capital of the kind that enables disadvantaged groups to improve their circumstances and relative position in society requires a third kind of capital, linking capital, which is cultural practices, knowledge, and relational abilities that enable them to negotiate with those in positions of power that affect their circumstances.

When this expanded definition of social capital was applied to the ILN project the following set of questions was generated:

- Does the ILN help participants support others in the same role within their local context (i.e. enhance or create bonding social capital)?
- Does the ILN help participants work in concert with others in nearby communities to extend best practice across the local authority (that is, enhance or create bridging social capital)?
- Does the ILN help participants work more effectively with those in positions of more power or authority in their local contexts (that is, enhance or create linking social capital)?

In order to address these questions, a member of the ILN facilitation team and two researchers came together to form the case study research team.

Design of the study

A case study approach was adopted that examined different kinds of evidence:

- course assignments;
- evaluation materials;
- records of participants' responses to course activities;
- observations of participation in ILN sessions;
- participants' responses to mapping tools administered by the researcher;
- transcripts from phone interviews with participants;
- e-mail survey responses.

Textual materials helped prepare the principal researcher to meet ILN participants and understand the observed activities. Attending sessions also provided an opportunity to describe the research and recruit individual members of the ILN for interviews, school visits and the follow-up survey. In selecting individual ILN members for interviews, care was taken, in consultation with the ILN facilitators, to draw on a representative range of contexts and perspectives. Textual materials were coded with the analytical themes generated by the AERS Social Capital Network as a framework and field notes were analysed for further insight into these same issues. The mapping activities were developed to provide a mechanism for participants to elaborate on a key term within the ILN, which at the same time revealed their understanding of the power dynamics at play within their local contexts. Responses to phone interviews and the e-mail survey were compared and analysed with particular attention to their relevance to bonding, bridging and linking social capital.

Findings of the study

Course materials and evaluations

A review of evaluations from each cohort provided strong evidence that the sessions had changed how participants thought and felt about themselves as change agents and about the kinds of tools and approaches they could use to encourage inclusivity. The evaluation responses of participants of the first residential course frequently mentioned that the sessions were emotionally hard work and some participants questioned the extent of the emotional involvement that particular activities exacted. While participants continued to refer to the emotionally demanding nature of the course, in subsequent years they conveyed a recognition that this work was necessary and beneficial. A change in tone also suggested that for many the course had widened perceptions or heightened sensitivity to the core values of what it is to be human. Many of the comments expressed in the final evaluation were of a profound, personal and relational nature, in contrast to the distant stance adopted by many in responding to the baseline assessment activity carried out at the beginning of the course, in which participants' goals had been couched in terms of policy objectives.

Observations of ILN sessions

Having analysed these evaluations, observations were made at three first-year residential courses and at one second-year research support session. Observing the emotional hard work in progress required emotional work on the part of the researcher who undertook the bulk of the data collection and a particular sensitivity to the emotional weather of the proceedings. At the session attended early in the course, the researcher observed subtle indicators that participants were coming from differing vantage points; this was indicated in body posture and paralinguistic features of participants' contributions to activities. Activities in these sessions sought to establish common ground by focusing on situations that all those in the session would have experienced personally. In the coffee session after this activity, the researcher observed an air of camaraderie and noted people talking in groups other than those they had been seated with. The researcher observed across sessions that presentations made to the group did not present a depersonalised organisational view, but were anchored within the individual stance of the presenter. Narrative was used more than expository prose. Participants were taken through what presenters felt and thought and the models presented were contextualised within this personal sense making. Listening to these narratives required emotional work. To the extent that all participants were doing this hard work together they gained a collective experience, a sense of having been through the narratives together with the presenter. By the researcher's third visit late in the course, a strong sense of group cohesion had formed. The researcher, as someone who had not participated in this collective experience in subtle ways, was now positioned as an outsider to the group, more so than at the first session she had attended, when the group were all relative newcomers. These observations, though limited, corroborated the centrality of the relational and emotional work to which the evaluations referred.

In the second-year research support session, the researcher observed participants using the reflective tools learned in the first year and making explicit reference to them. There was a sense of ease with which participants drew upon this collective repertoire. No strong differences were apparent between the way teachers, supporting professionals or parents approached the task or in the ways they related to each other.

Mapping activities

At one of the first-year residential sessions the researcher conducted an activity that explored the phrase which encapsulated the ILN's ethos: 'All in'. One of the premises that underpinned the work was a belief that improvements for pupils with support needs did not have to disadvantage anyone else in the education setting. This phrase was used to indicate a stance that moved away from the adversarial language of winners and losers that can characterise disability negotiations (Nespor and Hicks, 2005). To gauge the extent to which participants felt that their localities achieved this inclusion goal, they were asked to produce a diagram of how close to being 'All in' each different stakeholder in their locality was. The resulting maps revealed that participants' perceptions of their local context were quite different. Some mapped a state of disempowerment quite distanced from the 'All in' centre but a few stakeholders portrayed quite close working and learning relationships. Taking aggregate readings for each stakeholder across all maps, the picture that emerged was one in which teachers were positioned as the most powerful, the positions of parents and support professionals as variable, and the pupils as least empowered. In using the diagram, participants pointed out that there was a crucial difference between different members of the teaching staff. Learning assistants were important to include on the map, but they too were in a relatively disempowered position.

As a result of using the diagram, one participant then used the tool with the pupils with whom she worked. In addition a professional from an earlier cohort group volunteered to use the tool with pupils in her school. This provided the perspectives of 43 pupils on the same issue, both those with additional support needs and those without that designation. Pupils were asked to use a modified form of the tool. They mapped those who were significant to them in their learning setting and the degree to which each helped them feel 'All in'. There were some important reversals in their depictions. Other children were depicted as being more helpful than teachers. There were also differences in how pupils with additional support needs and pupils without identified additional support needs used the tool. Pupils without support needs did not often depict their parents as being part of their learning setting. Pupils with additional support needs without exception placed their parents on the map, and placed them as the most important person who helped them feel 'All in'.

While not providing information about the social capital formed within the ILN activity itself, this mapping activity did provide important background information about the varied contexts from which participants were coming and to which they returned. It also suggested that the dynamics within the contexts were viewed differently by adults and children, a finding which resonates with other studies (Badham, 2004, Lewis and Porter, 2004).

Conducting the mapping activity in schools also enabled some observations of school interaction to a limited degree. An activity in which young people were expressing their opinions rather than displaying their competence was in itself a departure from school norms and thus to a limited degree provided an example of including different dimensions of pupils' decision making and expertise. The activity allowed teaching staff to see pupils in a different light and also exemplified how inclusion relates to the personal and social development of all pupils. Some learning assistants expressed surprise at the degree to which young people could engage in the activity and the awareness of relations around them that they indicated.

Telephone interviews

Using common themes within ILN evaluation materials and observations of sessions as the basis for phone interviews, interviews with parents (two), teachers (two) and supporting professionals (two) were conducted to gather a range of perspectives. One of the strongest recurrent assertions by respondents was that the worth of the ILN approach resided in the mix of components and the extended period away from local contexts in which to experience them. This time allowed participants with different roles and therefore different perspectives to appreciate each other's concerns and dilemmas as well as their strengths and contributions. This sharing of perspectives did much to create a very positive ethos during course events. Given that a core aim of the project was to improve the ethos and relations in the localities themselves, it seemed important to trace how this sharing of perspectives affected continued practice or parenting experience once participants returned to their localities. Exploring this aspect of ILN impact also served as a means to investigate the extent to which linking and bridging capital initiated within the ILN sessions was transplanted back into the localities in a more durable form.

In these phone interviews, however, participants did not report that sharing perspectives across roles had continued in their localities. When parents expressed the belief that they now had someone to turn to, they named the course organisers. These relations are an instance of sustained bridging social capital.

ILN participant survey

Rather than surmise that what had been identified as a crucial feature of the programme had not been translated into local practice on the basis of the phone interviews, a short e-mail survey canvassed all participants, specifically asking to what extent this outcome of the programme had been developed. Five out of 60 participants responded, of whom none were parents. The professionals who did respond reported that they coordinated their work with other professionals more; they saw this as leading to benefits for pupils and felt that there was less slippage through the safety net for young people. In several instances, a meeting of all stakeholders was described as somebody else's responsibility to organise, or not of enough importance to squeeze into busy schedules. The degree to which such activity would sit at odds with prevailing structural practices comes across vividly in one respondent's remarks:

I have not been able to take this model forward – though I do feel that it would be valuable. The main reason is lack of time – as soon as I get back into school I feel swallowed up by the day to day stuff. Also I feel isolated and one small voice in the group of leaders in our school. We have tried to change our approach to parents and have had a good response as they feel valued and respected. There have been no specific meetings for groups of any kind. We have spoken about it as a department but it has not moved forward.

One professional reported that such a process would have been too contentious at a local level. However, one professional reported that she had taken the initiative to set up regular meetings for parents, support professionals and teachers, which had created a relaxed informal approach and were very beneficial. She described them as working very similarly to the informal components of the ILN course itself and creating the same positive ethos. Another professional reported that there were meetings for parents and professionals set up through other mechanisms and that more opportunities were being developed.

Discussion of findings in the context of social capital

Looking across the range of findings, it is important to consider what evidence emerges about the different kinds of social capital as framed in the core research questions: 'To what extent are bonding, bridging or linking capital evident in the ILN process?' 'To what extent are these kinds of capital transplanted back into local contexts?' We approach these questions by first summarising what the several kinds of data tell us about the different positions of those in school settings and how this impinges on the kinds of social capital they are party to.

The position of parents

Within the mapping tool, although parents' position averages out to be one of intermediate power, the individual responses were spread out quite widely over the spectrum, much more so than for teachers or young people. Narratives collected while observing sessions and within phone interviews with parents depicted a situation in which their position fluctuated significantly. A teacher whom they can work with one year can quickly be replaced by another in the next year with very little time or empathy for their situation. One of the benefits spoken about most commonly by parents participating in the ILN was the broader perspective of teachers that it had given them. An appreciation of the barriers and pressures that teachers face has improved the basis for communication and negotiation in several respects. One professional, in making recommendations for how inclusion work should continue, suggested that local networking meetings should include parents of young people without designated support needs, a possibility that would also broaden the support network and possibly mediate power dynamics for parents.

The position of non-teaching staff

One of the interesting features that the mapping exercise threw up was the importance of members of staff within the school with very little status, training or authority, but who had regular and sometimes crucially supportive contact with young people. A group of professionals working in the same region who took the opportunity of a gathering of all three year cohorts to confer with each other, articulated the perception that whether or not a child stayed included in a school when difficulties arose depended on the staying power and motivation of the learning assistant. They further related that women with lower socioeconomic status who provided the only income for their household stayed with difficult cases, whereas those who had some degree of choice about employment as part of double income households did not. In terms of a study concerned with the interactions between social and economic capital, the lack of inclusion of learning assistants in the ILN raised unsettling questions about learning assistants' own sense of empowerment and how that might be communicated to those with whom they work..

Although the ILN did not recruit learning assistants, some participants recruited as parents had employment in this capacity. Within the overall strategy, learning assistants were not assessed as being well placed to make decisions that could effect change on a larger scale. However, it does need to be asked: what is the significance of young people with additional support needs receiving the majority of their education from learning assistants? As one of the learning support teachers related in the course of an interview, 'lack of support' for learning assistance translated into their diminished ability to provide adequate support for the pupil and resulted in both being 'ground down'. This lack of support for learning assistants may result from immediate local factors, but also from larger structural and economic ones. Research that explores how learning assistants' resources and support networks affect the quality of relations with and service provision for young people with additional support needs is much needed. Examining the forms of social capital and how they are developed and utilised would be an important dimension to pursue in such a study.

The position of teachers

The mapping tool with ILN participants depicted teachers on average as having the most power in the educational context. Participants on the day were an even mixture of professionals working in allied services such as occuptional therapy and social work, as well as parents and teachers. As the ILN approach as a whole encouraged participants to suspend their identification with the roles they normally assumed in their local contexts, when facilitating the activity we did not ask participants to identify that role when completing the mapping tool. This limited our capacity to compare any differences in how participants used the tool. It would have been helpful to know if parents and supporting professionals were ascribing more power to teachers than teachers were to themselves.

It is also important to qualify this finding by questioning who the participants may have been representing. Was it classroom teachers, headteachers or learning support teachers they were thinking of? Although encouraged to expand and adapt the tool to most accurately depict their perspective, participants did not make distinctions between teachers, but between teachers and learning assistants. Nevertheless in the existing curriculum context, it is important to bear in mind that research reports teachers as feeling that they have had decreased autonomy and discretion in their classrooms under the effectiveness and attainment focus that has predominated in British education since the late 1980s.

It is also worth noting that there are other important stakeholders not included in the ILN process, but who play important roles in inclusion, such as educational policy makers, teacher educators and student teachers. In the independent study element of the second year of the course, some ILN members in cohort years one and two examined provision of inclusion issues within teacher education. They concluded that the coverage is scant and in many respects counterproductive, potentially reversing any of the gains the ILN may make within local authorities.

The position of supporting professionals

It is not easy to summarise the position of supporting professionals. ILN participants in the mapping activity noted that there are different kinds of support professionals who have markedly different relations with young people depending on the nature of their involvement, the frequency of their interaction with young people and the framework for collaboration between their service and that of the school. Support professionals revealed that the ILN improved their ability to understand and communicate. In the telephone interviews, a physiotherapist identified the changes to her practice as a result of participation in the ILN both in terms of understanding young people's and teachers' perspectives better:

> When I'm sitting in a meeting I relate physio goals not just to school but to [the young people's] wider life and having a life. (ILN participant, cohort 2)

> I can advocate for physio better because I connect: I can talk [the teacher's] language and recognise their barriers. (ILN participant, cohort 2)

The position of young people

As indicated earlier in the chapter, there was a tension between the stated empowering philosophy of the ILN, which the researchers also held, and the reality of young people's positioning within the educational contexts in which they were to be included.

Different kinds of power make social capital complex to assess. Young people had the power to befriend or exclude their peers while teachers could exercise power over the behaviour of the young people within school. The limited glimpse of these relations suggests that there is much more to learn about young people's social capital and the role this plays in inclusion as it is experienced by young people with additional support needs. Further work needs to be done to articulate the different kinds of power held by those in different roles and their simultaneous interaction with each other.

ILN outcomes and social capital: space for transitional social capital?

All of these roles and the relationships between them can be analysed in terms of social capital. In this section we first examine what a social capital analytic framework can help us understand about the relationships fostered within the ILN programme and the degree to which they transferred back to participants' specific localities. The issues that arise within this analysis, in turn, provide the impetus to think through the spatiality of social capital and in what ways social capital developed in a transient space can be transferred to more sustained contexts. We find that the success of such transitions is dependent upon a number of interacting larger social processes, which Dyson and Millward (1999) have argued is the case more generally for inclusion. In looking at the differences to relations that the ILN programme made, it is important to acknowledge that bonding, bridging and linking social capital are not discrete activities but often contribute to each other. Though parents saw the programme as making a big difference to their confidence, the emerging pattern seemed to augur better for professionals than for the parents involved (see Figure 2.1).

Figure 2.1: Social capital trajectories

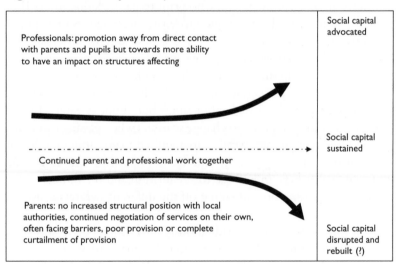

The bonding capital of teachers and professionals seemed to be strengthened. The linking capital was potentially enhanced by the fact that some ILN participants had moved into levels of regional responsibility and decision making. However, there was little evidence of retained links across regions, which means that any gains to bridging capital were localised within local authority power structures. Of all the goals of the ILN, improving working relations for parents was of particular importance, but this is where there is the least evidence that significant gains were made. Linking capital did not seem to be increased between parents and the range of professionals with power to influence the child's educational experience. What parents spoke most enthusiastically about, ironically, is the capital least apparent for professionals, that is the bridging capital with other parents in similar circumstances in different settings. Increased bonding capital with other parents in their own locality was also reported by one participant.

In order to examine the trends within Figure 2.1, a distinction needs to be made between social capital and the other kinds of portable capital that may be derived from it. Although the social capital may not have improved significantly for parents participating in the ILN and the professionals in their local contexts, there is evidence to suggest that some parents were using skills and strategies that the social capital generated within the ILN experience helped them to develop. A particular instance of this is highlighted in one of the resources derived from the course assignments. New legislation on lifting has added more technical requirements and regulations for people with restricted mobility. One parent, who prior to participating in the ILN training would have been tempted to write angry letters in response to difficulties encountered, had found a new way to articulate her experience. Instead of attacking people for being thoughtless, she sought out a means to help them better understand her situation through an analogy they could perhaps more easily identify with. Instead of a letter, she wrote a short story, not about slings but about sweaters. In this story, the family is required to change sweaters when passing through a door. Different coloured sweaters are required to go through different types of door. The story relates the encounters with staff at a range of facilities that have to enforce this regulation and the difficulty that finding and putting on and taking off the different sweaters causes:

> Jumpers may seem a ridiculously silly story but it was written instead of a raving letter. I wanted to write an angry letter. I wanted to rant on at anybody and everybody because it just made my blood boil. However having been fortunate enough to be on the Inclusive Learning Network I began to use some of the tools that had been shown to us on the course . . . I feel much better after writing a story than I would after writing an angry letter and there must be an element of HEALTH AND SAFETY in that! (Shankly, 2007)

The new skill illustrated above is different from having a template for how one can relate and situate oneself within the range of relations that are involved in interacting in an organisational setting. The extent to which social capital is comprised of transported social skills remains debatable.

Reflections on the process of studying social capital within transient shared space

An important strategy within the ILN was the use of a neutral shared space to provide participants with a different perspective on inclusion issues from those within their local contexts. The possibility of moving beyond immediate relations into a different space had the potential to foster linking social capital. Many of the research team's analytic discussions reflected on this potential, but the findings do not conclusively demonstrate how or even if this happened. Many of the participants in the ILN were themselves in transition, the professionals making transitions within their careers, the parents coping with their child's progression through the education system. Given the flux in participants' lives and the many factors shifting with these transitions, it was difficult to examine what effect the ILN may have had as distinct from other factors.

In studying shared space, we were drawn to reflect further on social capital as a shared asset. However, we found that it is difficult to retain foremost in our thinking that social capital is an asset that resides in the relational qualities among habitually interacting people. The grammatical possessive structure of European languages, as well as the prevalent individualisation within culture, limits our capacity to express or hold vividly in our imagination the collective state of social capital. It is easy to conflate it with the individual capacities derived from it.

Implications for policy and practice

In looking at what the ILN indicates about social capital, the findings highlight important considerations to take into account when assessing questions fundamental to the deployment of social capital as an analytic tool. We focus on three questions to illustrate this.

1. Can social capital relations be successfully or robustly improved without altering the access to power and resource allocation of its weakest members?

The ILN study highlights the importance of keeping clear the distinction between actual social capital that resides in ongoing relations and occasions to enact those relations, and what can be termed suspended social capital, that is, the capacity to reform social networks based on prior experience. For those with other flexible, easily transferable kinds of capital, that is economic and cultural means, suspended social capital may be valuable, as the opportunities to re-deploy it are more likely and more easily accessed. For those who may have experienced a temporary increase in social capital, but who are much more restricted in their social and economic manoeuvrability, suspended social capital may be much less of an asset; this finding is born out in other studies (Bagley and Ackerley, 2006).

The ILN study also highlights considerations in terms of the specific direct outcomes of social capital. Social networks may enable people to deploy, and have recognised, their professional skills. This kind of benefit is easily transferable. However, social capital may mean that people have someone who can provide a crucial care role for themselves or their dependent. Reliance on this help depends much more specifically on particular shared understandings and physical proximity. It is not an easily transferable benefit. This illustrates that the same experience of social capital can have very different trajectories of benefit for people placed differently in terms of their class and disability position within society.

2. Do we discount something crucial in social capital's incidental development by trying to create it intentionally?

In considering this question, it is important to reconsider Bourdieu's frequently quoted definition of social capital: 'the durable network of more or less institutionalised relationships of mutual acquaintance and recognition' (Bourdieu and Wacquant, 1992, p. 119). The key question is just how durable were the relations forged within ILN activities, given that they worked across rather than within institutionalised settings? Bourdieu and Wacquant understand institutionalised relations as those that are fairly frequent and stable due to the fixed social structures in which they take place. However, in saying that the relations are of mutual acquaintance and recognition, they appear to be describing relations that form incidentally to the core purpose of the institution or social space in which they take place. People get on because they share a work bench or coffee maker, not because their job description dictates that they do so. These are emerging relationships of parity or mutuality, often despite the hierarchical structures inhabited, as McGonigal et al (2007) also note. As one of the authors has examined (Cross, 2010), often funding for programmes designed to increase social capital, as is the case of the ILN, is relatively short term. The assumption seems to be that social capital, once it has been developed, will be self-sustaining after the resources, spaces and occasions in which it was developed are effectively withdrawn or scaled back. The ILN case study helps illustrate the dangers in this assumption.

3. Can social capital be intentionally fostered in order to produce other specific outcomes such as increased inclusion?.

In thinking through how successful the intentional fostering of social capital may have been within the ILN, we have recourse to a metaphor. The ILN may have acted as a greenhouse, providing the favourable conditions for tender plants to root and begin to develop. However, the degree to which these plants were able to mature and bear fruit was dependent upon the contexts into which they were transplanted. Some of the contexts were very fertile, while others resembled blasted heaths. In this respect, the ILN may bear strong resemblance to many of the other case studies and, indeed, any project which takes on a social capital development agenda, particularly if the intent is to do so in a transitory capacity.

Conclusion

Given these considerations, which together suggest that a cautionary approach be taken to any claims about social capital, we want to offer some metaphorical thinking about social capital that came out of the project. Implementing theoretical concepts requires not only analytic thinking but a more attuned sense of how we synthesise concepts into workable strategies, often in circumstances in which it is all too apparent that success will be against the odds. This aspect of practitioners' work often goes unrecognised and it is particularly helpful that researchers and practitioners within the AERS project had an opportunity to engage in dialogue about this way of deploying conceptual resources. This is one example of the research process drawing from the intellectual resources embedded within the practice setting, as the ILN frequently used images and metaphors to help its participants see issues and problems from different perspectives.

The following is a transcribed excerpt from one of the research forum sessions. In this, Dorothy McDonald, ILN leader and co-author of this chapter, examines the paradox of the transitory nature of social capital within ILN using a metaphor that drew on our thinking about the spatiality of social capital and our repeated attempts to answer the question, what kind of a space is shared space?

We were trying to think of a metaphor for the
relational investment people experience in going on the course
and we thought,
social capital – maybe it's like a beach.
You've got this beach,
a lovely flat beach full of sand
and people come along and build a sandcastle.
And the building of a sandcastle is a great experience
especially when you're five.
You put a huge amount of time and effort into it.
Everybody else that's round about you comes and helps you.
Other people start to join in sayin'
I've got a wee bucket
I've got this and the next thing
and you build this big elaborate sandcastle.

And then
you're building it as fast as you can
because the tide's coming in.
And then you walk up the beach
and you kinda look back
and it's just this pile of sand
and you kind of look back
and you think, well,
it's still there
you can see where it's been.
Or, ope! look the tide's come in again!
But eventually you're back to the smooth line of sand again
and you think to yourself,
well
maybe it's a bit like that.
We were thinking about time and investment.
You invest all this time into building a sandcastle.
Just because it disappears and it's flat again the next day,

does that mean to say it wasn't a worthwhile thing to do at the time?

No, it probably was a worthwhile thing to do at the time.

But is there any evidence that it's been there?

The only evidence that exists is in your memory

and the memory of the people that were there

. . .

So there must be some intrinsic value in the doing of it that benefits the people doing it.

Like the tide, schools have continual cycles of change. And yet these changes are unevenly distributed. Young people and their parents pass through; teachers, to varying degrees, remain. Thinking of the project of school as being like building a sandcastle invites a consideration of the positive dimensions of social capital as well as prompting important questions about the roles and nature of shared activity within schools. This is a useful resource to take away from the study.

References

Badham, B. (2004) '*How to ask us' learning pack: using multimedia methods to consult with disabled children and young people*, London: The Children's Society.

Bagley, C. and Ackerley, C. (2006) '"I am much more than just a mum": social capital, empowerment and Sure Start', *Journal of Education Policy*, vol 21, no 6, pp 717–34.

Bourdieu, P. and Wacquant, L. (1992) *An invitation to reflexive sociology*, Chicago, IL: University of Chicago Press.

Cross, B. (2010) 'Link or breach? The role of trust in developing social capital within a family literacy project', *Policy Futures in Education*, vol 8, no 5, pp 556–66.

Dyson, A. and Millward, A. (1999) 'Falling down the interfaces: from inclusive schools to an exclusive society', in K. Ballard (ed.) *Inclusive education: International voices on disability and justice*, London: Falmer Press, pp 152–66.

Lewis, A. and Porter, J. (2004) 'Interviewing children and young people with learning disabilities: guidelines for researchers and multi-professional practice', *British Journal of Learning Disabilities*, vol 32, pp 191–7.

McGonigal, J., Docherty, R., Allan, J., Mills, S., Catts, R., Redford, M., McDonald, A., Mott, J., and Buckley, C. (2007) 'Social capital, social inclusion and changing school contexts: a Scottish perspective', *British Journal of Educational Studies*, vol 55, no 1, pp 77–94.

Nespor, J. and Hicks, D. (2005) 'Segregated publics: Parents contesting special education practice', paper presented at the *Oxford Ethnography Conference*, September, Oxford UK.

Shankly, A. (2007) 'Jumpers', in J. Cochrane, D. McDonald and H. Simmons (eds) *Reflections and stories*, Glasgow: Equity in Education.

Slee, R. and Allan, J. (2001) 'Excluding the included: a reconsideration of inclusive education', *International Studies in Sociology of Education*, vol 11, no 2, pp 173–91.

THREE

Inclusion of pupils from refugee families

Geri Smyth, George MacBride, Grace Paton and Nathalie Sheridan

'Samah is a good friend. We've been friends since primary 2. She came in February and I came at the end of primary 1. We meet in the summer [holidays]. We ask her mum or my mum if we can go out to play. I live in the flats ... The lift sometimes gets stuck. I get a wee bit scared. My mum likes to come to the swings ... just in case of trouble.

'When I used to cry, and some [children] used to annoy me, she [Samah] used to come and say "What's the matter?"

'She [Samah] sometimes has trouble with primary 7 pulling her scarf [and asking] "Why do you wear it?"... and I help her.'

In the interview quoted above, Rodas, a 10-year-old girl whose family came from Turkey to seek refuge in the UK, talked to the researcher about the durability of her friendship with another Turkish girl. They have been friends for four years now and this friendship is marked by reciprocity in helping each other to cope in a new culture. Rodas expresses her and her mother's wariness about the possible clash of values in this new culture ('just in case of trouble') and indicates that she and her friend have experienced difficulties in school associated with cultural norms. These themes of durability, reciprocity, norms and values are the subject of the case study discussed in this chapter.

Introduction

Throughout this chapter we are using the term 'refugee' to apply to those children who have arrived in Britain, with or without their families, seeking refuge under the terms of the 1951 United Nations Convention on Refugees. This does not differentiate between those whose families have been granted refugee status and those who are still awaiting a Home Office decision regarding their case. Stead et al (1999) also adopted this terminology in their investigation of the education of refugee pupils in Scotland, and for simplicity, we adopt the same strategy.

The UK Home Office defines refugees as people who, as a result of their asylum applications, have either been awarded Exceptional Leave to Remain, a discretionary status allowing temporary permission to stay in the UK, or Convention status, which permits permanent residence in the UK. Prior to a decision being made, applicants and their families are referred to as asylum seekers.

The 1999 UK Immigration and Asylum Act led to the dispersal of asylum seekers around Britain, with Glasgow City Council the only local authority in Scotland which agreed to receive asylum seekers. The Glasgow Asylum Seekers' Support Project (GASSP) was established to provide housing, social work and education services for asylum seekers in Glasgow. One result of this was the establishment of GASSP Units in 27 Glasgow schools, with additional staff employed to support the pupils in English language acquisition and familiarisation with the Scottish curriculum. Children from refugee families were enrolled in mainstream classes but attended the units some of the time.

Rutter (2006) writes of the refugee pupil identikit, as opposed to that of other pupils, as being unannounced, traumatised, transient and insecure with no choice, no support and little cash. It is axiomatic that within a given community with refugees there is a great deal of heterogeneity, but needs and problems that may manifest themselves with significant numbers of refugee children include:

- interrupted education in the country of origin;
- horrific experiences in their home countries and during their flight to the UK;
- families who experience a drop in their standard of living and status in society;
- losing parents or usual carers;
- parents who are emotionally absent;
- families who do not know their legal and social rights in the UK, including their rights to basic services such as education and healthcare;
- speaking little or no English on arrival.

The Department for Education and Skills web page (DfES, 2006), which discusses good practice in the integration of refugee children in educational settings, argues that primary and secondary schools play a vital role in ensuring the integration of refugee children and families into the wider community and that 'developing support for refugee children is a whole-school responsibility'.

It is important for those working with refugee children to consider how they establish a relationship with their new external world and make social connections. Given the role of schools, it is necessary to consider whether schools actively pursue the making of connections for such children as part of their agenda and how durable and transferable any such connections might be.

Candappa et al (2007, p 40) indicated that good practice for refugee children in schools would be characterised, among other features, by 'fostering of friendships and socialising among students, good home–school links'. This would be a further indication of the relevance of social capital in this context. Lewis (2006, p 14) conducted an investigation of public attitudes to asylum seekers in Scotland for the Institute for Public Policy Research (IPPR) and found negative and intolerant attitudes to asylum seekers among young people across Scotland; however, conversely, Lewis also found that '[y]oung people who had attended an ethnically mixed school were likely to refer to these experiences as having had a positive impact upon their views about migration in general', highlighting again the important role of the school in fostering the development of trust and shared values.

Ager and Strang (2004, 2008) argue that social connections are one of the four indicators of refugee integration. The term 'integration' is itself contested, and in common parlance is often assumed to mean that successful integration will lead to immigrants becoming unnoticed and indeed losing their sense of self. Castles et al (2002, p 113) review the literature in relation to refugee integration and argue that 'minority groups should be supported in maintaining their cultural and social identities'. Consequently, the authors of this chapter considered it important for research with this population to address whether social capital practices in schools aim to create a homogenised melting pot where individual identities are squashed or a heterogeneous school community where diversity is the norm. This concern therefore informed the research design.

In common with Putnam (1996), Ager and Strang (2004) use the terms 'bonding', 'bridging' and 'linking' networks in their discussion of social connections, and these concepts have been adopted in this research. Smyth (2006) considered the perspectives of pupils in the GASSP units, and although this had not been the focus of that research, she unearthed a number of social capital building strategies used by both staff and pupils to enable integration of the pupils into the mainstream school. These strategies included enabling the pupils to use their home languages to negotiate meaning and utilising collaborative learning as a major pedagogic tool. Building on this earlier work, the aim of the research reported in this chapter was to investigate if and how teachers and pupils understand social capital, whether and what forms of social capital are consciously built by schools and if this affects pupils' networks outwith the school and their families.

The term 'social capital' is often used in policy, practice and indeed research without the user being explicit about its meaning. In considering the development of social capital in schools, it was important that, whether agreement is achieved or not, all participants made explicit their understanding of this concept. The researchers attempted to explain this understanding in the field to both young people and adults, and in some cases, this led teachers to further investigate the concept. The team drew on the work of Bourdieu (1986), Coleman (1994) and Putnam (1991) and the previous work of the AERS Schools and Social Capital Network (McGonigal et al, 2007) in evolving its understanding of social capital.

Bourdieu (1986, p 248) notes the connection between social capital and other capitals:

> The volume of the social capital possessed by a given agent [thus] depends on the size of the network of connections he can effectively mobilise and on the volume of capital (economic, cultural or symbolic) possessed in his own right by each of those to whom he is connected.

Putnam (1996, p 56) writes: 'by social capital I mean features of social life – networks, norms and trust – that enable participants to act together more effectively to pursue shared objectives'. Coleman (1994, p 98) defined social capital by its function:

> it is not a single entity, but a variety of different entities having characteristics in common: they all consist of some aspect of a social structure, and they facilitate certain actions of individuals who are within the structure.

In each of these cases, social capital is seen as located and acting within the relationships of human society. Social capital results from or is a feature of networks of social relations that are characterised by norms of trust and reciprocity but also by the realisation of these norms. Social capital does not inhere within a single individual but can only exist within a pattern of relationships. As noted above, Putnam (1996) described three forms of social capital as bonding, bridging and linking. As was outlined in Chapter One, bonding social capital exists in the connections between individuals with similar characteristics and has value in the promotion of solidarity between people sharing values. Bridging social capital occurs when people from different groups come together, while linking social capital exists in the connections between individuals who have different amounts of power and is often associated with a move into a new social context. Discussion of social capital has often been conducted in terms of the benefits to society, with its existence viewed as a prerequisite for sustaining civil society by enhancing the capacity to deal with challenges and problems, and as an important resource in supporting collective action. It is also implicit in this conceptualisation that the possession of social capital, especially bridging social capital, benefits the possessor.

Previous studies of social capital among young people have been concerned with what is brought to school by young people and this has been measured by means of a narrow range of indicators, such as family structure, parent–child discussion, or interaction with adults outside the family (Furstenberg and Hughes, 1995; Yan, 1999). These studies ignore the potential of schools themselves as sites for the production of social capital among learners, and neglect the active role that learners play in forming their own social capital. Additionally, they ignore opportunities to form social capital and to learn beyond the school.

As was indicated in the introduction to this chapter, writers on refugee integration, and specifically on successful integration of refugee children in schools, often refer, either implicitly or explicitly, to the need to consider the development of networks and friendships, so it is particularly relevant to consider social capital development for such pupils. In an increasingly performative school context however, it is also relevant to consider whether teachers are able to focus on the development of social capital in the face of examination and assessment processes. This tension is one possible reason for the different findings we report in the primary and secondary school settings.

Approach to the research

Exploring social capital in the school context through observation is a challenging activity and requires considerable reflexivity and respondent validation on the part of researchers. This is necessary to ensure accurate interpretation and to consider how far the possible indicators for social capital such as trust, reciprocity and bonding do in fact represent social capital which can be, to use Bourdieu's economic metaphor, 'cashed in' for goods. In the case of school pupils, these goods would include acceptance, integration and success in the school system.

The research set out to investigate the following questions:

- Does the school intentionally operate to develop social capital among its pupils from refugee families?
- What forms of social capital are developed by the school?
- Is the social capital transferable and sustainable?
- Do other capitals operate and interact with social capital development?

The team was very keen for pupil voice to be a major part in the data collected. The case study was focused on two schools with a small number of pupils in each school directly involved so qualitative methodology was most appropriate in this situation. Information gathered included analysis of policy documents; interviews and conversations with school staff and pupils; fieldwork in each school, observing teaching, learning and social situations; and photographic evidence collected by pupils themselves. Digital cameras were used in an attempt to give the children power over what they showed the researchers, because this technology allows young people to delete images that they reject. Photography also increased the possibility for children with limited English to have a voice in the research. Observations, field notes and photographs formed the basis for subsequent interviews.

In the primary school, twelve pupils from the final two years were chosen to be involved. All of them were from refugee families and all were fluent in the social use of English. The pupils came from a range of linguistic, cultural and religious backgrounds. The headteacher controlled the selection of pupils to whom the researchers had access and it was unclear if this selection involved discussion with the class teachers or pupils. The two researchers met the pupils as a group and discussed with them the purposes of the research, ensured that parental and their own consent forms were completed, explained the methodology to them and gave practical instructions on the use of the cameras. The pupils were asked to take photographs of areas, items or events within the school and its immediate environment which seemed to them to be important, interesting or significant. The photos were used as a stimulus for individual discussions with the pupils. These were recorded and transcribed and opened up the researchers' insights into the development of social capital among the children. Four periods of observation were conducted in each of the classes involved and field notes were used to initiate a discussion with the teacher about what had been observed and the means by which social capital was developed, consciously or otherwise. Observations were also conducted in the dinner hall and the playground and key points arising were discussed with the principal teacher with day to day responsibility for managing the project in the school. The headteacher, deputy headteacher and principal teacher were interviewed and the transcripts supplied to them for final consideration. Focus group discussions with children in primary 7 allowed more uninhibited discussion than individual interviews. The school agreed to follow up the focus group using tapes to allow pupils to express individual views. This enabled triangulation to take account of peer pressure and cognitive, linguistic and affective skills (Scott, 2000) but was perhaps limited by being mediated by a teacher rather than a researcher.

In the secondary school, the researcher made nine visits and conducted fieldwork in two mainstream classes and in the GASSP Unit. In the GASSP Unit the participants were approached one by one, and the project was explained with the help of the unit's English as an Additional Language (EAL) teacher or their peers. Access to both the mainstream classes and the GASSP Unit was negotiated with the support of the EAL teacher as gatekeeper. In the mainstream classes, the researcher introduced herself and explained the research to the whole class, with the support of the subject teacher. Further, a lunchtime photo club was established by one of the teachers. Not all of the pupils gave consent to use their pictures for the research. Using photography allowed access to parts of children's lives which would not otherwise have been possible within the frame of this study. Some of these pictures permitted an in-depth view of the space the children inhabit and their relationships in this space. Thirty-nine pupils were involved in the photo club, ten of whom were refugees. The main instrument in the secondary school was participant observation. This resulted in field notes and a series of informal interviews or conversations, most of which were noted during or immediately after the conversation. Within the photo club, the researcher established eight topics around which the children took pictures, although time permitted only two of these topics, spaces and objects of significance to be covered. In subsequent interviews, the children explained why they had taken these pictures, which gave insight into the networks and the quality of their relationships.

Discussion

This section discusses the findings of the research and also the research process, itself an opportunity to develop social capital among the research team. The overall aim of this research was to investigate how teachers and pupils understand social capital and how they can use these concepts to ensure valuable opportunities in school for children from refugee families. Some teachers in both schools had clear aims to help these pupils build social networks. While not often using the term 'social capital', they employed a range of practices which built bonding and bridging social capital. In exploring the associated concepts with pupils, researchers found an understanding of the importance of friendship and trust, and of cultural capital.

Schools were successful in developing bonding and bridging social capital among the pupils from refugee families and other pupils in the school. There is some evidence of differential access to social capital among participants in that primary school pupils had more consistent opportunities to develop and contribute to social capital than their secondary peers.

Within the primary school, this development of bonding and bridging social capital was effected through consistent, clear statements of the school's values of inclusion and multiculturalism: posters, displays of pupil work, assemblies and a range of consistent rewards; pupil–teacher verbal exchanges further illustrated these values. These values informed the norms to which pupils and staff adhered in the public areas of the school and in the classrooms observed. Within the secondary school, there were fewer clear public statements of values and the norms that operated in different areas of the school were not always consistent.

Practice at school level in the primary school (including buddies, lunch monitors and supported play at breaks) and pedagogy within the classroom operationalised these values and norms. Within this, each primary school class could be considered as a well-established community with its own explicit set of shared values and norms, reflected in pedagogy, in notices, posters and oral statements within the classroom, and in the relationship between teacher and children; in the observed classes, both mainstream and GASSP unit, these were consistent with whole-school values and norms. Within the secondary school structures, the composition of each class varied from subject to subject, which may have made the establishment of such a class ethos more difficult. Previous buddying projects in the secondary school had been abandoned.

While observation in the primary classes demonstrated that these values were explicit, it could be argued that this was easier in a context under the direct control of teaching staff. Although this control and explicit statements were less evident in the dinner hall and playground, pupils there demonstrated a culture of mutual responsibility, respect and care and of good order in which all seemed to participate. The contrast between young people's behaviour in the secondary school GASSP unit and in other classes within the school was clearer. It was thus evident that the expression of social capital was, at least to some extent, affected by the space, literal and metaphorical, within which children and young people were operating.

Acculturation and socialisation into the school were a strong focus within the GASSP units. This included explicit teaching about appropriate behaviour in the classroom and school and explicit life skills development. These units provided a close and intimate community where pupils were introduced to school values and norms, trust was established and close friendships flourished; the aim was to help the pupils to gain confidence to participate in and contribute to the wider school community.

It could be argued that school practice was designed (perhaps without reflection) to impose one set of norms and values on children from refugee families. This could lead to a perception that the development of bonding social capital (and possibly of bridging capital) was to address 'deficits' in the experience of refugee children; this would permit their participation in Scottish society but would not value diversity. However, within the schools, there was also explicit recognition of the value of the languages, cultures and faiths that these children and young people brought into the school. According to the age and emotional security of the pupils, events were organised such as religious festivals and celebrations, children's traditional games, music, and discussion of country of origin and asylum issues. These events and activities all enabled bridging social capital between the pupils to develop. There was evidence that children and young people maintained and valued their membership of cultural and faith communities outside the school. These communities provided further and different bonding social capital from that accessed within the school.

Within each school, it was evident that there were key people who facilitated access to social capital. In the primary school, senior staff provided leadership, which was willingly taken forward by a number of class teachers. There were indications of the role played by some members of support staff in developing social capital but these could not be fully investigated because of time constraints. Within the secondary school, staff employed to work specifically with the pupils from refugee families played a significant role in fostering networks but they did not have the same level of authority as key staff in the primary school and therefore had a less sustainable impact.

The extent to which staff in both schools explicitly attempted to develop linking social capital is not clear. With the exception of some individual work in the secondary school, there appeared to be little focus on the development of linking social capital that would enable networks and connections for the young people from refugee families with more powerful outside agencies. Senior staff in the primary school made positive attempts to develop links for parents with outside agencies, including those providing language classes, and offered advice on where to seek support.

There was some evidence that children's individual relationships which had been developed in school were maintained outside, but there is little evidence that this extended into bridging and linking across communities. It can be argued that skills development within the classroom contributes not only to bonding but also to bridging social capital. However, it is questionable whether this is sufficient or explicit enough to produce sustainable bridging social capital outwith the school. It was not possible to establish clear evidence about the transferability of social capital across transitions. These findings are discussed in more detail in Smyth et al (2010).

Researching social capital

As a research team, we considered that it would be appropriate and interesting to reflect individually as well as collectively on the research process and the opportunities it presented for collaboration and capacity building. The team had four core members who designed, managed, conducted and analysed the research. Additional peripheral membership, interest and inputs helped in shaping the research and building the collaborative knowledge. As the team members had not worked together before, the process itself involved the intentional building of bonding social capital between team members through collaborative discussion and research design. Norms, values and networks were an important feature throughout the research in terms of team collaboration, accessing and interpreting the research sites and responsibility of the researchers to reciprocate the trust given to us by the participants.

The processes of this research raise a number of issues worthy of discussion here:

- Scottish education is a small world. This may help to open doors but it has a possible disadvantage that teachers may have expectations about the dispositions of a researcher in their school, either through their awareness of her/his work or public views or through her/his association with a particular higher education institution. Further, this acquaintance may lead to an assumption on the part of adult participants that there are features of the school which do not require explanation, comment or reflection to a researcher, especially where those researchers are, or have been teachers.

- The resourcing of the project resulted in time constraints, which in turn affected the degree to which the pupils could be given ownership of the research and become more empowered researchers. In the primary school, the school assumed responsibility for contacting the children's parents to obtain consent, and as a result, the pupils' role could be interpreted as that of a captive audience, subjects of research who may find it difficult to refuse (Woodhead and Faulkner, 2000). Morrow (2005) has referred to this process as 'informed dissent' (p 36).

- The use of photographs taken by children was a new approach for the researchers and this raised a number of questions related to the primary pupils' ownership of the research. The most immediate was the need for equipment to be reliable and failsafe. More fundamentally, it was possible that the means by which children accessed the equipment (from an adult in the primary school) could have reduced their control and inhibited their responsibility. Even if they had free physical access, it may be that their freedom to record was constrained, implicitly rather than explicitly, by the ethos of classrooms and of the school. In the secondary school, the children were given control of the cameras for a week and almost half of the children brought in cameras from home to participate in the project. As a research instrument, the taking of pictures by the participants seems very powerful, particularly in combination with follow-up interviews about the pictures, which revealed meanings ascribed to the objects depicted, to which the researchers would not have had access without the input of the research participants.

- The fact that the research process was carried out in the domain of the school could have resulted in accentuating the pupils' vulnerability (Mayall, 2000). The individual interviews, particularly in the case of the more introverted primary pupils, may have inhibited free expression, whereas the primary school focus group appeared to allow a more relaxed and critical discussion about life at school.

However the researchers were aware of the potential risk of harming pupil–teacher relationships by the use of focus groups.

- The explicit focus on children from refugee families raises an important question in the context of research committed to inclusive principles. How does one ensure that a focus on such an identifiable group, and a public focus at that, does not, in the short term, put the participants under pressure and, in the longer term, encourage a group labelling, with the potential negative outcomes that are well attested (Malkki, 1992; Zetter, 1998; Turton, 2003)? Undertaking participant observation in the mainstream classrooms in addition to the GASSP Unit in the secondary school helped to ensure there was no labelling of the refugee children but made it much more difficult to follow them into mainstream classrooms. Both schools were keen to avoid this labelling, in the research and in their everyday practice.

- This research was stimulated by earlier work of the Principal Investigator, who had conducted research with refugee pupils in one primary school and found it difficult not to have a hands on research role in the current project. Her assumptions as to the success of the research were challenged by the very different nature of access to these locations and pupils.

- One result of engaging in minimally funded research was the competing demands on peoples' time, which led to difficulties in collaborative analysis.

- Collaboration in a team was very valuable both in helping to reflect on the events of the fieldwork and providing emotional support. Undertaking ethnographic work situated the researchers in the middle of the tensions and drama of the research participants. These included differing interpretations between teachers and the school management on education policies, or tensions between different pupils. However the emotional nature of the research, and indeed teaching in such a situation, became most apparent when one of the pupils was taken into a detention centre with her family as the researcher came into the secondary school.

Reflections on social capital as a construct

There is a need to further investigate the relationships between pedagogy and the development of forms of social capital and the implications of this for an extended understanding of the curriculum now used in Scotland and in other countries. There is also the need for continued debate about whether social capital is in itself something worthy of schools' consideration. The assumption of policy makers, practitioners and researchers often seems to be that the school or the education policy community needs to develop children's and young people's social capital. It may be helpful to consider also how schools can benefit from the social capital their pupils bring with them. Greater involvement of parents and families in learning could add value to vulnerable groups' social capital, rendering it more usable in schools than may currently be the case. This could also lead to greater transferability and durability of the social capital acquired in school.

The relationship between formal (often explicit) and informal (often implicit) practice merits further investigation if policy makers and teachers are to be effective in promoting social capital and in ensuring that children and young people develop their understanding of this and their ability to develop, share and use social capital. Possibly related to this is the view that social capital may not be transferable. When learners have developed their social capital within one community, schools need to consider how to build on this when the children are operating within another community. If social capital resides in reciprocal networks marked by trust and shared values, schools should explicitly seek ways to enable pupils to use their positive experiences of one such network to support or participate in another network. The means by which schools seek to build sustainable and transferable learning, in the context of pupils changing communities, would benefit from further enquiry.

Implications for policy, practice and research

The demography of Scotland is becoming increasingly diverse as a result of global political and economic change and there is a need for educational and social policy development to reflect this. This case study points to the need for more thoughtful and purposeful transition between education sectors to ensure continuity of support for young people from refugee backgrounds. Currently, there does not seem to be sustainability built in to the support provided, with much being dependent on individual teachers. Policy for the education of refugee pupils must have at its heart overcoming the insecurity which these young people have faced through their experience of forced migration. Sharing of practice between sectors could be beneficial in achieving this goal. The policy also needs to consider two-way integration, that is, not only the integration of refugee pupils into the Scottish education system, but also the adaptation of the system to the new reality of ethnic, cultural and linguistic diversity.

There is much good practice in schools, with teachers showing genuine concern for the welfare of their pupils from a refugee background, but teachers are perhaps not so well equipped to deal with the trauma resulting from pupils being removed or detained due to British immigration policy. While work is being done in schools to foster bonding and bridging social capital between pupils, more could be considered in terms of practices to foster bridging capital between the communities and linking capital with more powerful agencies.

There are questions about the possible impact on the research of the degree to which the gate-keeping role of the senior staff facilitated or restricted the researchers' access. Evidence suggests that the smaller primary school with a simpler internal structure not only facilitated a more consistent approach to developing social capital but was also more open to the researchers. However, this feature may at the same time have made it easier for the headteacher to 'manage' the research. The headteacher identified the classes to which the researchers had access and in so doing he made it explicit that he had selected teachers who would illustrate 'good practice' and who would also be likely to use the experience as a form of staff development. In the secondary school, changes in senior staff led to other staff postponing decisions on access and to changes in arrangements.

The methodology adopted was more successful in obtaining teachers' views than children's views. Although the views of the staff not involved in the research are not known, the methods appeared to allow expression of views by confident adult participants without inhibition. This was less clearly the case for children and young people. Given the complexity of determining the presence of social capital, there is a need to develop more effective means of obtaining the views of young people.

The relationship between school and community social capital also requires investigation. Time and access limitations prevented the research from investigating community social capital in the two settings and the possible impact of factors such as whether the communities had existed for generations or were transient. It was not possible to seek verifiable data about the opportunities for young people to take or use social capital developed in school into their wider communities as the research was school bound. Some community outreach projects were initiated by the GASPP Unit in the secondary school but the transferability of school-based social capital to these projects was not observed during the research period. The refugee population is mobile, with families changing residence when they are granted Leave to Remain, other families being detained or deported, and some families going into hiding for fear of deportation or detention. The local housing authorities also regularly exercise the option to rehouse refugee families, with little warning and without negotiation. We were unable in this research to investigate the effects of this mobility on the sustainability of any social capital practices.

It was not possible to make any connections between social capital and pupil achievement, although data did suggest that it affected pupil motivation to learn. This is an important issue, given the claims made for the impact of social capital on achievement. There is a related need for policy, practice and research to address explicitly the fundamental tension within the concept of social capital between its collective value to the local community (or indeed communities) and its value to the individual. School policy and practice has in general focused on the individual pupil and her or his achievement, which contrasts with the community values of some approaches to social capital.

In addition, policy, practice and research must consider how social capital can be developed and used both to recognise and celebrate diversity and to open up access to local economic and educational structures. There is a risk of reproducing one set of values and norms and indeed of reproducing inequality. Related to this is the need to consider what forms of social capital will be consistent with an education system which seeks to empower individuals and communities rather than to reproduce the structures of existing society.

We give the final words of this chapter to two 13-year-old Scottish-born ethnic majority pupils from the case study secondary school. The conversation reflects Lewis's findings (2006) regarding the important role of the school in fostering the development of trust and shared values between ethnic groups. A girl is talking to the researcher about a refugee pupil who has recently been taken into detention having arrived in Scotland via people trafficking ('the bad people') and a boy adds to the conversation on the emotional impact of his friend being removed. The children's awareness and empathy have been increased through the social networks created by the school:

> Girl: 'Jabaz did get here through the bad people. ... he is illegally here and now they are in this big prison cell ...'

> Boy: 'This is big c★★p. He was my pal. This is big c★★p man.'

References

Ager, A. and Strang, A. (2004) *Indicators of integration: final report*, London: Home Office.

Ager, A. and Strang, A. (2008) 'Understanding integration: a conceptual framework', *Journal of Refugee Studies*, vol 21, no 2, pp 166–91.

Bourdieu, P. (1986) 'The forms of capital', in: J. G. Richardson (ed) *Handbook of theory and research for the sociology of education*, New York: Greenwood Press, pp 241–58.

Candappa, M. with Ahmad, M., Balata, B., Dekhinet, R. and Gocmen, D. (2007) *Education and schooling for asylum seeking and refugee students in Scotland: an exploratory study*, London: Institute of Education, University of London.

Castles, S., Korac, M., Vasta, E. and Vertovec, S. (2002) *Integration: mapping the field*, London: Home Office.

Coleman, J. (1994) *Foundations of social theory*, Cambridge, MA: Belknap Press.

Department for Education and Skills (DfES) (2006) *The integration of refugee children: good practice in educational settings*, http://webarchive.nationalarchives.gov.uk/20090805000644/http://www.nrif.org.uk/Education/index.asp

Furstenberg F. and Hughes M. (1995) 'Social capital and successful development among at-risk youth', *Journal of Marriage and the Family*, vol 57, no 3, pp 580–92.

Lewis, M. (2006) *Warm welcome? Understanding public attitudes to asylum seekers in Scotland*, London: Institute for Public Policy Research.

Malkki, L. (1992) 'National geographic: the rooting of peoples and the territorialization of national identity among scholars and refugees', *Cultural Anthropology*, vol 7, pp 24–44.

Mayall, B (2000) 'Conversations with children: working with generational issues', in P. Christensen and A. James (eds) *Research with children: perspectives and practices*, London and New York: Falmer Press, pp 120–35.

McGonigal, J., Doherty, R., Allan, J., Mills, S., Catts, R., Redford, M., McDonald, A., Mott, J. and Buckley, C. (2007) 'Social capital, social inclusion and changing school contexts: a Scottish perspective', *British Journal of Educational Studies*, vol 55, no 1, pp 77–94.

Morrow, V. (2005) 'Ethical issues in collaborative research with children', in A. Farrel (ed) *Ethical research with children*, Maidenhead: Open University Press, pp 150–65.

Putnam, R. (1996) 'Who killed civic America?' *Prospect*, March, pp 66–72.

Rutter, J. (2006) *Refugee children in the UK*, Maidenhead: Open University Press.

Scott, J (2000) 'Children as respondents: the challenge for quantitative methods', in P. Christensen and A. James (eds) *Research with children: perspectives and practices*, London: Falmer Press, pp 98–119.

Smyth, G. (2006) 'Bilingual learners' perspectives on school and society in Scotland', in B. Jeffrey (ed) *Creative learning practices: European experiences*, London: Tufnell Press.

Smyth, G., MacBride, G., Paton, G. and Sheridan, N. (2010) 'Social capital and refugee children: does it help their integration and education in Scottish schools?' *Diskurs Kindheits- und Jugendforschung*, vol 2, pp 145–58.

Stead, J., Closs, A. and Arshad, R. (1999) *Refugee pupils in Scottish schools*, Spotlight Publication 74, vol 23, pp 40–6.

Turton, D. (2003) *Refugees, forced resettlers and 'other forced migrants': towards a unitary study of forced migration*, New Issues in Refugee Research, Working Paper no 94, Geneva: UNHCR.

Woodhead, M., Faulkner, D. (2000) 'Subjects, objects or participants? Dilemmas of psychological research with children', in P. Christensen and A. James (2000) *Research with children: perspectives and practices*, London and New York: Falmer Press, pp 9–35.

Yan, W. (1999) 'Successful African American students: the role of parental involvement', *Journal of Negro Education*, vol 68, no 1, pp 5–22.

Zetter, R. (1998) 'International perspectives on refugee assistance', in A. Ager (ed) *Refugees: perspectives on the experience of forced migration*, London: Continuum, pp 46–82.

FOUR

Social capital in the lives of young carers

Monica Barry

Introduction

Approximately three million children live in families affected by a chronic mental or physical health problem or disability in the UK. However, fewer than six per cent are officially recognised as young carers (Dearden and Becker, 2005).Young carers are often isolated, their caring roles leaving few opportunities for social and leisure activities, employment or friendship networks.The caring role can bring social isolation and mental health problems for young people (Dearden and Becker, 2005). Some rarely leave their homes except to go to school, and often young carers' school work is disrupted by their caring duties, leaving them disadvantaged in terms of educational outcomes. Some young carers are also vulnerable to being admitted to care if their family member is hospitalised or dies.

Becker (2000, p. 378) defines young carers as:

> Children and young persons under 18 who provide or intend to provide care, assistance or support to another family member. They carry out, often on a regular basis, significant or substantial caring tasks and assume a level of responsibility which would usually be associated with an adult.

With many families being in receipt of benefits and unable to work because of illness or disability, and with the majority of young carers living in single parent families, they are more likely to be living in poverty, thus exacerbating their access to social and other forms of capital. Low confidence and low self-esteem are also common among this group, making the formation of relationships outside the family even more difficult.Young carers are by definition living with difficult home circumstances. Their parents or siblings may be suffering from long-term ill health, disabilities, drug or alcohol dependency or mental health problems.

Community care policies often assume that care for ill or disabled relatives can be provided by other family members irrespective of age, or by friends and neighbours; in other words, relying on social capital within the local community. While there is a wider debate about the role of the state in providing such a service, the issue for young carers in particular is that they have limited access to social capital by dint of their age and status. They may take on an unprecedented amount of responsibility in childhood for the welfare of vulnerable adults within the family, which in itself may give them a degree of bonded social capital within the family. However, this is usually at the expense of access to bridging social capital within schools and the wider community. Two young carers (Henry and Morton, 2005) explained their role as being one of decision maker, cook, housekeeper and negotiator of services, and in so doing, they often had to conceal difficult and covert home circumstances from teachers or friends.

In 2007, a pilot study of young carers' perceptions of their families and wider networks was undertaken with the aim of developing a greater understanding of how those working with young carers could better identify their social and support needs and preferences (Barry, 2011). A particular emphasis was on social capital, both in school and in the community, and on theoretical and empirical aspects of social capital for young people more generally. Likewise, it was hoped that this research would better inform teachers and social care workers about how to promote social capital among young carers who might not feel able to make full use of the educational and social supports available within their local communities because of their caring commitments.

The research thus sought to answer the following research questions:

- To what extent do different forms of social capital impact on current and future opportunities for young carers?
- To what extent can various agencies and significant others (including teachers, young carers' projects and friends) help young carers to identify and build on the types of social capital they identify as important to them?

Methods

Four young carers' projects in Central Scotland provided a sample of 20 young carers, 10 male and 10 female, in the age range 12–23. In most cases, the researchers visited the projects and spoke to a group of young carers about the research. Those who were interested were given the opportunity to meet at the young carers' project for an interview before, during or after a group session, so as to make it more convenient and reassuring for them. One could argue that the researchers accumulated valuable bridging or even linking social capital from those discussions, in that the young people were able to inform the researchers about caring from a young carer's perspective.

Although the majority of young carers tend to be female (Dearden and Becker, 2005), it was seen as important to sample an equal proportion of young male carers, who might have less access than their female counterparts to social capital in childhood and youth (Barry, 2006). One-to-one semi-structured interviews were conducted with the 20 young carers who gave their consent to participate in the research. Given the sensitivity of the research questions, one-to-one interviews were deemed more appropriate than focus group discussions, especially in a pilot project of this size, and were felt to elicit more exploratory data than, for example, self-administered questionnaires. The initial proposal for the study was developed by Michael Gallagher and the fieldwork undertaken by the author and Maria Paredes during a six month period.

The concept of social capital is inherently difficult to define in academic circles, let alone among children and young people. However, the researchers attempted to explore with young carers issues relating to friendships, supportive relationships, and family and wider networks and to consider the 'dark side' of social capital (Field, 2003, p. 19) as well as its benefits. The fieldwork involved interviewing young carers about various aspects of social capital, including: their caring roles and their views and experiences of trust, networks, responsibilities and supports, not only within their families but also within the school, within social care organisations, among their peers and within the wider community. The discussions also covered young carers' past achievements, their future needs, aspirations, and expectations and the impact of their caring role on their actual and perceived need for such networks and support.

The types of illnesses or disabilities experienced by those cared for by the young people included mental or physical disabilities, mental health problems, alcoholism and physical illnesses. The types of caring role that they took on included looking after siblings (whether or not these siblings were the family members for whom they cared), shopping, doing housework, cooking, attending to medication or physical care tasks and offering emotional support. Sixteen respondents suggested that they cared for their mothers, fathers or both parents while the remaining four cared for one or more of their siblings. Often these young people cared for two or more family members with illnesses, disabilities or other problems, and on occasion, their caring role extended beyond the family home to friends, other peers and other relatives living elsewhere. This resulted in them often taking on multiple roles and tasks of a practical, medical or emotional nature with different individuals in different settings.

One young person described caring as "normally just a reaction ... an instinct" (15-year-old male) and another said: "It doesn't really feel like a chore, because rather than feeling I have to do it, I feel I want to do it" (16-year-old male). Several suggested that they had spent most of their young lives caring for a member of the family, with one saying that she had cared for her mother, and been at a young carers' project, since the age of 4, outlasting several of the project staff. These young people had taken on a range of responsibilities from an early age, and felt more protective of their families and more mature within themselves as a result, as one young man commented: "I'm 20 but I'm only 12." Several respondents mentioned not only the tensions arising from taking on a caring role within often tightly knit family circles, but also the tensions arising from being an adolescent growing up in a family affected by illness or disability.

The concept of social capital for young carers

The term 'social capital' combines rational action with social structure, including obligations, trust, expectations, norms and information-sharing (Coleman, 1988). Unlike Coleman, Putnam (2000) focuses more on civic community networks, a sense of belonging within a community, norms of reciprocity and trust, as well as positive attitudes towards, and engagement in, voluntary, state and personal networks. He also identifies two sub-categories of social capital: bonding social capital (exclusive and inward-looking group identities) and bridging social capital (inclusive and outward-looking group identities) which he describes thus: 'Bonding social capital constitutes a kind of sociological superglue, whereas bridging social capital provides a sociological WD-40' (Putnam, 2000, p. 23).

Putnam's concept of social capital is seen by many commentators as inappropriate to the experiences of young people, not least because they tend to be excluded from civic participation (Raffo and Reeves, 2000; Morrow, 2001) and develop their own individualised social networks. Morrow (2001, p. 55) also argues that Putnam's concept is 'a woolly, catch-all category' and ignores the historical and economic context, is gender blind, is culturally specific to the USA only and tends to ignore individual agency in generating one's own social capital. Despite these reservations, she suggests that young people from more disadvantaged communities tend to draw on bonding rather than bridging social capital and as a result can only get by rather than get on. Webster et al (2004, p. 30) comment on the adversarial nature of some sources of bonding social capital, notably in relation to young people, which can 'exclude, marginalise, constrain and entrap' them, and MacDonald and Marsh (2005, p. 203), like Morrow, suggest that there is a 'paradox of networks', where poorer areas can lack bridging social capital but are nevertheless a major source of support and legitimate opportunities for young people.

The French sociologist, Pierre Bourdieu, attempts to bridge the gap in social theory between agency and structure, without losing the 'major contribution of the structuralist legacy to social science' (May, 1996, p. 125). Bourdieu suggested that individual and collective constructions of the social world are not developed in a vacuum but are reproduced by, and in turn reproduce, social structures and are thus subjected to structural constraints. There is a constant interplay between structural constraints and individual choice, and the importance of time, space, agency and the individual's capacity to change are all implicated in the construction and reconstruction of the social world (Bourdieu, 1990). He stresses personal networks and power relationships and focuses as much on agency and sociability as on structure and institutionalisation. He argues that individuals accrue capital – social, cultural, economic and symbolic – through their social practice, starting with social capital, which he describes as:

> the aggregate of the actual or potential resources which are linked to possession of a durable network of more or less institutionalized relationships of mutual acquaintance and recognition – or in other words, to membership in a group – which provides each of its members with the backing of the collectively-owned capital, a 'credential' which entitles them to credit. (Bourdieu, 1986, p. 51)

In other words, social capital consists of valued relations with significant others and is generated through relationships which in turn bring access to resources from networks and group membership. To Bourdieu (1986), social capital includes not only social networks but also 'sociability' – 'a continuous series of exchanges in which recognition is endlessly affirmed'. His focus on 'sociability' seems to suggest that social capital theory is less relevant to young people and their families in that he sees familial ties as producing more cultural than social capital; he argues that social capital comes more from wider social relationships. Equally, Bourdieu's approach to social capital is somewhat utilitarian in nature and does not allow for reciprocity or the 'giving back' to others of social capital that one has already accrued.

Young carers in particular may have a natural proclivity to give more than they receive but equally value reciprocal relationships with others, notably their friends, through trust, loyalty, keeping secrets and being mutually supportive. However, social capital can be constrained by the strong bonds developed within families marred by illness, marginalisation and death; by the negative perceptions that many young carers have of 'supportive' professionals such as teachers or social workers; and by their resultant recourse to self-sufficiency and responsibility taking. Young carers represented in this study may take on more family responsibilities than most young people in childhood and may have to cope with often adverse reactions from peers, professionals and the public not only as a result of their family circumstances but also because of their status as 'young people'.

Nevertheless, like many young people, they demonstrate a high degree of resilience and build coping mechanisms to protect themselves, their families and their close friendships during this period of transition. Transitions for them may be familial (from two-parent to one-parent families) or from diagnosed illness/disability to stability, recovery or even death; educational (from primary to secondary school); developmental (from adults caring for them to them caring for adults); and/or social (from familial dependence to wider friendship networks). These transitions can be fragmented and disrupted, and yet they are rarely supported by the external world but negotiated primarily by the young people themselves, bolstered by the support and encouragement they draw from their accrued close friendships, family cohesiveness, however tenuous, and the young carers' projects.

The significance of others for young carers

Young people were asked about the people who were significant to them – whether positively or negatively – in their daily lives. These people mainly comprised family members (both living and deceased) and peers. The number of significant others identified ranged from four to 19 and all but one respondent identified family members, including parents or step parents, grandparents, siblings, cousins, aunts and uncles.

In addition, all identified friends/peers, teachers and young carers' project workers. However, the most commonly cited people were friends/peers and family. Cree (2002) found that young carers tended to share their problems mostly with their friends, with their mothers, and with young carers' project staff, and these categories of significant people in their lives are explored further below.

Friends/peers

The significance of peers in the transition to adulthood is evident, with Coleman (1990) suggesting that friends take on a greater significance in adolescence than the family, and that many young people worried about upsetting or endangering those often tenuous but positive friendship ties. Friends featured large in the lives and loyalties of these young people and they tended to choose their friends because of common interests, common experiences (such as being a young carer) or feeling that they could trust and confide in certain of their peers rather than others. 'Having a laugh' was a significant factor in the common bond between friends, and although some felt that moving away from an area or a school might lessen the bond between them, others felt that the friendship was strong enough to cope with distance. One young man felt that one friendship had remained strong even though they lived further away from each other, and that leaving school would not create a barrier to continuing to meet: 'we've already bridged that gap.'

The constraints on young people's social and geographical mobility has been highlighted by a study of territoriality in the UK (Kintrea et al, 2008), where it was found that this can lead to isolation, fear and violence for those innocently caught up in such practices, while for the perpetrators, territoriality created a 'darker side' of social capital through group affiliations, solidarity and identity. One young person suggested that she could not visit a certain friend because her parents felt that the neighbourhood in which that friend lived was unsafe. Several other respondents mentioned peers whom they either disliked or wanted to avoid, because of a fear of violence, harassment and bullying.

The vast majority of respondents spoke highly of their friends as having a positive impact on them. Many said that friends helped them to take their mind off the caring role or the family situation and they were often torn between their home commitments and their desire to be out with friends. Often they needed to juggle their responsibilities at home with the time available to see friends and this could result in emotional tension and feelings of guilt. This often meant that going to school provided an ideal opportunity to meet friends during the day. Although many were close to their families, they never seemed to tire of being with friends, as one respondent commented: "you'd think if you spent that much time with someone, you'd hate them" (15-year-old male).

While their friends were often supportive of their role as a young carer, knew the family situation or were confided in about their friend's caring role, some respondents felt uneasy about inviting friends into the family home because of embarrassment or wishing to protect the feelings of other family members. Two young carers whose mothers suffered from alcoholism commented about their friends: "I wouldn't want [them] to see my mum" (16-year-old female), and "[they] never came up when she was ill … I'm quite happy to invite them up now [that she's better]" (12-year-old male).

There seemed to be no difference between male and female respondents about their attitude to friends, although the young women mentioned the emotional bond of friends more than the young men, whereas the young men cited leisure pursuits with friends as being an important bonding mechanism.

Family

Eleven of the twenty respondents stated that their parents had separated or divorced, but that they still kept in touch with the other party living elsewhere. There tended to be a lot of movement between family members living in different locations, for example, where parents were separated or where grandparents or siblings lived elsewhere, albeit usually locally. Fifteen of the twenty respondents (ten young men and five young women) mentioned that they were particularly close to their mothers, including one who had died, and nine (six young men and three young women) suggested that they were particularly close to their fathers, again including one who had died, although six people did not mention their fathers. One respondent felt that he was close to his stepfather, but another – a 12-year-old young man – stated that his stepfather treated his mother "like a piece of rubbish … He's got no right talking to my mum like that."

However onerous the caring task may seem to these young people and however worrying in terms of what the future might hold for that family, being a young carer was seen as a definite bonding mechanism between the young person and his/her family. None of the respondents seemed to resent the role that they had as a young carer, although it may at times have caused arguments or tension within the household. While five respondents were only children, others spoke affectionately about their siblings, and despite some arguments, they tended to confide in and support them, whether they lived with them or not. Grandmothers were also spoken of highly.

Three respondents mentioned having experienced the death of a close family member within the last five years. It may well be that there were more young people who had experienced the death of a relative or friend, but those who mentioned it at interview suggested that it had affected them greatly. One young man whose aunt had recently died described her as "more of the woman figure in my life" (14-year-old male) and one young woman's mother, for whom she had been caring prior to her death some years ago, was described as: "my best friend, my sister, my mother, all in one ... my mum was my life" (22-year-old female). Two further respondents mentioned that a parent or other family member would, in the foreseeable future, die as a result of their illness, and one feared that her parents might again attempt suicide as a result of their ill health. Some respondents seemed torn between their caring role at home and their desire to keep in touch with other family members living elsewhere. In one case, where a young man's estranged father was seriously ill, he felt guilty about going to see his father when he should have been caring for his disabled mother.

Teachers

School was not only seen as a place of education but as serving a primary function as a meeting place for friends. However, whether the school setting is of greater importance in this function for young carers (who may not be able to leave the family home during evenings and weekends because of their caring role) than for young people in general is beyond the scope of this research. School was also seen (perhaps fortuitously) as a centre of education and learning, as one young man surmised: "If it wasn't for school, we wouldn't have an education" (14-year-old male). However, overall the comments about schooling and teachers per se were more negative than positive, with eight respondents citing negative facets of school, nine citing positive factors and three expressing mixed views. The main criticisms were levelled at the attitude of teachers rather than the quality of education. For example, several found it difficult to justify the aggressive or authoritarian approach of some teachers, as the following quotation illustrates:

'They think they can do whatever they want. They think they can shout at you and give you more work, but I just

> can't take it ... There was one teacher that was really getting
> on my nerves and I just shouted at her. But she chucked
> me out of the class, so I never got a chance to shout at her
> properly.' (16-year-old female)

Some young people felt that teachers were not supportive enough of
pupils who were behind or struggling with the workload and a few
respondents suggested that teachers could do more to encourage pupils
to enjoy being at school:

> 'I never hated anything more in my life ... I hated it, it was
> horrible ... It's just, if they give you the right help and they
> make it interesting, then you'll pass and you'll do well, but if
> you're bored with it and they just shout at you or whatever,
> you're just going to be like, whatever.' (15-year-old female)

Of the young people who enjoyed school, most suggested that it was
certain teachers or the ambience of a particular school that helped them.
One young woman who resented moving to a third high school by
the time she was in the fourth year (because of family ill health) was
now feeling more positive about school: "I actually do enjoy school,
it's quite scary!" (16-year-old female) and she had decided to stay on
until the sixth year. This change of attitude came about partly because
of the friends she had made at her most recent school, but also because
she felt her school work was improving following the further help she
had requested from her new teachers.

   School bullying is a concern for pupils, teachers and policy makers
alike and seven respondents said that they had been bullied themselves
in primary or secondary school. Most of the others had indirect
experience of it and could comment on the issues involved. Bullying
was said to result from various factors: being overweight, being a
carer or having a disabled sibling, coming from a minority ethnic
background, having attention deficit hyperactivity disorder (ADHD)
or just being outwith the friendship circle of the bullies. One young
woman suggested that girls rather than boys were more prone to
bully others, because "girls hold grudges". Six young people said that
teachers did not respond constructively to reports of bullying and
told those experiencing such harassment to either fight back or take
evasive action. While one respondent asked to be moved to another
school because of bullying, another did not want to move because of
having established friends in the current school. One young woman
who had been suicidal as a result of such bullying felt that the school's

response was "diabolica", noting that violence had to be "seen" before the school would take action against bullies.

The role of school for young carers can be an ambivalent one: partly it can be a safe haven away from the worries of the caring role, but also some respondents suggested that they wanted to keep school separate from their caring role, almost so as not to 'contaminate' that safe haven. One young man explained it as: "my personal life is not in school. In school is school"(12-year-old male). Several respondents also suggested that they purposefully did not want the school to know they were young carers either because they might get preferential treatment, which they did not want, or because they might be treated more harshly, and the following quotations illustrate this dichotomy:

> 'My guidance teacher, he knows a lot about my situation which other teachers wouldn't, so when I've no time to do homework or whatever, he'd be able to sympathise with me and make some sort of agreement with me, whereas other teachers just say "oh, no, you're just at it now" sort of thing.' (14-year-old male)

> 'I'd rather them not know [I'm a carer] ... If I was late and there was a reason I was late, then I can't just sit there and go "it was because of this," because they're not going to believe me ... [or] they might treat me different, and I don't want them to ... they might give sympathy and I don't want it. I just want to be the same as everyone else.' (16-year-old female)

Some respondents singled out specific teachers who knew their situation and were supportive, understanding and would give an extension for homework if there was a change in the circumstances at home that prevented the young person from doing school work. Nevertheless, some teachers were either not adept at understanding, or perhaps were not given the discretion to accommodate the needs of young carers, as the following quotations suggest:

> 'There's a wee bit more understanding [at school] about young carers but there is still room for improvement. School was brilliant *when* my mum died. They understood everything ... "oh, your mum's died, oh we can do this, we can do that, and we can do the next thing for you." Eh? What happened *before* my mum died? ... I think it's more

sort of black and white when there's a death.' (22-year-old female)

'With teachers, you're always conscious if you say something, it'll get blown out of proportion or they'll go and phone your mum or something ... teachers try too hard to relate to pupils instead of relating to pupils' problems ... they're trying to be like us rather than understand us.' (15-year-old female)

This latter quotation highlights the dilemma perhaps for teachers as being 'mentors' and yet also 'agents of the state' in terms of child protection, education and discipline. These young carers were probably more wary of confiding in teachers about their problems, because they felt that teachers could not be trusted in the same way as a friend could, or alternatively that their request for help might be taken out of their hands and dealt with by adults without consulting them first or obtaining consent: being 'listened to' (in a consensus building way) is not something that young people generally feel happens in their dealings with adults (see, for example, Franklin, 2002).

Other professionals

Few young people mentioned other professionals in their lives or those of their families, but it could not be ascertained whether this was because they themselves were unaware of other agencies' involvement with the person(s) being cared for or whether other agencies were not involved because the family was seemingly coping on its own. The stigma associated with disability or mental illness, for example, is always prevalent in the minds not only of young carers but also often of their families, and each seeks to protect the other from resultant discrimination and embarrassment. Banks et al (2002) noted that some young carers and their parents are reluctant to engage with formal services because of such stigma and intrusiveness and also because of fears about the response of services to their requests/needs.

Two types of professional support were mentioned by respondents. Support for the person being cared for specifically included, for example, a befriending service, medical or health professionals, or social work support. Professional support for the young carer specifically included counselling or learning support at school, a young carers' project, a psychologist, social work support or a job skills agency. The support offered to these families included respite care, help with shopping, counselling and health advice, but these young carers suggested that such help was minimal, either because services had been withdrawn because of funding or health and safety (of home care workers, for example), or because the agencies did not specialise in or necessarily understand certain diagnoses or needs.

Neighbours

Putnam (2000) suggests that the community in which one lives is a crucial source of social capital, and yet increasingly communities are being eroded by factors such as social mobility, employment constraints, housing policies and greater use of the internet. Equally, within the context of community care, neighbours could be seen as a crucial source of social and human capital, serving as a bridge between those who may be housebound and the wider community through shopping on their behalf, holding a spare set of house keys or offering practical support in the home when requested. Nevertheless, neighbours were often not mentioned by these young people as featuring significantly in their families' lives, and where they were mentioned, they did not seem to be viewed in a particularly positive light, either because they knew too much or enquired too much about the family. However, equally, one young man mentioned that "neighbours come and go" (23-year-old male), even though his own family had lived in the same house since his early childhood.

Young carers' projects

Because the sample had been accessed through young carers' projects, and all respondents were active members of such projects, it is understandable that they mentioned gaining a great deal of support and comfort from project involvement. This section therefore focuses on the views and experiences of these young people, notably about their involvement in the five young carers' projects in Scotland from which the total sample was drawn, and about their perceptions of the caring role.

Young carers' projects were seen as helping these young people, both in offering support of a practical or emotional kind to the young people and in dealing with other family members' issues as well as their own. The projects that these young people attended, albeit often only once a fortnight or once a month depending on project funding and staffing, were spoken highly of by all respondents. The reasons why they viewed these projects so positively were threefold, namely:

the sociability aspect of attending; feelings of 'respite' from the home situation; and the emotional support they received. These three factors are explored in greater detail below.

Sociability

Undertaking activities and going on outings with friends through the project was seen as one of the primary attractions of attendance at a young carers' project. Outings and activities are a common bond and vehicle to relieve boredom for young people with few alternative leisure opportunities, but perhaps more so for young carers who are depended on within the home on a regular basis: "I like it. It helps me get out and that … my mum worries when I go out … she knows when I come here, I'm safe and I'm with friends and that, so I like it" (14-year-old female).

These young carers often described their young carers' project as 'a laugh' and somewhere where they could meet new people as well as existing friends. They also spoke highly of the staff, who were 'there for you' when needed. While some young carers used the project for advocacy support, most just wanted the sociability that came from meeting other young people in similar situations to themselves and from participating in leisure and respite activities with them.

Feelings of respite

Not only was a young carers' project somewhere where young people could meet socially, enjoy new networks and activities and be offered emotional support, but it was also somewhere divorced from the family situation and the caring role, and this enabled these young people to get out of the house and into new and supportive surroundings, if only once a month. Many young people spoke of the 'respite' element of attendance, as the following quotations illustrate: "You come here to forget about it all really. It's just in the back of your mind, but you know if you did have to talk to someone, they would be happy to talk about it … they know the situation I'm going through" (16-year-old female) and "They always take us places and get us out of the road for a wee while, so it takes your mind off all the stuff at home" (14-year-old male).

There were mixed feelings among respondents about whether or not they wanted to use the project as a means of forgetting or confronting their caring role, with some saying they did not like to talk about caring at the project, but used it as a form of release, but with others suggesting that talking about it to staff or other young people was in itself a form of release.

Emotional support

The emotional support offered by the project was seen as an important aspect of attendance for many young carers, through talking about problems/issues with both staff and other young people and through being able to empathise with people in similar situations to themselves, something they could not easily do with friends in different family settings:

> [At the project] there are lots of people that are in the same situation as you. And friends at home, they don't understand that you have to go home and care for your mum and dad, because their mum and dad actually care for them. But here, many people are in the same situation so it's a lot easier to talk to people. (16-year-old female)

> When I was younger, it was a lot harder to explain to people why I couldn't do things and why I couldn't go out, because I was embarrassed to explain my situation … you kind of felt like there was nobody out there in the same situation as you. But when I came to young carers I realised that I wasn't alone. (15-year-old female)

As mentioned earlier, it is perhaps not surprising that these young people spoke so highly of the young carers' projects, since they had been referred to and actively wanted to attend such projects. Nevertheless, the strength of their commitment to and appreciation of the staff and fellow participants at these projects highlighted the importance of social capital in their young lives. There was a strong sense of self and social identity at young carers' projects which was perhaps aptly demonstrated in the young people's perceptions of themselves, as explored further below.

Perceptions of self

The young people at interview were asked how they would describe themselves or how their friends might describe them. Seven respondents described themselves in terms of the skills they had, for example being able to cook, sing, dance or play football. Others described themselves in terms of personality traits, being what could be summed up as self-sufficient (four respondents), confident (three respondents) and non-violent (two respondents). Other personality traits, mentioned by one respondent each, were popular, friendly, a joker, shy and too passionate: "My mum said I'm too passionate. When Rangers got kicked out of the last 16 of the European Champions League, I think I was the only person in the place crying!"(14-year-old male).

> 'It's quite hard for me, because I'm quite shy just now, but I'm more confident. It's just like in school situations ... it's hard to meet people you've known from a different area. But if I'm out and about skating and stuff, it's dead easy and you can just go and talk to them, because they don't know your history and they can't judge you or anything ... the fact that I was really, really shy.' (16-year-old female)

Yet other respondents described themselves in relation to other people, namely that they could give good advice (seven respondents), that they were protective of others (three respondents) and that they were trustworthy (two respondents). Part of this advice giving, protectiveness and trustworthiness came from their role as a carer, which may have become part of their persona, as one young woman explained:

> 'I'm that used to caring that I care for everybody ... probably if you had to take everybody away and just leave me, I would struggle 'cos I couldn't care for somebody else. Caring for myself is just a basic instinct, whereas caring for someone else is something that I know I can do, if that makes sense ... once you stop caring for them, you sort of need to find somebody else to care for.' (22-year-old female)

Whether the caring role that these young people took on heightened their sense of responsibility for others is beyond the scope of this research, but nevertheless, all these young people felt a strong sense of responsibility for others. Nine said that they felt responsible for one or both parents (to protect them from harm), eight for siblings (to offer a role model, activities, a feeling of being safe, or an education) and six for friends (to be there for them when needed).

When asked about what these young people would like to be doing in the future, the vast majority focused primarily on doing well at school, passing examinations and going to college or university. In terms of future professions, their main employment preferences were artistic/ creative, caring or health-related professions, teaching sports or other subjects, or joining the police or other professions. Some mentioned wanting to have their own house but realised that they might still be needed to take on a caring role within the family. Indeed, the caring role was seen as the most likely 'obstacle' to achieving their desired goals, because either they were the only carer or because of the seriousness of the illness/disability of their family member. The stronger the familial bond, the greater was the likelihood that this might restrict their opportunities in the future. Other obstacles to achieving their goals included having no money, current bullying at school, their lack of confidence in their capabilities or capacities, and having no links with the world of employment.

Social capital in the lives of young carers

The prevalence and relevance of social capital in the lives of these young people is evident from the research. These are discussed below under the following headings:

- bonding and bridging social capital
- the mobilisation of resources
- the durability of social capital in transition.

Bonding and bridging social capital

Holland et al (2007) argue that staying within the 'comfort zone' of the caring role and the family network is often a positive, not a constraining source of social capital for young people and that they positively choose to remain within that closed or narrow network. However, having said that, some of the young people that these authors interviewed suggested that bonding social capital was stifling and that they wanted more social mobility (getting on) than was available within the home environment (getting by). The young carers in this study often cited their caring role as a barrier to their future aspirations to make something of their lives, and equally tended to use school and friends as a welcome relief from the confines of their familial role.

These young carers seemed to move between two very strong, but totally separated bonding groups: the family and the friendship group. But friends were also a 'bridge' *away from* the family, assuming a bridge can be an escape route from one bonding group as well as a link to another bonding group. In other words, friends offered them an alternative lifestyle and respite from the caring role, which arguably could be called bridging social capital. However, because young carers may not want to bring friends home with them, and because parents may not interact with the activities of a young carers' project, there may be a reduced availability of bridging social capital for these young people. Family, friends and young carers' projects were all kept separate (whether by design or choice), and social capital was kept contained within, but not between, each of these three social circles.

The enclosure of each of their family, friendship and young carers' project groupings might make bridging more difficult, as might these young carers' perception of themselves as being self-sufficient in order to cope. They also had limited involvement with, or trust in, outsiders such as teachers, doctors and social workers, exacerbated perhaps by their desire to protect the family from outside interference or scrutiny.

The mobilisation of resources

Bassani (2007) argues that social capital theory is limited and under-theorised in respect of youth studies, partly perhaps because close-knit families do not generate much transferable social capital and young people cannot easily mobilise family resources to produce social capital themselves. There is a distinction between a 'resource' (for example, parents) and capital (the end product of that resource, for example, trust or security). A resource only becomes capital if it is mobilised through a combination of structural and functional social resources (Lin, 2001). Bassani (2007) suggests that only through the mobilisation of parental resources can young people create positive social capital. However, she tends to place the responsibility for mobilisation on to the young person, rather than suggesting that the parents themselves, or others, should mobilise their own resources for the benefit of young people, and she also stresses the importance of a healthy family relationship for mobilisation of parental resources to be effective. Nevertheless, it is arguable that the relationship needs to be more reciprocal and mutually proactive to produce social capital. Because families tend to be closed groups, they are often seen in the literature as curtailing or even preventing the building of wider social capital in outside groups.

Although not focusing on social capital, two studies of young carers in Scotland have uncovered the need for support for this group to enable them to make better choices and have greater access to opportunities as young adults. Cree (2002) interviewed 61 young carers in Scotland and found that the vast majority felt a need for greater support in their caring role as well as in their role as emerging adults. Likewise, Banks et al (2002) identified four key needs of young carers in Scotland:

information on medical conditions and services; individual support and counselling; practical help; and social contacts/activities.

While young people in this study seemed to offer to, and receive from, their peers certain resources which could result in social capital such as trust and confidences, they had mainly negative or dismissive views of 'outsiders', such as teachers or other professionals; this suggests that these adults either did not have the resources to mobilise on behalf of young carers or did not use those resources in the interests of young carers. Likewise, young people in the transition to adulthood may not wish to mobilise the resources of others as this may be seen to be a sign of weakness or dependence. Markers of adulthood for young people include accepting responsibility for themselves and others and becoming independent of adults. Sennett (2003) suggests that self-sufficiency gains one respect through not being seen to be a burden on others. However, he realises that self-sufficiency can go against the need to belong to a group through mutual ties of interdependence and sharing. In wanting to become adult and to gain respect, young carers may not fully grasp the importance or value of seeking help or acknowledging their limitations. They may therefore not identify with, or grasp, the significance of social capital in their own lives.

The durability of social capital in transition

Bourdieu suggests that capital has to be durable in order to be effective (Bourdieu, 1990; Bourdieu and Wacquant, 1992). However, durability is almost by definition *absent* in the transition to adulthood, where youth is a liminal phase and young people's resources are constantly changing and uncertain. This uncertainty (or lack of durability) for young carers is also evident in their concern about the health and future of the person they are caring for, making their own futures tenuous as well, and bereavement can also undermine any sense of permanence or sustainability that young carers may have had in the past. Likewise, friends tend to lack durability at that age and the transition from primary to secondary school does not help to sustain earlier-formed friendships. Holland et al (2007, p. 102) imply that one needs existing friends in order to make new friends, and that young people need existing friends who move to the same schools as them: 'having a stable base of bonds enabled many to bridge out to new friendships'. Although some of the young carers mentioned having friends in secondary school who had also been close to them in primary school, most gave the impression that affiliations changed over time or that the move to secondary school precluded their continuing relationships with former primary school friends. While many young carers seemed to have tenuous ties with friends at school or in the community, their friends in young carers' projects proved perhaps the most durable over time, irrespective of moves of school or home.

Conclusions

As mentioned above, social capital is inherently difficult to conceptualise, let alone to operationalise. Equally, social capital is difficult to accumulate, not only for young people but also for researchers who wish to access it for research purposes.

Without the help of the young carers' projects, the process of contacting these twenty young people would have been virtually impossible, not least given the sensitivity of the topic and their 'hidden' status as young carers. Although this particular study was limited to a small number of respondents, the narratives of these young carers have nevertheless thrown light on the issues and challenges faced in understanding social capital in relation to minority or vulnerable groups, such as young people taking on high levels of responsibility as carers of family members. These young people's social and spatial networks were restricted not only because of their age and status as children and young people but also because of their additional roles as carers of other family members. The role of young carers can exacerbate already limited networks for young people and limited access to geographical, leisure and civic spaces which may be more accessible for adults. Their social and spatial networks were predominantly confined to the home and the school environment, restricted by structural constraints on their choice of where and when to meet friends and when to be with their families.

Taking Bourdieu's four concepts of social, economic, cultural and symbolic capital together, there seems to be a tension for young carers as a vulnerable group in accruing and sustaining all forms of capital, not just social capital. Their desire for cultural capital (through academic qualifications) and eventual economic capital (through viable employment) is in direct competition with their desire to maintain the social and symbolic capital accrued within the family through the bond established in the caring role and the loyalty that results from such responsibility. Likewise, the social and symbolic capital accrued within the friendship group is in direct competition with that of the family, and loyalties are stretched between these two social and spatial networks.

The status of children and young people generally in the transition to adulthood restricts their access to durable friendship networks, as a result of the transience of youth and their rapid developmental changes. Young people tend to experiment with both adult and peer relationships at this time in their lives, and perhaps more often than adults need the feedback from others to develop their own sense of self and social identity. The challenges for social capital theory are in extricating these individual narratives about social networks from the structural constraints that envelop them, including their responsibilities as carers, their liminal status as young people in transition and the dichotomy for them of 'getting by' rather than 'getting on'.

Implications for policy, practice and research

There are three main implications for policy and practice which could improve young carers' access to social capital and the support that derives from that. First, relevant agencies – education authorities, social work departments and health boards – need to work more closely with young carers and their families to ensure that their needs are met and that they are encouraged, *with* other professionals, to build durable, positive and transferrable social capital for young people in transition. Secondly, young carers' projects need to be given the resources and time to engage meaningfully, regularly and over longer periods with young carers, and to fulfil their wishes for greater support in practical, emotional and educational terms. Finally, young carers themselves need to have the opportunity within confidential spaces to voice their concerns about their caring role, their family circumstances, their developmental needs and their futures.

The implications for research relate primarily to the current lack of understanding of the role of social capital within the general population, let alone in relation to young people. However, research also needs to find ways to operationalise the concept of social capital in respect of young people whose social and spatial networks are already limited by dint of the fact that they lack status, recognition and support in an otherwise adult-oriented society. Vulnerable or marginalised groups such as young carers have an even greater need for the recognition and support that social capital can offer, not least because the role they have assumed in the family is one which would, if undertaken by adults, be seen as valuable and responsible.

References

Banks, P., Gallagher, E., Hill, M. and Riddell, S. (2002) *Literature review of identification, needs assessment and service provision for young carers and their families*, Edinburgh: Scottish Executive Central Research Unit.

Barry, M. (2006) *Youth offending in transition: the search for social recognition*, Abingdon: Routledge.

Barry, M. (2011) '"I realised that I wasn't alone": young carers and social capital', *Journal of Youth Studies*, vol 14, no 5, pp 523–39.

Bassani, C. (2007) 'Five dimensions of social capital theory as they pertain to youth studies', *Journal of Youth Studies*, vol 10, no 1, pp 17–34.

Becker, S. (2000) 'Young carers', in M. Davies (ed.) *The Blackwell encyclopaedia of social work*, Oxford: Blackwell, pp 378 –9.

Bourdieu, P. (1986) 'The forms of capital', in A. H. Halsey, H. Lauder, P. Brown and A. Stuarts Wells (eds) (1997) *Education: culture, economy, society*, Oxford: Oxford University Press, pp 46–58.

Bourdieu, P. (1990) *In other words: essays towards a reflexive sociology* (trans. M. Adamson), Cambridge: Polity Press.

Bourdieu, P. and Wacquant, L. (1992) *An invitation to reflexive sociology*, Cambridge: Polity Press.

Coleman, J. (1988) 'Social capital in the creation of human capital', *American Journal of Sociology*, vol 94, S95–121.

Coleman, J. (1990) *Foundations of social theory*, Cambridge, MA: Harvard University Press.

Cree, V. (2002) *Under pressure: a study of mental health needs of young carers*, Edinburgh: Edinburgh Young Carers' project.

Dearden, C. and Becker, S. (2005) 'Growing up caring: young carers and vulnerability to social exclusion' in M. Barry (ed) *Youth policy and social inclusion: critical debates with young people*, Abingdon: Routledge, pp 251–66.

Field, J. (2003) *Social capital*, London: Routledge.

Franklin, B. (ed) (2002) *The new handbook of children's rights: comparative policy and practice*, London: Routledge.

Henry, J. and Morton, B. (2005) 'Postscript on young carers', in M. Barry (ed) *Youth policy and social inclusion: critical debates with young people*, Abingdon: Routledge, pp 26–9.

Holland, J., Reynolds, T. and Weller, S. (2007) 'Transitions, networks and communities: the significance of social capital in the lives of children and young people', *Journal of Youth Studies*, vol 10, no 1, pp 97–116.

Kintrea, K., Bannister, J., Pickering, J., Reid, M. and Suzuki, N. (2008) *Young people and territoriality in British cities*, York: Joseph Rowntree Foundation.

Lin, N. (2001) *Social capital: a theory of social structure and action*, Cambridge: Cambridge University Press.

MacDonald, R. and Marsh, J. (2005) *Disconnected youth? Growing up in Britain's poor neighbourhoods*, Basingstoke: Palgrave Macmillan.

May, T. (1996) *Situating social theory*, Buckingham: Open University Press.

Morrow, V. (2001) 'Young people's explanations and experiences of social exclusion: retrieving Bourdieu's concept of social capital', *International Journal of Sociology and Social Policy*, vol 21, no 4/5/6, pp 37–63.

Putnam, R.D. (2000) *Bowling alone: the collapse and revival of American community*, New York: Simon and Schuster.

Raffo, C. and Reeves, M. (2000) 'Youth transitions and social exclusion: developments in social capital theory', *Journal of Youth Studies*, vol 3, no 2, pp 147–66.

Sennett, R. (2003) *Respect: the formation of character in a world of inequality*, London: Allen Lane.

Webster, C., Simpson, D., MacDonald, R., Abbas, A., Cieslik, M., Shildrick, T. and Simpson, M. (2004) *Poor transitions: social exclusion and young adults*, Bristol: Policy Press.

FIVE

Youth club connections

Marion Allison and Ralph Catts

Introduction

The effects of social capital on the development of opportunities and aspirations for participants in a Scottish youth club, based in an urban area of deprivation, were investigated over a period of fifteen months. The youth club operated from the community wing of a new build primary school on Friday nights and was given financial support by the local authority. The club was primarily run by parent volunteers and local authority sessional staff with a janitor present. Most of the young people lived in the community where the club was located. At any one time about half the participants were boys and half were girls and their ages ranged between 12 and 14 years.

New participants attending secondary school were allowed to join at any time but were particularly recruited in the final weeks of their primary schooling. Those who continued normally remained engaged for the first two years of secondary schooling. The club had a natural turnover as some moved on and others joined. Most young people who joined continued regularly for at least six months and some for more than two years. The youth club offered a place where young people could develop their social networks with peers and also their connections with trusted adults. Eighteen young people, including three who were involved with the club for just one week, voluntarily participated in this study.

The key purpose of this research was to examine how connections among young people and volunteers in a youth club affect their immediate and medium-term social, economic and cultural needs. Other research questions included whether the youth club provided benefits as a social amenity to the community, encouraged a reduction in territorialism and provided those involved with positive choices and chances, as stated in the Scottish Government's More Choices, More Chances policy (Scottish Government, 2006). Consideration was also given to how the policies of the local authority are implemented and the effect they have on the operation of a youth club.

Background

Generally, it is accepted that peer groups are important influences on successful transition for young people in early adolescence (Holland et al, 2007) and that peer support is correlated with school attainment after controlling for prior achievement (Azmitia and Cooper, 2001). Three elements of peer support were identified as significant for young adolescents by Veronneau and Vitaro (2007). First, they noted that young people need one or more secure friendships through which they share and develop generalised trust. As defined by Uslaner (2002), generalised trust involves an expectation that one will receive fair treatment and reciprocate in kind. Secondly, young people need affiliation with one or more peer groups, and they separately need not to be rejected by an influential peer group. Finally, through peer groups and significant adults young people can access positive role models and adopt norms and values consistent with community expectations.

Family and community networks also play a crucial role in the formation of aspirations by young people (Salmela-Aro and Schoon, 2009). If there is little access to experiences of employment and further education in the family and neighbourhood, the information young people require to both form and inform their aspirations is not readily available. Elliot et al (2006) have suggested that the limited flow of information into poor neighbourhoods restricts access for adolescents and their families to reliable information about labour markets, schools, apprenticeship opportunities and financial markets. Young people from families where no one works are less likely to be positive about their own future and more likely to struggle to find employment (Goodman and Gregg, 2010). Youth clubs are social sites where the need for information can be addressed, opportunities for further education and for avenues to employment and community participation can develop and access to opportunities through linking social capital can occur. As will be shown later, this is most important at this age because many young people form their employment aspirations during this period.

The role of social capital

This study was conducted using social capital as a construct through which to explore the social networks of the young people and the adult volunteers. In an attempt to draw together Bourdieu's forms of capital (1986) and Putnam's understanding of social capital in terms of the civic society (2000), we modelled a conceptual framework. The model presented in Figure 5.1 seeks to describe how we conceive the effects on outcomes for young people of macro socioeconomic factors, including neighbourhood influences, access to infrastructure and community social characteristics on the one hand, and the immediate physical, social and economic circumstances of the family on the other. In the model, we also recognise that there are individual psychological and physical characteristics that affect the resilience of individuals. We postulate that youth development depends primarily on young people feeling safe and secure in their home, in their neighbourhood, and in their school and other institutional affiliations. We argue that individual, economic and family factors all contribute to youth well-being (safety) and hence to youth development. The assumption we make is that any person who feels insecure will be at a distinct disadvantage in utilising available opportunities at school and in their neighbourhood. Hence youth safety is in the centre of the model presented in Figure 5.1 and this is shown as a prerequisite for youth development through learning.

This approach differs from the view adopted by some policy makers who have focused on individual competencies as the framework through which to prepare young people and disadvantaged adults for employment and further education. The approach we have adopted is a more holistic view of the individual and we have sought to explore how access to social networks may result in the transmission of advantage or disadvantage from one generation to the next.

Figure 5.1: Social, economic and cultural capital and the development of young people

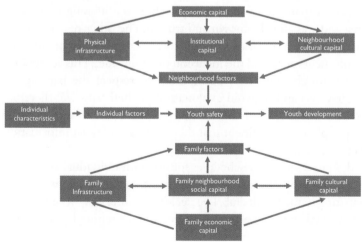

Methodology

This case study involved a form of 'impact evaluation' (Owen and Rogers, 1999, p. 54) which is appropriate for a settled programme and involves an investigation of the processes and outcomes; the aim is to provide insight into the way a programme (a youth club in this case) actually operates and what effects it has on the lives of participants. The process component of this method focused on the way in which social capital was formed, changed and utilised, and how these processes affected the opportunities for the young people both within the youth club and beyond. This was done primarily by the researchers working as additional adult volunteers over a period of 15 months in order to observe the peer group processes and the interactions of the young people with adults. As participant observers, we drafted field notes to record significant events, and these were used to inform and verify matters that were raised when after 12 months we carried out interviews.

Consideration of the effectiveness of the youth club process included the level of attendance and the level of participation in the activities undertaken. The nature of benefits reported by the participants allowed us to identify what they considered to be the outcomes and benefits of the youth club, and to compare these with the local authority objectives. It also allowed us to identify opportunities to enhance and consolidate outcomes. Finally, a focus group of participants was used to confirm and elaborate the findings.

There was careful consideration of the ethical implications of becoming embedded and trusted by the community. Issues addressed included gaining trustworthy evidence, and in this regard we had an advantage in that one of the two researchers is a lifelong resident of the area and was already known and trusted. The other researcher was accepted both by association with the local researcher and because the adult volunteers accepted the inclusion of an outsider. This acceptance however brought with it responsibilities to respect the participants and their views and to avoid exploitation of their trust. We therefore negotiated well ahead of the interview days to make sure that the young people were confident that they understood what information we were seeking.

We designed interview schedules for use with individual volunteers and a parallel protocol for use with pairs of young people who were participating in the youth club. The decision to interview young people in pairs was taken both because it offered them a sense of security and support from a peer, and because it helped us to explore their social networks through the interchange of ideas among young people.

Once we had compiled our findings, we fed these back to the young people who were attending the youth club in a focus group format. We presented summary statements and asked them what they thought of these findings, what they thought should be done in response, and who should take responsibility. This produced responses from the young people that demonstrated a substantial and nuanced grasp of the complexities of the issues we identified.

By conducting the study over 15 months, we not only accumulated a substantial amount of information from participants and stakeholders, but we also had opportunities to verify the trustworthiness of the information. For instance we gained insights into what occurs in practice in youth clubs and were able to compare this with what is considered 'common knowledge' about how youth clubs operate. In particular, this enabled us to highlight where council policies are effective and possible gaps in services. We were also able to match our observational data with the information derived from interviews. Because we had shared experiences with the young people, we were well positioned to verify the issues that they brought up in interviews. The local knowledge of one of the interviewers meant that verification included local information gathered vicariously in the community. As a consequence, we have confidence in the trustworthiness of the data.

In summary, the data sources accessed were observations at the youth club and in the community, a review of local authority policy documents, observations of youth club activities, interviews with the participants and with key stakeholders in the community, and a final focus group with eight of the participants who were still attending the youth club.

Findings

Using our model of social capital outlined in Figure 5.1, the findings from the case study are summarised in relation to the effects of space and territories and the importance of key people in the neighbourhood and among the peer group who broker access to social capital. We also considered the different levels of access to youth club participation, the durability of social networks and the effects of social capital in the formation of aspirations and the personal and social development of the young people. First, we explore how the physical infrastructure in the neighbourhood and at the youth club venue, as identified in Figure

5.1, affects the social capital processes. We then consider how family and neighbourhood social capital influences access to the youth club.

Space and social capital

Most interviewees had absolute views about only attending a youth club in their immediate neighbourhood and did not see their answer as one that required any explanation as summed up in the following brief exchange:

Interviewer: 'Would you go to a youth club in another area?'

Hamish: 'Naw [No].'

Both the lack of inclusion of young people from beyond the immediate neighbourhood, and the territorial limits of the informal power of the adult volunteers raise organisational challenges and also raise issues for enriching information accessible in small communities. A council officer suggested that the local authority could not afford to subsidise a youth club in each neighbourhood, but this probably means that some young people will be denied access to a youth club. This territoriality means that information accessible to participants is limited to that available in the immediate neighbourhood unless a sessional worker from the local authority can be present.

The community in which the youth club operated is undergoing regeneration of the housing stock and the rebuilding of the primary and secondary schools. It is widely accepted that one of the components required to enhance economic and social opportunities for young people from disadvantaged backgrounds is to build new schools with modern facilities, and to provide sound housing in which people can live safely. However, we found that the process of regeneration of physical infrastructure is not only expensive, but can also be disruptive.

The secondary school that the young people attended was rebuilt on the playing fields of the old school during the period of the case study. Once the new school was completed, the old school was torn down and much of this space was used to build new housing in order to recoup the cost of the new school buildings. One of the effects on young people was the loss of much of their school playing fields. In the primary school where the youth club was situated, a 'brown field' site was utilised to build a new school, but playing fields where the youth club participants could play outside during summer were not available for more than a year after the new school opened. There was also a loss of public space in the neighbourhood. Most of the participants in the youth club lived in rented public housing. When the redevelopment of the old housing estates commenced, it was the open spaces such as playgrounds and parks which were used first for new housing. Further, the remaining open spaces marked for subsequent development were allowed to deteriorate.

Most of the young people made comments about the lack of public space and the impact on their neighbourhood activities. They reported that there were no safe places in which to kick a ball or to gather to talk with friends. It meant that their main option was the streets and the culture of the streets that involved underage drinking and other antisocial behaviour. The youth club was one of the few safe outlets in their neighbourhood. Hence, a generation of young people were without much open space in both their school and their neighbourhood. With the loss of open space in the community, permission to access the school community wing by the youth club was of benefit. One of the local authority managers suggested that the youth club provided a sense of stability during the upheaval of relocation. As one young person explained:

> **Stewart:** 'It was my ma that was saying, cause we were bored because they were building the houses where we used to play football and then she says, go down to the youth club.'

The new build facilities in which the youth club was housed were appreciated by most of the participants. Two of the boys explained the benefits as follows:

Angus: 'A lot better than what they were in the old school. There's more to do, there's room as well.'

Stewart: 'Lots of space. You can go and out and play football and that.'

However, while they appreciated the space in the school grounds once it became available, there were limitations to the indoor space imposed by the local authority rental policies for the new build facilities to which the youth club had moved. The interior space was substantially smaller than in the old school and did not include the gymnasium. The hall rental fees for the new facilities meant that renting the gymnasium involved a separate fee and this was not affordable on a regular basis.

Even when the gymnasium was rented, indoor football could not be played.

Some younger members felt that the limited space in the main community room meant that they could not undertake their own activities. On occasions and especially on wet nights, some young people went out into the hallway to get some space for themselves. One of the younger girls, when asked why more space was needed, explained as follows:

Maggie: 'To have two dance spaces. Like the older ones could have one and the younger ones could ...'

Interviewer: 'Okay and why would that be an advantage?'

Maggie: 'Because sometimes the older ones ... they can just like turn it over onto ... like another song and then the younger ones don't really get a choice.'

Social capital and issues of access

A further component identified in Figure 5.1 as influential in the development of adolescents was the role of family and neighbourhood social capital. It was evident in the youth club setting that both family bonds and bridging social capital networks in the immediate community were influential in determining access to the youth club.

Young people joined and regularly attended youth clubs if they had friends or family who had a positive experience of accessing these services. To confirm this we asked participants a question about how they heard of the youth club and why they either continued or dropped out of it (three girls who were interviewed attended the youth club only once). All respondents indicated that they had heard about the youth club by word of mouth through their peers, family and/ or neighbourhood links, and most were prompted to join by poster promotions in the final weeks of primary school. However, they all went to the youth club because of a connection such as a friend who was going, or because they knew the community volunteers who worked at the club, or because they had a relative who had gone or was still attending the club. The following examples are typical of the explanations provided.

Interviewer: 'And so how did you find out about being allowed to start?'

Sadie: 'Because of Isla cause she was already going. She said that I could go cause the primary sevens were allowed to start, so I started, cause she was already going.'

Interviewer: 'And is Isla one of your friends?'

Sadie: 'Uh huh [yes].'

A further example is given by the following:

Interviewer: 'How did you find out about youth club, Donald?'

Donald: 'Big brother told me.'

Interviewer: 'Did he used to go to the youth club?'

Donald: 'Aye, ages ago. Basically him and his pals used to go.'

These examples illustrate how peer and family networks provide young people with information about the youth club, and also provide an initial contact with a youth club participant. In other cases, the link was through parental friendship with a youth club volunteer, indicating that family, neighbourhood and peer social networks support access. Thus social capital facilitates access through the provision of information about the youth club and through the support of a personal contact.

The youth club was a territory with distinctively different norms and values from school because all participation was voluntary. The youth club had come to represent an attractive territory to the young people between the ages of 12 and 14, whose adherence to, enactment of, and even policing of the norms and values contributed to the maintenance of the youth club as a distinctive territory. In many ways, the youth club was a safe space where they were removed from antisocial street behaviour such as drinking or gang conflict. There was a divide between most of the young people who attended the youth club and those who 'hang out' in the streets, although two of the boys were torn between the two contexts and on at least one occasion, one left when a cousin texted him to join a group involved in a gang dispute between adjoining neighbourhoods. For most participants, the youth club gave them a refuge from such behaviour. The distinction between the street and youth club cultures was a genuine perspective held by the young people as is indicated in the following response:

Interviewer: 'Can you tell me a bit more about why you don't talk to them anymore?'

Stewart: 'Cause they're hanging about with all the "numpties" in [local area] you know, they're a bit mental.'

It was the young people, rather than the adults managing the youth club, who sanctioned the entry into the club by selecting those whom they invited, and those with whom they interacted. This was evident in our observations and also in several of the interviews, and was raised with the participants who attended the focus group to discuss the findings. They pointed out that not all people get on in the area and there would be little point in inviting people with whom they would get into a fight.

The durability of social capital

Early adolescence is a period when young people develop their individual identities, and many commentators agree that social networks play a significant role in this process. We observed changing patterns in the social connections among young people in the youth club over the 15 months of our participation. The following dialogue provides an insight into how adolescent relationships change over time. Donald starts by telling us how he is currently friends with Gordon and Hamish, with whom he formed friendships at the youth club, although he also knew them from school and his local neighbourhood. However, these two boys were not his initial reason for joining. The friends who introduced him to the youth club no longer attend, although he regularly does. He appeared embarrassed when talking about his friends' departures.

Interviewer: 'Why did you decide to go to the youth club?'

Donald: ' 'nstead of sitting in the house all day on a Friday, I just went cause my pals were going so, I went.'

Interviewer: 'Which pals were going?'

Donald:	'James and Danny were going at the time cause they're in the same year as me, then the year after that, Gordon and Hamish started going and that, so.'
Interviewer:	'So Gordon and Hamish are in first year. So how did you feel when Danny decided not to go to the youth club?'
Donald:	'Didn't bother me.'
Interviewer:	'Because you had other friends?'
Donald:	'He's coming back but.'
Interviewer:	'Is he?'
Donald:	'Aye, I don't know when. It's supposed to be this week but don't know yet.'

As was the case with the transition case study reported in Chapter Nine, we became aware that some young people can have two social networks, one that represents the people with whom they actually engage, and another group with whom they aspire to engage. We term this second category 'aspirational social capital'. Donald pursued Danny and Jamie for a few weeks to try to persuade them to rejoin the youth club. One never came back and the other only popped in sporadically before leaving for good. Hence Donald's reciprocated network included Gordon and Hamish, but his aspirational network included Danny and Jamie.

Another participant, Hannah, provides an example of how young people who have weak links can make new friendships and remain in attendance at the club. Like Donald, Hannah joined the youth club along with her friends. Over time, these relationships broke and new ones were formed. Both Donald and Hannah have used the youth club to build new friendships that have helped them in the transition to secondary school by enabling them to establish new connections with peers as previous links faded.

Interviewer: 'Yeah. So how did you decide to come?'

Hannah: 'Because we got a ... somebody came to the school and gave us a letter about it and then I heard that some of my friends were going to it. So I just decided to go.'

Interviewer: 'Which friends?'

Hannah: 'Maggie and Mary and Ruby.'

Interviewer 2: 'Did any of your (current) friends go to the youth club back when you first started?'

Hannah: 'Yeah, well ... I've kind of fell out with Jessie, she used to go and Maggie used to go and I think Mary and Ruby went.'

Interviewer: 'So, are there other people at the youth club that you've got to know better?'

Hannah: 'Isla and the other girls.'

Interviewer: 'And you knew Isla before?'

Hannah: 'No.'

Interviewer 2: 'So, you've made new friends at the youth club?'

Hannah: 'Yeah.'

Interviewer 2: 'And you still ... are you quite happy to go to the youth club with your new friends?'

Hannah: 'Yeah.'

Hannah is an exception to the rule that the youth club is the preserve of one community. She lives in a different neighbourhood from the one in which the youth club is situated and all the other participants are drawn. She is the only young person who explicitly said that her reason for going to the youth club was to make new friends. Although Hannah joined because she knew a group of friends who attended, she was keen to make new ones and this goal was supported by her parents. The youth club provided the platform for her to form links with a new group of young people with different and possibly more positive aspirations. Our observation notes indicate that she was usually a follower of the initiatives of others, and hence her inclusion seemed to be predicated on her willingness to join in activities initiated by others.

In the focus group where we presented our findings to participants, after they confirmed the conclusions we asked them what if anything we could do when young people fall out. The consensus was that these things happen and adults only make it worse when they interfere. This poses a dilemma for youth workers since those isolated and excluded lose access to information and if they do not forge new friendships, they are likely to leave and are then vulnerable to the street culture of underage drinking and smoking.

Neighbourhood social capital

We deliberately interviewed three girls who attended the youth club on only one occasion, which happened to be early on in the study when we were seeking the consent of young people and their parents to conduct the study. These three were friends from another primary school nearby. One lived in the local area for the youth club and the other two were from a neighbouring community and said that they did not feel affiliated with the youth club neighbourhood. Connection to the local area was considered important because the youth club was seen by most participants (but not by all council officers) as the 'property' of a particular community. When interviewed these three young people made it evident that they did not feel connected to the neighbourhood of the youth club because their peer group had defined a different area as their neighbourhood, even though one of them lived in the catchment area for the youth club. Their response emphasised that how neighbourhood social capital was defined by the young people is significant in enabling young people to access opportunities for information and learning through the youth club.

As youth clubs are maintained by local volunteers and youth workers who normally live in the local community, there is a significant opportunity through the youth club for family and neighbourhood social capital to interact. This is a mechanism through which reciprocal sanctions can operate to curb antisocial behaviour and potentially to enhance local authority goals, including healthy living and access to opportunities for employment and further education. The volunteers explained that because they were known and respected by other parents, the young people knew that unless they accepted the standards of the youth club, their parents would be involved in sanctions. One of the volunteers identified a particular example of the capacity of these local sanctions to influence the behaviour of young people who are at risk of harm:

> 'at the very beginning we did have, you know a few young people that turned up like under the influence of drink and drugs and what have you and you had to say to them, "Sorry, you can't get in here tonight, you can't come in here." You know. And they then in turn, came back. One of them in particular came back the following week, totally sober, and which was very unusual for him, and said, "Can I get in now?"'

The participants also identified the issue of alcohol abuse as a complex problem and in the focus group where they considered the findings they agreed by consensus on a nuanced view of how to address the problem. After considering what the responses of their own parents would be were they to find out that a young person was allowed to attend the club drunk, and the consequences of turning a drunk adolescent away, the participants recommended a short ban but an opportunity to return in future weeks, thus confirming the appropriateness of the strategy successfully adopted by the local volunteers.

Neighbourhoods are a primary source of support for young people and the bridging social capital can support them to join a youth group. In the present study, with one exception, all the young people who attended regularly shared some connections through their immediate neighbourhood and their extended family. Neighbourhood hence has some synergy with the notion of space, but neighbourhoods are also mental constructs that embrace norms and values. This is why neighbourhood social capital occurs in Figure 5.1 alongside family social capital, and why neighbourhood physical infrastructure occurs alongside other physical resources. According to Gwynne (2005):

> residence in neighbourhoods characterized by strong social organization may increase the likelihood of interaction with adults outside the family who can provide valuable encouragement and information about post-secondary educational opportunities. It is also possible that residence in these neighbourhoods may be more likely to stimulate the activation of cultural capital within the home, thereby supporting and enhancing access to family-based knowledge useful in the pursuit of [post-secondary destinations].

Formation of aspirations

Our findings concur with others who found that prospects for post-school education and employment are in the main not informed by what happens in schools, but from the expectations they develop from their home and by sharing among their peers (Liddell, 2007). All the young people in the youth club had formed ideas about their careers and most were able to identify a family or neighbourhood member from whom they had drawn inspiration for their nominated interest. Thus their extended family social capital was a primary source of information. For instance, one explained her career goal as follows:

Interviewer: 'What do think you would like to do when you leave school?'

Jessie: 'Be a vet.'

Interviewer: 'Be a vet, oh fabulous! And do you think you need to go to college or anything for that?'

Jessie: 'Yeah, you need to spend … it's five years or something like that, cause my mum … my dad's friend … his girlfriend and she's a trained vet.'

Another example was as follows:

Interviewer: 'How long since you wanted to be a mechanic?'

Donald: 'From I was wee. 'Cause I like motors.'

Interviewer: 'Is there anyone else in your family who's a mechanic?'

Donald: 'My big brother. He wanted to be a football player but he didn't get it so, he wanted to be a mechanic and he got it.'

We noted three young people who identified medicine as a preferred career, suggesting that at least at this stage some had high aspirations. The following is one example where the young person sounds quite determined on medicine as a career choice:

Becky: 'I would like to be a surgeon. And I know it does really … that would require college and university and a lot of really hard work.'

Interviewer: 'And why do you think you would like to be surgeon?'

Becky: 'I don't know, when I was five, I just … started wanting to be a doctor. I must have watched a show or something and ever since I was five, I've been telling my mum and dad I wanted to be a doctor.'

This young person went on to describe how her mum had discussed her aspirations with their local medical practitioner, who had offered to give her a work experience placement in due course. Although the connection in this case came from family social capital, the other two youth club participants with an interest in medicine thus became aware of the possibility of a placement with their GP.

It is the aspiration of many young men to become professional footballers. This ambition can sweep aside other aspirations and can have a negative impact on young men's development if they are unsuccessful in their initial trials, or are subsequently denied progress to the more advanced levels. The opportunity to be selected for a development team is much sought after. We noted one example where a male volunteer linked a young person up with an opportunity to try for a place at a second club that was more distant from his home after he missed selection for his first choice team.

Those who make a squad also face potential loss of social capital because training takes them away from their youth club peers. They may then be isolated if cut adrift in a subsequent year by the club. We noted an example from one young male whom we interviewed who had left the youth club because it clashed with training times for the development squad in which he had been selected. We noted some anxiety about his future, which was more in the tone of voice in which he explained his situation:

Interviewer: 'You said you got a contract? … What does that mean?'

Angus: 'I play for the team for a year and then get a new contract if I do well.'

Missing out on a development squad can also have negative consequences. One young male was most despondent and became more difficult to manage at the club after his best friend made a development squad and he missed out. He had taken time to show one of the authors some basic football skills and had been quite proud of his capacities, but his self-esteem took a heavy blow and he pronounced himself "no good at football" once the squad selection had occurred.

Implications for practice, policy and future research

Many of the young people told us that they will have 'grown out of' the youth club by the age of 15 to 16 years as by that time they will 'be doing their own thing'. This is another key transition period in young people's lives and from other council data, we know that, there are many incidents of antisocial and risk-taking behaviour at this point. The young people agreed that they would welcome some of the older ones being trained and staying on as 'mentors' in the youth club. This would not be for everyone, but we noted one example where an older brother had been encouraged to contribute in such a role.

Youth services staff suggested that structured and targeted provision such as the Bridges Programme, a community-based education programme for youth at risk of leaving or being excluded from high school where referrals come from the school, could help to support young people who are disengaging from formal education at this stage. Youth work programmes, including youth clubs, provide an opportunity to support young people, their families and the wider neighbourhood through the transition stages by developing bridging and linking social capital.

There is also an opportunity to share good news stories between schools and neighbourhood youth clubs. Young people welcomed the idea that their teachers might be told if they were doing well in the youth club and felt that this would give teachers and parents the opportunity to see them in different contexts. This was strongly endorsed by young people in relation to individual teachers whom they felt did not value them. Conversely, improved information sharing could help youth workers encourage better support for young people who are at risk of dropping out of school and are as a consequence in danger of losing their social networks, as was observed in the Get Ready for Work case study described in Chapter Seven. Although social capital is not transferable between social networks, evidence that in a different social context, behaviour is positive might alert the school guidance staff to investigate whether there were barriers to progress in the school setting. Because youth club attendance is voluntary, unexplained drop outs may indicate a move to disconnect from supportive peers and community before this is identified by schools. We observed one such case where changed behaviour at the youth club was followed within months by difficulties at school.

The local adult volunteers were much respected, but one was on sickness benefit and the other, after many years as a carer, secured a casual supermarket job during the course of the study. Neither therefore had a wide range of social contacts with people in work or further education, and hence they did not have access to bridging social capital to open up a wider range of opportunities for young people. The presence of the researchers as participants provided opportunities for linking social capital. For instance, many of the girls enjoyed dancing and theatre so as part of our contribution, we arranged for the participants to visit a theatre where they were shown all the types of work associated with live theatre, thus opening up awareness of avenues for future employment. While volunteers might know some of the more obvious theatre positions, they were not familiar with some of the backstage roles. Hence, as participant volunteers, we provided access to linking social capital through which the participants became aware of wider opportunities for their future career options.

The young people attending the youth club were not in the main the most disadvantaged in their community and some had quite optimistic expectations about their future choices. We note however that in a study by the Prince's Trust, one sixth of young people whose family worked reported that their parents did not have the knowledge to help them find a job, and a quarter of those from families where no one works expressed the same view (Goodman and Gregg, 2010). There is a need therefore for additional information from trusted sources. The neighbourhood youth club can provide such sources, but only if community development staff provide wider access to information and role models. Our proposition is that access to information is best provided within the youth club. We suggest therefore that for schools to play a more effective role in expanding and developing aspirations for employment and further education, teachers and school guidance staff need to better interconnect with the primary sources of advice for young people, namely their homes and their neighbourhood.

Findings from this study also inform a wider analysis of the role of social capital in the development of opportunities for young people to explore the worlds of education and employment. Results indicate that young people rely on the adult volunteers at the youth club for advice and role models, and evidence shows that the youth club provided an opportunity for isolated young people to maintain affiliation with a community peer group.

Potential benefits that were not fully realised in the youth club included learning about healthy living and a reduction in smoking; extending networks for youth and volunteers, especially through linking social capital to adults with information about education and employment opportunities; and extending curriculum outcomes through volunteering and through feedback to schools on success in youth group activities.

The adequacy of social capital as a construct

Social capital is an imperfect construct but as Field (2003, p. 43) noted the 'issue is not whether a concept can be applied loosely, but whether it leads to new insights when applied finely'. Social capital is generally perceived as an inherently 'good' practice with a 'dark' side (Field 2003, p. 71) and while the body of knowledge pertaining to it is constantly being refined, nonetheless, as illustrated above, we found it to be a valuable tool for exploring social processes and practices.

Morrow (2001) claims that Putnam's version of social capital as it is operated in policy is not broad enough to incorporate a wide variety of factors that impinge upon young people's lives. Both Holland et al (2007) and Morrow (2001) reject the notion that children are passive recipients of social capital as was implied by Coleman (1994) when he defined access to social capital for young people in terms of attributes of their family status. In contrast, Morrow (2001) claims that social capital needs to be able to accommodate a range of different identities, which, based on our experience, is a view we share.

Hayes and Kogl (2007) claim that social capital is useful for dealing with the dilemma of collective action, such as arose in this study with the issue of underage drinking. If the response to issues also provides additional information through bridging and linking sources of social capital, then it is possible to also address underlying causes such as social injustice and inequality, which were the concern of Bourdieu (1986).

The model we constructed and presented in Figure 5.1 allowed us to examine the different perspectives of Bourdieu (1986), Coleman (1994) and Putnam (2000). We found common ground, which included the importance of access to information, the distinction between bonding, linking and bridging networks, and the importance of sanctions in realising the benefits of networks. Indeed, sanctions were one of the crucial elements that bound the youth club together, but they could also have been a barrier to accessing more diverse information. Had our roles not been accepted by the youth club community our information would not have been trusted and the access we provided to sites for learning beyond the immediate community would probably not have been utilised. The more we discovered about how networks operate among young people, the more we learned about social capital practices. For example, one participant told us how she asked her maths teacher for support material for her mother who had a new job and needed help with maths work. These were the kind of social capital practices that could enable the recipients to 'get on'.

Conclusions

Findings from the study were shared with the local stakeholders and nationally. The volunteers were briefed informally about the results during a youth club planning meeting so that they could consider the implications for the future leadership of the youth club. This reinforced their perception that the participants needed to take part in excursions and led to a joint activity with a neighbouring youth club. We also provided information to the school cluster group meetings involving primary feeder schools and the two high schools in the region, and to the head of the youth and community learning section of the local authority, and invited their responses. This helped teachers and managers to identify the benefits of youth work in terms of the overall education of young people in the immediate area. The ideas also informed the development of the community education inspection model introduced by the Scottish education inspectorate in September 2008. In addition, the findings helped to lay the foundation for partnership work in relation to the local implementation of Curriculum for Excellence, a Scottish policy initiative. One example of this was the use of older siblings as mentors, mentioned previously. We therefore suggest a more systematic approach, including fitting near-peer mentoring into school and community award and recognition programmes. This has now been implemented through the Youth Achievement Awards in this local area. We conclude that the notion of social capital can inform an analysis of how community education and development programmes can contribute to policy and to practice.

References

Hayes, R.A. and Kogl, A. (2007) 'Neighbourhood attachment, social capital building, and political participation: a case study of low and moderate income residents of Waterloo, Iowa', *Journal of Urban Affairs*, vol 29, pp 181–205.

Azmitia, M. and Cooper, C. (2001) 'Good or bad? Peer influences on Latino and European American adolescents' pathways through school', *Journal of Education for Students Placed At Risk*, vol 6, nos 1–2, pp 45–71.

Bourdieu, P. (1986) 'The forms of capital' (R. Nice, trans.), in I. Richardson (ed) *Handbook of theory and research for the sociology of education*, Westport, CT: Greenwood Press, pp 241–58.

Coleman, J. (1994) *Foundations of social theory*, Cambridge MA: Harvard University Press.

Elliott, D., Menard, S., Rankin, B., Elliott, A., Wilson, W. and Huizinga, D. (2006) *Good kids from bad neighbourhoods: successful development in social context*, Cambridge: Cambridge University Press.

Field, J. (2003) *Social capital*, London: Routledge.

Goodman, A. and Gregg, P. (2010) *Poorer children's educational attainment: how important are attitudes and behaviour?* Joseph Rowntree Foundation, www.jrf.org.uk/sites/files/jrf/poorer-children-education-full.pdf

Gwynne, J. (2005) 'Post-secondary plans of Chicago youth: the roles of schools and neighbourhoods', *Dissertation Abstracts International A: The Humanities and Social Sciences*, vol 66, no 6, p 2402A.

Holland, J., Reynolds, T. and Weller, S. (2007) 'Transitions networks and communities: the significance of social capital in the lives of children and young people', *Journal of Youth Studies*, vol 10, no 1, pp 97–116.

Liddell, R (2007) 'Developing social capital for working class students'. Paper presented at the *British Educational Research Association Annual Conference*, Institute of Education, University of London, 5–8 September, 2007, (cited with permission of author) www.leeds.ac.uk/educol/documents/168093.doc

Morrow, V. (2001) 'Young people's explanations and experiences of social exclusion: retrieving Bourdieu's concept of social capital', *International Journal of Sociology and Social Policy*, vol 21, nos 4/5/6, pp 37–63.

Owen J. and Rogers P. (1999) *Program evaluation: forms and approaches*, 2nd edition, Crows Nest, NSW: Allen and Unwin.

Putnam, R. (2000) *Bowling alone: the collapse and revival of American community*, London: Simon and Schuster.

Salmela-Aro, K and Schoon, I. (2009) 'Youth development in Europe: transitions and identities', *European Psychologist*, vol 14, no 4, pp 372–5.

Scottish Government (2006) *More choices, more chances: a strategy to reduce the proportion of young people not in education, employment or training in Scotland*, Edinburgh: Scottish Government, www.scotland.gov.uk/Publications/2006/06/13100205/0

Uslaner E.M. (2002) *The moral foundations of trust*, Cambridge: Cambridge University Press.

Veronneau M.-H. and Vitaro, F. (2007) 'Social experiences with peers and high school graduation: a review of theoretical and empirical research', *Educational Psychology*, vol 27, no 3, pp 419–45.

SIX

Commentary: social capital and inclusion: implications for practice

George MacBride

These four insightful analyses of evidence provided by young people and parents (Chapters Two–Five) suggest that, while the phrase 'social capital' is today not uncommon in Scottish education, there is a need to develop our critical understanding of this concept, theoretically and practically. Barry points out (in Chapter Four) that social capital is difficult to define in academic circles, let alone among children and young people, and the researchers have tried to explore both the 'dark side' of social capital (Field, 2003, p. 19) as well as its benefits.

These studies, explicitly and implicitly, raise a number of overlapping questions: To what extent do individuals own their social capital? To what extent is social capital bound to the context where it has been created; how transferable is it? Is social capital primarily an instrument for benefiting individuals or is it an indicator of social cohesion? Is it a means of asserting control through setting social norms? Is it a weak substitute for planned and resourced state provision? Is it a discourse used by policy makers to avoid responsibility for inequality by blaming those at risk of social exclusion for their lack of social capital?

In recent decades the phrase 'social capital' has been used with a range of interpretations, not always fully explicit, sometimes ill-defined or self-referential; some uses of the phrase are inconsistent with others; and it seems difficult to measure social capital, even when well-defined, in any meaningful way. Schuller et al (2000, p. 1) begin their analysis of the concept of social capital by suggesting that it 'has an immediate intuitive appeal' but quickly identify inherent problems. Stolle and Hooghe's (2004) review of competing claims about the decline of social capital leads one to conclude that a more clearly defined concept, with a stronger theoretical basis and one more open to analysis, would be less likely to lead to mutually conflicting research outcomes. The complexities inherent in measuring social capital are illuminated by Haezewindt's analysis (2003), whereby the extent of a group's social capital depends on the measures employed; by some measures, particular vulnerable groups (for example, lone parents) are, contrary to received wisdom, rich in social capital. The Office for National Statistics (2001, p. 21) raises the fundamental question:

> After reviewing the definition, measurement and research studies of social capital, one inevitably arrives at the 'so what' question. How does the evidence translate into policies which can make a difference?

The ONS authors give no conclusive answer.

Such questions are important for teachers who are contractually bound (Scottish Negotiating Committee for Teachers, 2001) to carry out their 'important work ... within the framework of social inclusion', professionally obliged (General Teaching Council for Scotland 2006) to 'show in their day-to-day practice a commitment to social justice' (p. 14), and legally required to promote equality (HMSO, 2010; Equality and Human Rights Commission, 2010). Practitioners may ask whether the concept of social capital ultimately adds anything to the analyses offered. Cross et al's research questions (Chapter Two) were:

- Does the Inclusive Learning Network (ILN) help participants support others in the same role within their local context (i.e. enhance or create bridging social capital)?
- Does the ILN help participants work in concert with others in nearby communities to extend best practice across the local authority (i.e. enhance bridging and linking social capital)?
- Does the ILN help participants work more effectively with those in positions of more power or authority in their local contexts (i.e. enhance or create linking social capital)?

Practitioners may not see the words in parentheses as adding anything to the questions. Runge (1971) provides an account of the creation by young people of networks based on trust and shared norms; this makes no reference to any concept of social capital. Regine, aged 17, is quoted:

> There's a girl in our class who's got four younger brothers and sisters. Her mother had to go into a chest clinic and the girl had a lot of housework to do. We sorted it out quickly so that once every week two of us went round to help her: we got the beds changed and did the shopping and things like that so that she could relax a bit. ... Lots of

people in our class were not doing well in physics ... we were worried about this and one of the guys who's really good at physics ... said he was ready, once a week, to ... go over the stuff again with those who hadn't got it ... (p. 306) (translated by G. MacBride).

Unfortunately for proponents of social capital as a marker of liberal democracy, Regine attended school in the German Democratic Republic and this makes some theoretical approaches to social capital problematic.

The studies address this lack of clarity. The difficulty of so doing is revealed by Smyth et al (Chapter Three), where the elision of the views of Bourdieu, Coleman and Putnam avoids considering fundamental differences among these authors. Smyth and colleagues each made their understanding of social capital explicit to each other and drew on the earlier work of the AERS Schools and Social Capital Network (McGonigal et al, 2007) in evolving their understanding of social capital.

These accounts strongly challenge views that social capital is irrelevant to practitioners. They consider the role of social capital for learners and its potential for making a difference in relevant contexts: Cross et al (Chapter Two) research a government funded initiative; Smyth et al (Chapter Three)analyse school practice; Allison and Catts (Chapter Five) examine social capital within a youth club; and Barry (Chapter Four) considers the social capital created by young carers. There are common features to all four. Networks located within specific communities (the school, friends, or semi-official networks) were important to individuals, as were high levels of trust and shared norms within these networks; the role of the school was, in different ways, problematic in each case; the learners in each study were members of groups who were vulnerable and likely to be failed by current practice.

Recent Scottish legislation, in the form of the Education (Additional Support for Learning) (Scotland) Act 2004, has broken away from the traditional categorisation, identification and labelling of learners in terms of their difficulties, and encourages the view that additional support needs may lie in circumstances in which the learners find themselves, rather than arising from or inhering in the individual. Within this moral and legal commitment to inclusion, addressing the needs of such vulnerable groups may be seen to reflect the need to address the injustice, identified by Bourdieu (1986), that social capital, like financial and human capital, is inequitably distributed in our society. However, the relationship between social capital and social justice could be examined in more depth. Otherwise, some practitioners may take the view that social capital is an issue only for a minority of learners and is unimportant for teachers or for the majority of learners. Indeed, this focus may risk sustaining a view that the responsibility for failure should be attributed solely to individuals, a view rejected by commentaries such as that by the OECD (2007). Smyth et al (Chapter Three) recognise this concern, arguing that the explicit focus on children from refugee families raises an important question in the context of research committed to inclusive principles. They asked how one ensures that a focus on such an identifiable group does not, in the short term, put the participants under pressure and, in the longer term, lead to the labelling of that group.

All four studies recognise the potentially problematic nature of the relationship between social capital and state provision. Smyth et al report that staff recognised the value of the languages, cultures and faiths which the refugee children and young people brought into the school. However, they note that school practice elsewhere may seek to replace children's own social capital with a passive acceptance of the school's (indeed the state's) norms. Those who refuse to value existing real social capital justify this in terms of the need for the school to develop social capital to address alleged 'deficits' in children that prevent their 'fitting into' Scottish society. The young people in Barry's study (Chapter Four) expressed clear awareness of the downside for them of attempts to coerce them into the school's norms. There was an expectation, among the young participants in the youth club case study (Chapter Five), that they would soon 'grow out' of the youth club, even if they were currently benefiting from its networks and norms. The participants in the ILN, perhaps because they were adults, seem to have been more able to develop their own norms without submitting to external imposition.

The networks described in Chapters Two and Four may be needed because the state has failed to promote social justice or even provide a minimum of necessary support to vulnerable groups. This may well become a major issue for practitioners in some UK jurisdictions as the rhetoric of the 'Big Society' employs ill-considered and vague references to social capital to justify an abdication of responsibility by the government and state for the welfare of society.

Political debate within the UK, through the use of the phrase 'social mobility', avoids to a large extent addressing meaningfully the fact that young people grow up in one of the most unequal societies in Europe. In this discourse, social capital has an instrumental value: improving individuals' life chances, especially career prospects, which will encourage upward mobility. This argument is built on the false assumption that, like house prices, social mobility is unidirectional – upward. Unfortunately, if some move up, it is likely that others must move down. However, upward social mobility is likely to be blocked as advantaged families use their capital resources (of all types) to maintain their social advantage. More fundamentally those promoting social mobility as a substitute for equity ignore, wilfully presumably, Tawney's (1964, p. 105) scathing rejection of this 'tadpole' philosophy of social justice. It is inconsistent to espouse simultaneously a concept of social capital as a marker of an inclusive society and a concept of education as a commodity (in an unfair market) intended to promote individual competitive advantage.

The authors of these studies refuse to accept such limiting instrumental conceptions of social capital and provide powerful accounts of mutual support, both emotional and practical. However, they do not resolve the tensions between concepts of social capital as benefiting society and as advantaging individuals. As Barry recognises (Chapter Four), young people themselves may have internalised this individualistic view of society. She cites Holland et al (2007), who argue that staying within the 'comfort zone' of the caring role and the family network is often a positive, not a constraining, source of social capital for young people. They point out, however, that some of the young people that these authors interviewed suggested that bonding social capital was stifling and that they wanted more social mobility (getting on) than was available within the home environment (getting by).

These accounts recognise the role of the school and other local networks in building bonding social capital while failing to build much bridging or any linking social capital. Allison and Catts, however, illustrate in Chapter Five the importance of the youth club volunteers in bridging the young people to the wider world and broadening their horizons. Unlike financial and human capital, which are in some senses 'owned' by the individual and transferable from one context to another, social capital is by definition more bound, either to a specific context or, more generally, to interaction with others. The relationship between the individual's skills, attributes and dispositions and the support afforded by the social infrastructure or context (local or extended) requires further consideration if we are to avoid the traps of attribution approaches (Kennedy, 2010). These tensions and the need for further enquiry, both theoretical and practical, are noted in the studies. Barry, following Bourdieu (1990), notes in Chapter Four the constant interplay between structural constraints and individual choice in the construction and reconstruction of the social world. Smyth et al (Chapter Three) point to the need for policy, practice and research to address explicitly the fundamental tension between the collective value of social capital to the local community (or indeed communities) and its value to the individual.

These accounts raise an issue ignored by some who claim that social capital is in decline. Those who argue this frequently portray social capital in terms of local community activities (neighbourliness, participation in community groups) or of formal citizenship (voting, petitioning). They fail to recognise that communities are not limited to territorial communities, although Allison and Catts' case study (Chapter Five) reveals the importance of neighbourhoods and the territories they covered. There are communities of interest and of language, culture and faith. There are communities which are obligatory (school or workplace) and communities freely chosen (face-to-face, online or global). These young people belonged to a variety of communities.

The studies describe prosocial networks, generally aligned with the stated aims of school education, even where school education was failing to carry these out. For many practitioners, social capital may, however, be associated with cultures which are troubling in some way: antisocial and anti-school (for example territorial gangs); distracting (for example Goths); or generally prosocial but opposed to aspects of school culture (for example Moravian Brethren expectations of girls' roles).

The authors' interest in service users (children, young people, parents) precludes in-depth examination of the role of bonding social capital in sustaining and developing the habitus and acculturation of practitioners (within a staff room, a subject interest group, a trade union), policy makers (within a government agency or a local authority directorate) and researchers. This may reinforce the view that social capital is an issue for (disadvantaged) young people and sustain a culture in which practitioner, policy and research communities do not expose themselves to considered scrutiny. Related to this is the limited extent to which learners were included as active partners in planning and carrying out the research. This is attributed to practical constraints (Chapter Three) or to the unwillingness of practitioners, policy makers and parents to facilitate the active participation of young people (Chapter Two).

The relationship between Bernstein's concept of restricted codes (1973) and bonding social capital may be worth consideration. Both have to some extent negative connotations. Restricted codes are sometimes associated with communities marked by low aspirations and close horizons; similar suggestions have been made about the operation of bonding social capital, evidenced by the Office for National Statistics (2001). However, restricted codes can be associated with 'high status' communities (for example, a church) which are self-referential and sustained by bonding social capital – networks, trust and shared norms. The significant factor in accessing both elaborated codes and bridging and linking social capital may be support for learners to develop awareness of the value of operating in new contexts and their capabilities to plan their own learning – skills and attributes as well as knowledge. This clearly has implications for school practice.

Smyth et al (Chapter Three) comment directly on classroom practice and pedagogy; Barry (Chapter Four) does so less directly. Linking social capital to policy and practice in curriculum, pedagogy and assessment is essential if practitioners are to consider this matter further. This may contribute helpfully to developing practical definitions of social capital. In Scotland, links between Curriculum for Excellence (CfE) and social capital practice can be established. CfE affords learners opportunities to develop not only the knowledge and understanding but also the skills and perhaps, even more importantly, the attributes and capabilities which will support the development of social capital in ways which recognise not only benefits to the individual but also to society.

Two of the four capacities fundamental to CfE (successful learners and confident individuals) can be readily associated with individual aspirations. However, the Curriculum Review Group's report (Scottish Executive, 2004) makes it clear that even within these two capacities learners will demonstrate skills and attributes related to practice associated with social capital:

> Successful learners with ... openness to new thinking and ideas ... will be able to
>
> • learn independently and as part of a group
>   link and apply different kinds of learning in new situations
>
> Confident individuals with ... self-respect ... secure values and beliefs will be able to
>
> • relate to others and manage themselves
> • achieve success in different areas of activity. (p. 12)

The other two capacities (responsible citizens and effective contributors to society) explicitly recognise that education relates to social as well as individual benefit. More categorically, this document makes clear that some of the connections referred to in social capital literature should be features of learning in Scotland's schools:

> Respectful and constructive relationships are the starting
> point for successful learning. Schools and other educational
> settings can foster respect, responsibility and tolerance by
> living out their values, practising them within their own
> communities. (Scottish Executive, 2004, p. 13)

These early aspirations have been developed within Curriculum for
Excellence through a move from a concept of education defined
primarily as content to one of education articulated in terms of learning.
This requires the education system formally to recognise young people's
learning in contexts beyond the school and in ways beyond those
typical of previous school education. The concept of achievement
now extends beyond traditional models of attainment which focused
on the reproduction of knowledge and the demonstration of narrowly
defined skills, validated through national and local qualifications systems.
Education is no longer limited to a passive reproduction of the past but
rather challenges and supports young people to contribute actively to
planning their learning and, therefore, their future.

Building the Curriculum 5: a framework for assessment (Scottish
Government, 2011; –original version published in 2009) and the
associated document (Scottish Government, 2010c) outline the
means by which learners become active participants in planning and
reviewing their learning through a range of assessment activities,
including personal learning planning, profiles, learner statements, self-
assessment and peer assessment. These are not simply a set of easy to
apply techniques. Rather they imply different roles for the learner and
for the teacher from those to which we have been accustomed. The
learners' active role involves not only developing a wider range of skills
and attributes but also ensures that they are aware of in control of, and
responsible for their learning, in partnership with their teachers and
others. Government funded research (Scottish Government, 2010a and
2010b) into the recognition of achievement concluded that learners
can be supported to reflect on their learning and gather evidence of
all kinds of learning and achievement. They can use this to reflect on
and better understand their learning, to explain their learning to others
and to prove their achievement against formally recognised standards.

The principles underpinning the recognition of achievement,
profiling and reporting (Scottish Government, 2010c) require that
practices:

1. relate to the full range of achievement in learning
2. are appropriate to the learner's age, stage, individual needs and interests, and support further learning
3. are fair, inclusive and manageable
4. promote learner ownership through reflection by learners and dialogue with learners as central features
5. focus on the progress which the child or young person has made and take account of the breadth, challenge and application of learning. (p. 5)

These developments in assessment which challenge and support learners' self-awareness and responsibilities are closely related to developments in pedagogy (for example, critical thinking, collaborative learning) which promote the learners' responsibility not only to themselves but also to their peers.

These developments are not limited to classroom practice. The move to recognise the range of contexts in which learning takes place, the extended range of learning and the range of achievement was recognised at an early point by the statement in *Progress and proposals* (Scottish Executive, 2006) and reinforced in *Building the curriculum 3: a framework for learning and teaching* (Scottish Government, 2008, p. 3) that learning takes place through:

- the ethos and life of the school as a community
- curriculum areas and subjects
- interdisciplinary projects and studies
- opportunities for wider achievement.

The recognition of learners' multiple communities, including local communities, online communities and communities of interest (formal and informal), as valued sites for learning extends the range of knowledge, skills and attributes recognised by the education system to include those which are built into the social context of the learner's life. This approach may promote models of learning distinct from those that stress the centrality of the individual. It extends learners' understanding both of how they learn and of what learning is. Schools, through valuing the contribution to their learning of the communities of which learners are members, value the bonding social capital of these communities. Further they build links with their communities which may afford opportunities for the development of bridging and linking social capital across the school and communities.

The move from focusing primarily on knowledge and understanding to enhancing skills, attributes and capabilities encourages schools to support learners to be more aware of the need to be critical of the pressures of acculturation while being more able to use their learning in a range of contexts. Insofar as social capital can be related to the individual's skills and attributes and separated from a social context, then it seems clear that these skills and attributes must support the development, maintenance and enhancement of social relationships which can be extended beyond the immediate 'comfort zone'. This requires learners to be able to continue learning, to meet new challenges. The clearest statement of the role of the school in promoting the sorts of skills, attributes and capabilities which may be associated with social capital is provided in the statements of experiences and outcomes in health and well-being (Scottish Government, 2008, p. 1):

> I can expect my learning environment to support me to:
>
> * develop my self-awareness, self-worth and respect for others
> * meet challenges, manage change and build relationships
>   ...
> * understand and develop my ... social skills ...
> * understand that adults in my school community have a responsibility to look after me, listen to my concerns and involve others where necessary ...
> * acknowledge diversity and understand that it is everyone's responsibility to challenge discrimination.

The specific statements of experiences and outcomes related to mental and emotional well-being and to social well-being provide some detail of how these expectations can be operationalised. Examples include:

> * I know that friendship, caring, sharing, fairness, equality and love are important in building positive relationships
>   ...
> * I contribute to making my school community one which values individuals equally and is a welcoming place for all
> * Through contributing my views, time and talents, I play a part in bringing about positive change in my school and wider community
> * I value the opportunities I am given to make friends and be part of a group in a range of situations. (Scottish Government, 2008 p. 3)

These are the responsibility of all staff. The ethos of the school expressed through relationships and symbols becomes as important as the concepts of pedagogy, assessment and curriculum.

While these developments recognise the social aspects of learning, they do not in themselves deal with social inequality. This matter is recognised most explicitly perhaps by Barry (Chapter Four). If we accept Bourdieu's thesis that social capital is distributed as unequally as financial capital and that those who hold social capital will, like those who hold financial capital, use this to maintain their advantaged position, then we are forced to consider again the powerfully argued conclusion by Bernstein (1970) that education cannot compensate for society. Too much 'compensatory' education has focused on blaming (whatever the euphemism employed) individuals for their alleged personal failings. Education becomes no more than a palliative, ameliorating the worst symptoms of the inequality of our society by allowing a few people to 'escape from their backgrounds'.

As noted above, Scottish schools and teachers are explicitly obliged to promote inclusion and social justice. The Educational Institute of Scotland (EIS), as a trade union and professional organisation, has consistently argued that education must provide a model of a more just society and must prepare learners to work for such a society throughout their lives, but has argued as strongly that the successful achievement of a more just society requires that barriers to equality must be removed. The *Breaking down the barriers* series of publications has developed this; the most recent, following AGM 2008 decisions, is *Poverty and education* (Educational Institute of Scotland, 2010).

It is, of course, important that teachers develop the skills and capabilities required for their pupils to be active and critical members of society, to develop the individual attributes which support the creation of social capital. Curriculum for Excellence moves towards this. At the same time teachers must pursue the development of a more just society to ensure a more equitable distribution of all types of capital, including social capital; this is a precondition for ensuring that all young people can use their skills and attributes to their own benefit and that of society.

References

Bernstein B. (1970) 'Education cannot compensate for society', *New Society*, vol 15, no 387, pp 344–47.

Bernstein B. (1973) *Class, codes and control, vol 1*, London: Routledge and Kegan Paul.

Bourdieu P. (1986) 'The forms of capital', in J. E. Richardson (ed) *Handbook of research for the theory of sociology*, Westport, CT: Greenwood Press, pp 241–58.

Bourdieu, P. (1990) *In other words: essays towards a reflexive sociology* (trans. M. Adamson), Cambridge: Polity Press.

Educational Institute of Scotland (2010) *Poverty and education*, Edinburgh: EIS, www.eis.org.uk/images/pdf/povertypaper2010web.pdf

Equality and Human Rights Commission (2010) *What equality law means for you as an education provider: schools*, London: EHRC, www.equalityhumanrights.com/advice-and-guidance/new-equality-act-guidance/equality-act-guidance-downloads/

Field, J. (2003) *Social capital*, London: Routledge.

General Teaching Council for Scotland (2006) *The standard for full registration*, Edinburgh: GTC, www.gtcs.org.uk/web/FILES/the-standards/standard-for-full-registration.pdf

Haezewindt P. (2003) 'Investing in each other and the community: the role of social capital', *Social Trends*, no 33, London: Office for National Statistics, pp 19–27.

Holland, J., Reynolds, T. and Weller, S. (2007) 'Transitions, networks and communities: The significance of social capital in the lives of children and young people', *Journal of Youth Studies*, vol 10, no 1, pp 97–116.

HMSO (2010) *Equality Act,* London: HMSO, www.legislation.gov.uk/ukpga/2010/15/contents

Kennedy, M.M. (2010) 'Attribution error and the quest for teacher quality', *Educational Researcher*, vol 39, pp 591–8.

McGonigal, J., Doherty, R., Allan, J., Mills S., Catts, R., Redford, M., McDonald, A., Mott, J. and Buckley, C. (2007) 'Social capital, social inclusion and changing school contexts: a Scottish perspective', *British Journal of Educational Studies*, vol 55, no 1, pp 77–94.

OECD (2007) *Reviews of national policies for education: quality and equity of schooling in Scotland*, Paris: OECD.

Office for National Statistics (2001) *Social capital: a review of the literature*, London: Office for National Statistics, www.ons.gov.uk/ons/guide-method/user-guidance/social-capital-guide/the-social-capital-project/index.html

Runge, E. (1971) *Reise nach Rostock*, Frankfurt am Main: Suhrkamp Verlag.

Schuller, T., Baron, S. and Field, J. (2000) 'Social capital: a review and critique', in S. Baron, J. Field and T. Schuller (eds) *Social capital: critical perspectives*, Oxford: Oxford University Press, pp 1–38.

Scottish Executive (2004) A *curriculum for excellence: The Curriculum Review Group,* Edinburgh: Scottish Executive, www.scotland.gov.uk/Resource/Doc/26800/0023690.pdf

Scottish Executive (2006) A *curriculum for excellence: progress and proposals,* Edinburgh: Scottish Executive, www.scotland.gov.uk/Resource/Doc/98764/0023924.pdf

Scottish Government (2008) *Building the curriculum 3: a framework for learning and teaching,* Edinburgh: Scottish Government, www.ltscotland.org.uk/Images/building_the_curriculum_3_jms3_tcm4-489454.pdf

Scottish Government (2008) *Curriculum for excellence: health and well-being experiences and outcomes,* Edinburgh: Scottish Government, www.ltscotland.org.uk/Images/hwb_across_learning_experiences_outcomes_tcm4-540905.pdf

Scottish Government (2010a) *Recognising achievement: literature review and model for managing recognition processes, Edinburgh: Scottish Government,* www.scotland.gov.uk/Resource/Doc/303752/0095220.pdf

Scottish Government (2010b) *The national evaluation of the collaborative enquiry projects on recognising achievement, Edinburgh: Scottish Government,* www.scotland.gov.uk/Resource/Doc/303888/0095293.pdf

Scottish Government (2010c) *Building the curriculum 5: a framework for assessment: recognising achievement, profiling and reporting, Edinburgh: Scottish Government,* www.ltscotland.org.uk/Images/BtC5RecognisingAchievement_tcm4-641217.pdf

Scottish Government (2011) *Building the curriculum 5: a framework for assessment, Edinburgh: Scottish Government,* www.ltscotland.org.uk/buildingyourcurriculum/policycontext/btc/btc5.asp

Scottish Negotiating Committee for Teachers (2001) *A teaching profession for the 21st Century, Edinburgh: SNCT,* www.snct.org.uk/library/278/2001%20Teachers%20Agreement.pdf

Stolle D. and Hooghe, M. (2004) Review article: 'Inaccurate, exceptional, one-sided or irrelevant? The debate about the alleged decline of social capital and civic engagement in Western societies', *British Journal of Political Studies,* vol 35, pp 149–67.

Tawney, R. (1964) *Equality,* London: George Allen and Unwin.

Part II
Social capital in and out of school

SEVEN

Social capital transitions of 'Get Ready For Work' trainees

Janine Muldoon and Ralph Catts

Introduction and context of the case study

This chapter presents findings from a case study of six young people in Glasgow, Scotland, who enrolled on a course designed to help them move into employment, further education or training (EET). When this study was carried out in 2007/2008, the 'Get Ready for Work' (GRfW) programme was viewed as an important contributor to the Scottish Government's commitment to social justice (Scottish Executive, 2006). Until its inception, most previous policy interventions had an employability focus and did not specifically address the various risk factors that make positive outcomes hard to achieve (York Consulting Ltd, 2005). The young people targeted are those who face multiple barriers related to economic disadvantage and educational disaffection, such as poor physical and mental health and low attainment (Raffe, 2003; Thomas et al, 2008).

Access to social capital is likely to be particularly important for these young people, helping them to overcome or become more resilient to the problems they face. Social capital has been described as the best predictor, after poverty, of children's welfare. Families with high social capital are more likely to have children who have good mental and physical health, educational attainment and subsequent employment (Ferguson, 2006). However, an inward-looking tendency is said to characterise people who live in deprived areas (Atkinson and Kintrea, 2004). Therefore, bonding social capital on its own may intensify a sense of 'us and them' and limit opportunities to develop bridging and linking social capital.

The authors were aware, from their discussions with staff at the centre prior to the course, that people in the local area lacked confidence and tended not to venture too far from home. Safety, as an important constituent of community social capital, was a particular concern. In the most disadvantaged areas of Glasgow, the presence of male gangs who perpetrate violent acts defines territories and boundaries that must not be crossed (Kintrea and Suzuki, 2008).

Weller (2009, p. 874) argues that social networks are particularly important for young people as they are implicated in identity formation: 'different forms of social capital can enable the creation of new identities or the (re)affirmation of particular aspects of self'. As the quality of our relationships and the provisions they yield affect the way we feel about ourselves, interactions with others are inherently emotional (Lupton, 1998). If young people have difficulties forming relationships or are unable to understand and manage the emotions they experience, they are unlikely to be able to learn effectively and therefore move on in life (Goleman, 1996).

GRfW was designed specifically to address barriers to EET outcomes through 'holistic' support and tailored 'strands' to suit particular groups of individuals. The case study reported in this chapter was based in a community centre in Glasgow that was contracted to run the introductory level 'Life Skills' course. Its focus was on helping young people socialise and participate, get back into a routine and attend on a regular basis, as well as supporting them to move on to another strand of the programme or to other opportunities appropriate to their needs.

The main aims of the study were to identify social capital that participants brought to the course and to track any changes in social capital and associated effects as a result of being on the course. The following questions guided the research:

- What kinds of social capital resources did these early school leavers have access to when they made their entry into community learning activities?
- What were their recollections of schooling and how have family and school life contributed to current social capital and emotional well-being?
- What role did social capital play in participants accessing and remaining on the course?
- Did young people form new social capital during the course and how did this help them access further opportunities?

Methodology

The cohort involved in our case study commenced their 12-week course in April 2007 and the authors monitored their progress during the course and over the subsequent 7 months with the last interviews occuring in January 2008. Although the principal method was the collection of life histories from volunteer participants, data were also generated from documentation, interviews with parents and stakeholders, and regular observations of sessions as participant observers. This chapter focuses on the data from six participants (three male, three female) and three parents (two male and one female). The authors decided (as one female and one male researcher) to interview young people of the same gender. Each participant was involved in up to three interviews during the course and three contributed to follow-up interviews carried out 3–4 months and 6–7 months after course completion.

A staged-interview process (outlined below) was used to enable insight into the ways in which social capital had operated in the young people's lives. Interviews were also divided into segments with a break for refreshments, and simple pen and paper exercises were used to trigger discussion, because the authors were aware from pilot interviews that some participants would be reluctant to talk openly. The same degree of information could not have been captured if this process had been rushed.

The first brief interview in the third or fourth week sought information on how the young people came to be on the course and who had played a role in this decision. A Health Score Sheet was administered to get a sense of their self-perceptions and general feelings about life. A mapping exercise was also used to identify important people in their lives and those with whom they spent time. The second and longer interview in the seventh or eighth week used a life history approach to ascertain prior experiences at school, at home and in their community. Their experience of the GRfW course was also discussed. The third interview, carried out during the last two weeks of the course, examined how social capital had developed during the course and how they felt about moving on. The Health Score Sheet and mapping exercise were repeated to help identify outcomes related to the course.

The follow-up interviews were carried out ten to twelve weeks after the course, and then again just over six months later. These interviews were concerned with their overall progress in securing employment, education or training outcomes and how they were faring emotionally. The main aim was to identify whether the social capital they had accessed during the course had improved their prospects.

Measures

In the light of the links between social resources and mental health, the Health Score Sheet was designed to provide a snapshot of participants' views about themselves and their life at the beginning and end of the course. The authors were keen to examine how social capital developed and to assess whether enhanced social capital was related to improved emotional well-being. Therefore, measures from the Scottish Health Behaviour in School-aged Children (HBSC) study (Griebler et al, 2010) were used to assess self-rated health and subjective well-being (happiness and life satisfaction). The Mental Health Index (European KIDSCREEN Group, 2006) and a measure of shyness which we adapted for use with this group (Crozier, 1995) were also employed because the course tutors had concerns about social anxiety and inferiority experienced by young people in the local area. A further measure was taken from the HBSC study to assess the supportiveness of the centre where the course took place. This is important in terms of the young people accessing the social resources available. The measure includes perceptions of participant autonomy, support from peers and tutors, and perceived demands. The wording was altered slightly to change the context from a school to a community centre environment.

Findings and emergent themes

The young people attending the course

Although the centre was expecting 11 participants, only one female and three male trainees attended on the first day. The other seven participants arrived at different times during the first two weeks, although two of these (male) participants withdrew after initial contact and another was asked to leave in Week 4 after a court conviction became known to staff. The six participants we interviewed had left school between 6 and 18 months before starting the course and all had been unemployed since leaving school. Only one person had succeeded in any further education, but had not progressed beyond an initial course. The impetus to join the community centre course stemmed either from the enthusiastic portrayal of the centre by Careers Scotland advisers, or because the participants knew people who had attended previously. In all cases, there was encouragement from immediate family and the small stipend for attendance was also a motivating factor. The participants had not been in receipt of any welfare or job start allowance before commencing the course.

The Health Score Sheet (HSS), used in the first interview, revealed some interesting insights into the young people's evaluations of themselves and their lives. First, the life satisfaction scores were particularly striking. In contrast to the general population of 15 year olds, 85% of whom score six or more on the zero-to-ten scale (Currie et al, 2011), these young people rated their life to be four or five. When asked what would improve things, if they could change one thing, the responses highlighted the significance of family circumstances, learning difficulties and problems managing feelings.

> 'Ma [my] reading and writing.'
> 'My anger … sometimes I snap, sometimes I flip, but well I didn't have a problem with my mum breaking with my dad at first but then when [boyfriend] moved in … my anger just kind of rules a wee bit.'
> 'Never smoke hash … I used to when I was young, it affects your memory.'
> 'My family … yeah actually there's a lot about my family that I'd like to change.'
> 'Not get angry … I'm like a volcano.'
> 'To go out more often … I'm always babysitting for my big sister … 'cause she can no [cannot] cope.'

Underlying these comments was the respondents' lack of either peer social capital or influential adults beyond their immediate family, perhaps explaining why four of the six participants reported feeling sad to some extent and four out of five who responded to the question said they felt moderately or very lonely. Other contributory factors included negative experiences in the past, boredom associated with lifestyle patterns and negative perceptions of self in relation to achievements, academic or otherwise.

Family life, social capital and emotional well-being

Families with high social capital are more likely to have a two-parent structure with a paternal figure (Ferguson, 2006), but all the young people in this case study were living in single-parent homes either alone or with siblings. Two girls were living with their mother and one with her father, and likewise two of the boys were living with mum and one with dad. In most cases, there had been conflict, and either strong negative emotions (resentment, anger) were directed at the parent or parental figure who had left the family home, or they did not want to mention the departed parent at all. Sympathy for what the parent they lived with had been through was also apparent, suggesting that these single parents had also experienced difficulties coping. In each case the family trauma had occurred just before or after they had entered secondary school and this disruption appeared to be associated with the difficulties they encountered in secondary school, especially when they had moved to a new school in a new area. One boy's father confirmed that his divorce had been the main reason for his son leaving school and was still continuing to hold him back: "the way that the marriage broke up, that really devastated him and [sister] as well you know, but we've obviously learned to go on from it, whereas [participant] hasn't."

Ryan (2002) found that emotional health suffers when family structure changes are associated with weakened affective bonds between parents and children. This was the case in relation to the absent parent for this group of young people. However, in most cases the separation appeared to generate stronger bonding social capital with the remaining parent, so much so that this appeared in some cases to restrict linking or bridging social capital. Family demands and loyalty or responsibility limited social capital formation. A strong sense of duty was evident in the girls' descriptions of their home life. Two described a strong bond with a parent and referred to 'looking after' them. One of the girls described her mum as the only friend she had and her references to other family members suggested that there had been conflict in the past and that she and her mum were somehow separate from the rest of the family. The other female participant with close family ties was the second youngest of five girls, but, according to her dad, was unlike the others (and more like him) in that she liked to stay at home. Consequently, she had become the main carer of both her dad and her sisters' children when they were working, shopping or in ill health. She also had a chronic health condition.

Poor relationships with parents and extended family were apparent for another girl who described having lots of 'dads' but only viewed her biological father favourably. Perhaps unsurprisingly, she did not get on well with her mum, with whom she was living when the course commenced. She welcomed wholeheartedly the relationships she was developing with her boyfriend's family and her commitment to them was very strong in spite of difficulties she was having due to his drug and alcohol usage.

Perhaps the most important finding relates to the paucity or even complete absence of people in their lives that they would call 'friends'. All of the girls had a boyfriend but all the boys with the exception of one said they did not have a girlfriend, but would like one. None of the boys had any male peers whom they identified as friends. The absence of age peers is undoubtedly linked to leaving school early (Audas and Willms, 2002) but also to spending a great deal of time at home or in the immediate local environment. One female participant talked about living in a dangerous area and so didn't go out at night and this was a reason for not attending the final interview as she would be getting back home in the dark. Most of the group said they spent time at local shops, McDonald's and the cinema, but did not go into the city centre. Interestingly, one of the participants' fathers explained why his daughter spent most of her time in the local areas:

> 'with [sisters'] boyfriends and husbands and that side of the family, you really don't need to go very far to mix socially... most of the people in our district have not moved out, they've mostly stayed here and took up housing beside us.'

In other words, the close bonding of family and local community, while positive in many respects, can lead to networks that are limited in terms of bridging or linking social capital.

For most participants, no immediate family members were employed, and in all families the parent or sibling they lived with was unemployed. This meant that they had limited access to networks of people in employment or further education. There was one exception where a member of the extended family who was employed offered opportunities to access a course. However, this generated stress because the participant did not feel competent enough to succeed and allowances were not made for her health problems.

Life since school

The majority of participants had left school early, but the reasons for this had to be inferred as in most cases there was a reluctance to discuss this time in their lives; perhaps as one participant explained, there was no desire to look back: "can't remember ... I left school and then I shut it off." Only one female participant had fond memories of school; she left early because she was offered a place (recommended by teachers) on a college course. For the others, descriptions of life since school were vague. Every participant said that prior to the course they had been doing 'nothing'; however, it was clear from the interviews that the girls were supporting their families, through babysitting siblings' children or looking after parents who were unwell or could not manage certain tasks. The girls appeared to have cultivated a strong identity in relation to their caring roles within the family, or in one case, a 'surrogate' family that had been developed through her relationship with her boyfriend. All of the girls referred to doing housework and looking after a parent, or in the latter case, her boyfriend as a result of his drug and alcohol abuse. The boys, by contrast, had no current peer networks and said they spent most of their time playing Xbox or computer games at home.

Participants' explanations that they had been doing 'nothing' or 'sitting on my arse' since leaving school appeared to stem from feeling that they had made no progress and this was linked to a lack of work or college experience. Pressure from parents, siblings living in the home or extended family to 'do something' and perhaps contribute financially as well as practically to the home exacerbated the tendency to view themselves in negative terms. Efforts appear to have been made by all participants to gain a college place or apply for jobs, although details were provided in only two cases. It is possible, as with their recollections of school, that perceived failure to secure employment, education or training led to a tendency to shut out and forget these attempts. On the other hand, their lack of success may have resulted from a failure to identify opportunities available to them, as knowledge about career pathways was vague or distorted. One girl, for example, thought it would take six years to become a hairdresser and that you would need to be skilled in chemistry. They viewed themselves very negatively and as incompetent academically and these self-perceptions had fostered a sense that there would be no opportunities for them. There was certainly a reluctance to think about attending college because of its association with school, as well as identity concerns because they did not identify with being a college student. In contrast, all expressed a desire to move on in life, earn some money, support a family and secure independent housing.

In summary, on commencing the course, bonded family social capital was at the centre of the young people's experiences and the principal or only source of social discourse. This was in marked contrast to young people involved in other case studies who were exploring peer networks. Relationship breakdown and the loss of a parental figure had also generated significant emotional harm.

Perceptions of the course

The course included modules on basic skills (literacy and numeracy), employability (CV construction and job search) and healthy living (exercise, gardening, cooking and alcohol awareness). These were provided within the community centre and in the case of exercise classes at a local leisure centre. In addition, multimedia sessions were delivered at a local college. Trainees were taken on excursions to help them feel more confident moving beyond their immediate neighbourhood and there were opportunities for leisure activities (pool, computer games and table tennis) within the community centre.

The course and centre were rated very highly in respect of informal activities and relationships with staff. Importantly, one of the parents confirmed the advantage of the local community centre explaining that this was a place his son felt safe. As argued in the case study of the youth club (Chapter Five), safety is a prerequisite for learning, and it is clear, location aside, that certain members of staff created safe spaces during the course that allowed young people to express themselves.

> 'His home from home, sort of thing, you know, he feels safe, entirely, that's what I would say, he feels safe here you know.' (father of participant)

More formal aspects of the course, such as the basic skills, multimedia and alcohol awareness, appeared to trigger anxieties which were linked to negative perceptions of competence. These were exacerbated when the sessions used examples/models with which young people could not identify. Informal skills the young people possessed, such as caring for children or adult family members and budgeting, were not identified as relevant for employment. Being singled out to respond in class sessions also triggered anxiety for some, as did tutors (external to the centre) who were considered unapproachable or 'teacher-like'.

In terms of participation, it was easy to observe reluctance, standing back, boredom and sometimes anger or forthright refusal to take part. Although this was linked to apathy or lack of motivation by some stakeholders, interviews with participants revealed the extent to which they felt anxious in certain situations as a result of past experiences. These had led to entrenched negative self-perceptions, particularly in terms of basic skills and social competencies, and therefore to stubborn and defensive responses. Examples from the interviews included:

> 'I never feel like I've achieved anything.'
> 'I'm not very smart ... my head's empty.'
> 'I'm an idiot, I'm stupid.'
> 'I can't go into places.'
> 'I'm shy in front of people.'

An example of the way negative self-perceptions could manifest themselves in behaviour and participation was evident in one girl's response to the question 'is there anything you can do now that you couldn't do before the course?' She replied "no, because that spelling and maths thing, I couldn't do that," and explained angrily that when she refused to do the work set, the external provider threatened to get one of the centre's staff. Her refusal was linked to her perception that she was unable do the task and felt that the tutor was helping everyone but her. Similarly, in a numeracy workshop, one of the other female participants explained that she had not taken part in the session, even though there was only her and another trainee present. "I'm rubbish at maths," she said, as an explanation for not taking part.

Lack of confidence in numeracy was observed among the whole group in a session on alcohol awareness. When asked to calculate the number of alcoholic units in particular drinks, trainees appeared embarrassed and looked to other group members to respond. On two other occasions, one male participant whispered to one of the researchers that he wasn't confident to ask for help and welcomed intervention from the researcher in order to obtain support. Discomfort was also observed in early sessions, where participants were asked to interview each other using a microphone that they had just been taught to use. Yet another example was where they had to construct an individual CV. Taken as a whole, these incidents highlight the anxiety of the young people about their limited skills, which required a sensitive and nuanced approach rather than a traditional classroom model.

Several participants also expressed boredom as the course progressed. For some, the pace was too slow in certain sessions and there was a lot of sitting around and waiting for sessions to commence. While providers thought they were asking too much of such a group whom they felt lacked motivation to participate, trainees' comments suggested that at least for some not enough was expected.

Social capital development during the course

Several participants rated the course very highly and described it as 'better than anything else I've been to'. One participant said she couldn't 'fit in' to other courses she had attended, as they were too similar to school and consisted of people who were older than her. All participants appeared surprised at the degree of 'fun' they had experienced and found aspects of the course that were largely informal far more enjoyable and useful than those more formal sessions which, in contrast, staff felt would help them most. Sessions at the leisure centre, outdoor activities and pool sessions in the hall were viewed positively and it was clear from observation that these were the sessions in which participants really got to know each other and further developed their social skills, often in the context of feedback from tutors in relation to competitive etiquette, supporting others and treating others fairly. This is especially important given participants' negative evaluations of their own ability to socialise and talk to people at the outset. These sessions also facilitated connections with the centre tutors, who adopted a relaxed and informal approach which one participant described as "not like teachers".

By the end of the course, although participants found it difficult to pinpoint how it had helped them improve their 'skills', four of the six described the social impact of the course as its most positive feature. 'Meeting people' who were 'a laugh', 'nice', 'friendly' led to the outcomes highlighted below. Rather than describe these, the young people's comments about the ways in which they felt they had changed or improved are highlighted and linked to notable changes on their HSS.

As indicated in Table 7.1, all but one participant showed improvements on the HSS, and the one participant who showed deterioration explained that this was due to the course coming to an end " 'cause I've had laughs here and we probably won't see each other again." His father confirmed this change in his demeanour: " 'cause he's sitting round the house, he's watching the telly now and he's starting to laugh and all that sort of stuff, which he wouldnae [would not] do before, you know." The problem of endings was echoed by another participant's father:

> 'The nine weeks here gives them the basic skills to look for job employment and gives them team building as well. It makes them dependent on each other, and they know there is someone else that's in the same boat. But then again, the problem with that is that you get a course like this, you build a team, and then they've got to break from that team and go into the other environment and it's ... there is a certain group that, if you're going to help, then I think you should push that wee bit further.'

No further achievements or improvements, apart from confidence and routine, were recognised by participants, and this is undoubtedly due, in part, to poor procedures for monitoring progress and the problems identified in the previous section relating to low expectations and poor recognition of participants' anxieties and their antecedents.

Table 7.1: Matching respondent comments with HSS scores

Participant 1 (Male)
'[Staff member] says I'm interacting more', 'my brother says that I'm getting on with people and that', 'it's helped my confidence, meeting people', 'it's getting me up in the morning', 'I feel healthy ... get more sleep ... just go to my bed early'.
HSS: Felt happier, rated health more positively and showed improvements in mental health and shyness.
Participant 2 (Female)
'Dad says I'm a bit louder', 'I'm more confident', 'I can talk to different people easier than I used to'.
HSS: No Interview 3 data available.
Participant 3 (Male)
'My sense of humour ... I cannae [cannot] stop laughing', 'I think my confidence goes up each time I do this course', 'I think my confidence grew because there are such a lot of people here and they're quite friendly'.
HSS: Negative change in happiness, increase in sadness and loneliness
Participant 4 (Female)
'Mixing with the others, talking to them', '[Better at] participating', 'joining in', 'I talk more, my confidence has been building – well sort of', 'mum thinks I'm happier ... she says I'm 'glowing'. '[Can] talk to people now'.
HSS: Life satisfaction moved from 5 to 10; reduction in shyness and positive changes in mental health.
Participant 5 (Male)
Reported improvement in being able to use a computer software package (video).
HSS: Rated health 'good' rather than 'fair' and showed improvements in mental health, though slight increase in shyness.
Participant 6 (Female)
Reported no improvements.
HSS: No Interview 3 data available.

Most of the comments above identify the formation of new social connections, even though they were in the main short lived. In their exit interviews, Participants One to Four placed at least one other participant and a staff member from the centre on their map, whereas Participant Five only mentioned one trainee who was a 'pal' and Participant Six did not mention anyone at the centre. Participant Six started the course late and also attended infrequently. The others explained their greater confidence in terms of the social connections they had made, and these changes were evident for four of the five on the shyness measure. The three male participants bonded the most easily and their friendship was the only bond to last beyond the course.

One of the three also linked well with a volunteer at the Centre and subsequently joined him as a volunteer. All three attended the first day of the course, unlike the girls, who arrived at different points and tended to get on with one or two but not all of the others.

Course outcomes and social capital

Only one (male) participant was able to attend both follow-up interviews three and six months after the course and one of the other boys attended the first of these. It was impossible to secure individual follow-up interviews with the girls, although one did come along to the interview with her father. As far as the boys were concerned, significant positive changes could be observed in terms of their confidence, appearance and overall demeanour. One explained how he had finally sought support for a personal problem he had struggled with for a long time and that had prevented him engaging in social interaction. The improvement, achieved in a short space of time, was clearly evident at the three-month post interview and was surprising to the researcher. This participant had also joined a gym and had a new haircut, both of which stemmed from an increase in confidence and "my mood changing" as a result of feeling more competent socially. Referring to the course he said, "that's helped me get in the gym, from the [provider]. It's one thing I wouldn't have done." He told the researcher "I feel good" and described how his mum was "happy to see me getting on". Through his key worker, he registered with a national charity providing training and work opportunities for people who are disadvantaged in the labour market. Through a contact there, he had secured a place on a computing course two days a week, had completed forklift training and had literacy support. He explained that if he hadn't attended the GRfW course, he wouldn't have been assigned a key worker and would therefore not have established a link to the charity which was proving to be a gateway to a range of opportunities. The key worker was the vital 'bridge' between services. These positive changes were also evident on the responses to the HSS questions in the first follow-up interview. Improvements in feeling happy and in good health, evident in the end of course interview, were retained, life satisfaction had increased and, having felt very lonely up to this point, he now reported not feeling lonely at all. This participant had agreed to attend the second follow-up interview but did not arrive and explained subsequently by phone that he had met a friend on the way to the Centre. This in itself was a sign of progress in terms of peer networks because at the start of the course he named no peer friendships. However, this event may also tell us something about the role of reciprocity in his relationships with others. Perhaps he saw a new friend as someone with whom he could continue to build a relationship outside the family, whereas the researcher had made it clear that this would be the last meeting.

The participant who attended both follow-up interviews also appeared more confident socially. During the course, he had demonstrated an interest in volunteering opportunities and had managed to secure a short-term volunteer position in the centre where the course had been run. At the first follow-up interview he explained that he had also joined another GRfW course but left after one day: "I didn't enjoy it." His key worker put him in touch with A4E, an international business working with government, private and third sector organisations to design, develop and deliver frontline public services: "they get you in placements and in college, so I've got a placement and I start on Monday." In spite of this positive news, he explained that splitting up with a new girlfriend had led him "downhill ... I'm kind of going back to my old self." He had started drinking again and taking drugs, which eased his feelings of depression. Apart from positive changes in shyness (in particular, no longer feeling shy in a group), his responses on the HSS revealed very low life satisfaction and less positive mental health (mean score on a 5-point scale from 3.22 to 2.67). Negative changes in other relationships were also apparent. In particular, having responded on other occasions that it was easy to make friends and having said that it was not true that he only talked to one or two friends, he now felt the opposite.

However, by the six-month follow-up interview, the situation had changed again with reported improvements in mental health and life satisfaction. These changes appeared to be due both to resuming his close relationship and also progress with the work placement. He had moved past his 4-week trial and had been on a 13-week placement. Not only had he received positive feedback from management staff, but he had also been trusted to take on different roles within the organisation to fill in for permanent staff members who were on leave: "I was quite nervous at first but now I'm not ... I'm just used to it because I've been there so long." This experience had given him greater direction in terms of choosing a career and someone at his workplace had offered to speak to a company to 'find more contacts'. It was evident that he had now established bridging social capital with people who were able to help him connect with opportunities for employment. He also reported not having had a drink for a while, inspired by his girlfriend. He subsequently contacted one of the researchers to report that he had secured a part-time job.

As far as the girls were concerned, while all three were keen to remain involved in the research and seemed to want to sustain contact with the researchers, it was very difficult for them to identify appropriate times to meet or they were so preoccupied that they forgot the appointment. Immediately after the course, one of the girls became pregnant and so could not meet at three months as she was suffering from morning sickness and at seven months was nearing the birth date. She had begun another course, but had to leave as a result of feeling ill. Another girl had moved on to another strand of the GRfW programme. Clear changes were apparent in terms of the confidence with which she spoke to the researcher over the telephone. The full-time nature of the course, in combination with her concern about arriving home after dark to a dangerous area, prevented her attending the three-month follow-up interview, while she forgot to attend the six-month interview, as she was with 'pals'. Although this was disappointing for the research, it represented a significant development and finding in itself. On commencement of the Life Skills course, she had only identified mum as a friend, having lost contact with friends from school as they left the area one by one. During the course, she developed friendships with participants (particularly two of them) and cited this as the reason behind her developing a further friendship outside the course. Given the social anxieties and defensiveness displayed at the beginning of the course, this improvement is considerable, especially within the timescale. She talked enthusiastically about the new course and was reluctant to miss any of it to meet with the researcher.

The researcher was also unable to secure follow-up interviews with the third female participant. However, on request, her father agreed to participate in the research and attended with his daughter. This proved particularly useful because it shed light on the extent to which concerns about this group of young people involve not just the individual but the family. Clearly a supportive father, he talked of the frustration he encountered at the poor responses of employers and college administrators to the efforts his daughter was making. She had continually applied for jobs but to no avail, which was undoubtedly due, in part, to her social capital being restricted to family and family contacts, few of whom were employed. However, her father offered another explanation for her lack of success and in doing so, provided feedback for GRfW providers:

> 'I think it should be part of a six or nine month or even a year thing. If you do the initial part, which is the hardest part, to get them into the routine and get them into the

> thinking about work, and then to try to transfer it, into maybe a work-related course ... that way the transition is not so abrupt.'

He suggested that, although valuable, the course didn't really prepare them for the world of work and that without the next transitional phase, this was not enough. Some work experience within the local community, he felt, would help to expand networks, so that the young trainees would not become so dependent on people connected to the centre. Keeping these young people connected to further opportunities is vital to keep the momentum going:

> 'You could send them to work places but I think a lot of kids now would need that six months of maybe having that. If you can do it in the community, and you can have the back-up that you have got here anyway, then it can help ... She needed help and she needed an incentive but I think that making that transition into the work based environment or social environment or anything like that, interacting with other people outwith the basic training team, might make it more helpful.'

In summary, the experiences the authors shared with the participants were notable for the ways in which location enabled or disrupted social capital. In their prior experiences, many had lost peer networks due to family upheaval and relocation. Their early departure from school and hence loss of the school as a place for accessing networks led to both a paucity of peer networks and a lack of access to significant (non-parental) adults when they commenced the course. In this context, the community centre provided a safe location in which to explore new friendships. Although in the main these did not last after the course finished, the young people had gained confidence and all those whom we were able to contact after the course was completed had made new friendships. Thus the bridging social capital experience during the course, although not durable, had been a new beginning.

Researching social capital

This chapter has highlighted some of the difficulties of researching the social networks of young people with multiple forms of deprivation who live chaotic lives. The study is necessarily limited by the difficulties of making contact and following up with young people who have negative self-perceptions and lack confidence. However, it was interesting to note the transformations over time in the ways in which the young people interacted with the authors. Insights were gained from informal discussions with them while waiting for the course to begin or during break times. Some of the centre tutors noted the strong bond two of the participants had with the researchers, reflected in a gift given by one of the girls. The authors also found that the girls and two of the boys tended to 'clam up' within the recorded interviews. This was in marked contrast to their talkativeness outside this situation. Although the techniques and the developing trust in the researchers meant that this improved in later interviews, a more systematic approach to the production of field notes would have captured the informal responses of these individuals to the course and to their transition experience. Any element of 'formality' appears to be a major barrier to engagement.

This group of young people were notable for their lack of either peer networks or connections to significant adults. In this regard, they were atypical of the young people in the other case studies reported in this book. One consequence for participant observers of this lack of social capital was that as supportive adults, the authors had a significant impact on some of the group in the absence of access to other sources of social capital. Information and advice was provided that in at least one instance helped a young person move away from the influence of a drug dealer. This means that the authors could not be considered detached from the lives of the participants. Indeed, it is highly unlikely that such young people would participate in large-scale surveys or even one-off interviews. Hence the embedded strategy adopted in this study seems to be the only way to obtain an understanding of how to support progress for individuals with multiple causes of disadvantage in accessing further education and employment.

Implications for policy and practice: managing transitions

In a period of just 12 weeks, the young people were expected to make two significant transitions. The first was the transition into a programme that required regular attendance, formal learning activities and interaction with strangers. The second was the transition from the course to other employment or training options. These transitions represented significant challenges for the young people. Their school and post-school experiences, with one exception, were largely negative and related to learning difficulties and problematic relationships with peers and teachers. Networks of support were also disrupted when pupils changed school and when they moved to a new community. Indeed, an unsuccessful transition to secondary school, coupled with family breakdown, appeared to be the catalyst for a lack of peer and school social capital. Thus, a consequence for policy is how secondary schools can identify and respond to the needs of newcomers from another community who have multiple sources of disadvantage. The lack of community social capital, combined with delays in recognition of the needs of these vulnerable young people, meant that they quickly fell out of favour in the educational system and became alienated and detached from school.

Given this experience, the transition into the GRfW course was an opportunity that required sympathetic and careful management by the provider. These vulnerable young people can slip through the gaps in service provision where multiple providers are involved. The key worker was essential to provide the linking social capital that enabled these young people to access the multiple services they required. Therefore, the second conclusion for policy is that for those young people with multiple disadvantages, the key worker role is an essential element in the provision of support.

Finally, young people needed support and direction to progress beyond the 12-week course and this requires closer collaboration between the funding agencies and the community provider. Parents, young people and the community provider all supported the idea of a further 12-week course to build on the success of the initial programme, possibly subject to satisfactory attendance and participation in the initial programme. This should have been a guaranteed outcome for those who demonstrated success, but for most young people there was no immediate further avenue available. There also needs to be greater monitoring and flexibility to respond when young people show willingness to progress. The fact that work experience could not be offered to a particularly successful participant on this course was a missed opportunity.

Elliott, et al (2006, p. 299) suggest that the absence of 'a flow of information into poor inner-city neighbourhoods [will] restrict ... access to reliable information concerning labour markets, schools, apprenticeship programs, and financial markets'. Therefore a question of particular interest is whether structuring experiences of young people to deliberately enhance and strengthen the formation of bridging and linking social capital can improve the opportunities for young people to form and realise their aspirations. Some studies have reported success from such interventions with adolescents (e.g. Kay and Bradbury, 2009; Raffo, 2003). Raffo found that work placements can enable new social capital, which, in turn, influences aspirations and opportunities for employment and further education. Our findings endorse the view that developing bridging social capital improves young people's employment, education and training prospects, and their social and emotional development.

Despite the limitations associated with the implementation of the course, there were positive effects for three of the young people in terms of their emotional well-being. Greater confidence to interact with others and participate in community activities that they would not have considered is clearly a very positive foundation for the development of social capital. This highlights the importance in the early stages of re-engagement of recognising and focusing on what *individuals* can realistically accomplish in a positive way, rather than emphasising skills that participants feel they will never achieve. An initial skills focus only serves to shut down opportunities (Yates and Payne, 2006). If we are to sustain young people in further education, employment or training, it is also imperative that those working to support them develop an understanding of each young person's self-perceptions to help remove self- imposed restrictions on their prospects for further education and employment.

References

Atkinson, R. and Kintrea, K. (2004) 'Opportunities and despair, it's all in there: practitioner experiences and explanations of area effects and life chances', *Sociology*, vol 38, no 3, pp 437–55.

Audas, R. and Willms, J.D. (2002) *Engagement and dropping out of school: a life-course perspective*, Ottawa: Applied Research Branch Strategic Policy, Human Resources Development Canada.

Crozier, R.W. (1995) 'Shyness and self-esteem in middle childhood', *British Journal of Educational Psychology*, vol 65, pp 85–95.

Currie, C., Levin, K., Kirby, J., Currie, D., van der Sluijs, W. and Inchley, J. (2011) *Health behaviour in school-aged children: World Health Organization collaborative cross-national study (HBSC): findings from the 2010 HBSC survey in Scotland*, Edinburgh: Child and Adolescent Health Research Unit, The University of Edinburgh.

Elliott, D., Menard, S., Rankin, B., Elliott, A., Wilson, W. and Huizinga, D. (2006) *Good kids from bad neighbourhoods: successful development in social context*, Cambridge: Cambridge University Press.

European KIDSCREEN Group (2006) *The KIDSCREEN questionnaires: quality of life questionnaires for children and adolescents: handbook*, Lengerich: Pabst Science Publishers.

Ferguson, K.M. (2006) 'Social capital and children's well-being: a critical synthesis of the international social capital literature, *International Journal of Social Welfare*, vol 15, pp 2–18.

Goleman, D. (1996) *Emotional intelligence: why it matters more than IQ*, London: Bloomsbury.

Griebler, R., Molcho, M., Samdal, O., Inchley, J., Dür, W. and Currie, C. (eds) (2010) *Health behaviour in school-aged children: a World Health Organization cross-national study: internal research protocol for the 2009/10 survey*, Vienna: LBIHPR and Edinburgh: CAHRU.

Kay, T. and Bradbury, S. (2009) 'Youth sport volunteering: developing social capital', *Sport, Education and Society*, vol 14, no 1, pp 121–40.

Kintrea, K. and Suzuki, N. (2008) 'Too much cohesion? Young people's territoriality in Glasgow and Edinburgh', in J. Flint and D. Robinson (eds) *Community cohesion in practice: new dimensions of diversity and difference*, Bristol: The Policy Press, pp 199–218.

Lupton, D. (1998) *The emotional self: a sociocultural exploration*, London: Sage Publications.

Raffe, D. (2003) *Young people not in education, employment or training: evidence from the Scottish School Leavers Study*, Centre for Educational Sociology Briefing 29, Edinburgh: University of Edinburgh, Centre for Educational Sociology, www.ces.ed.ac.uk/PDF%20Files/Brief029.pdf

Raffo, C. (2003) 'Disaffected young people and the work-related curriculum at Key Stage 4: issues of social capital development and learning as a form of cultural practice', *Journal of Education and Work*, vol 16, no 1, pp 69–86.

Ryan, S. (2002) 'Poverty, social context and adolescent emotional health', *Dissertation Abstracts International, The Humanities and Social Sciences*, vol 62, no 11, p 3950A.

Scottish Executive (2006). *More choices, more chances: a strategy to reduce the proportion of young people not in education, employment or training in Scotland*, Edinburgh: Scottish Executive, www.scotland.gov.uk/Resource/Doc/129456/0030812.pdf

Thomas, J., Vigurs, C., Oliver, K., Suarez, B., Newman, M., Dickson, K. and Sinclair, J. (2008) 'Targeted youth support: rapid evidence assessment of effective early interventions for youth at risk of future poor outcomes', in *Research Evidence in Education Library*, London: EPPI-Centre, Social Science Research Unit, Institute of Education, University of London.

Weller, S. (2009) 'Young people's social capital: complex identities, dynamic networks', *Ethnic and Racial Studies*, vol 33, no 5, pp 872–88.

Yates, S. and Payne, M. (2006) 'Not so NEET? A critique of the use of "NEET" in setting targets for interventions with young people', *Journal of Youth Studies*, vol 9, pp 329–44.

York Consulting Limited (2005) *Literature review of the NEET group: enterprise and Lifelong Learning*, Edinburgh: Scottish Executive Social Research, www.scotland.gov.uk/Resource/Doc/77843/0018812.pdf

Acknowledgements

We would like to thank the young people who participated in the research and shared so much about their lives with us. We are also grateful to the staff at the centre for providing space for us to carry out interviews but, most of all, for their time. Thanks are also due to the parents who took part in the interviews, to members of the Schools and Social Capital Network for continual feedback over the course of the research and to Pamela McGibbon for administrative support.

EIGHT

Social capital, diversity and inclusion: lessons from one primary school

Rowena Arshad and Susan Maclennan

Many have written about the possibilities and limitations of social capital as a concept (Garmanikow and Green, 1999; Dika and Singh, 2002; Smyth, 2004). Some suggest that the term is so ubiquitous that it is now not clear if the concept is an 'analytical tool or a clingfilm wrap' (Schuller, 1999; Shucksmith, 2000) and it is difficult to distinguish between what is meaningful and what is nonsense (Garmanikow and Green 1999). However, social capital 'has been identified as having significant potential for reducing disadvantage, improving educational outcomes and enhancing health and well-being' (Allan et al, 2009 p. xiv) and it has been acknowledged that 'child development is powerfully shaped by social capital' (Putnam, 2000, p. 296). When this concept was being introduced into the education communities in Scotland through the Applied Educational Research Scheme (AERS), a primary school (which we shall now call Fairforall Primary) provided an interesting example from which to explore the concept of social capital as well as its potential for promoting inclusion and social justice.

Fairforall Primary: background

Fairforall Primary has 280 pupils and a staff of 18 and is located in an area where individuals face multiple discriminations at personal, cultural and social levels. The primary issue affecting pupils in the school's catchment area is poverty. Over two thirds of the pupils are on free school meals. Many are in cared for or fostered situations and the school regularly receives pupils with interrupted education. The nursery has the largest number of free full-time places in the local authority. While poverty is the main issue other social issues exist related to ethnicity (racism) and gender (domestic violence), as well as drug- and alcohol-related problems.

The school is a product of the merger of two schools with falling roll numbers. Within five years of merger, when this study took place, the new school looked as though it had successfully built a whole new culture where staff, parents and pupils were developing productive friendships, partnerships and networks. In this chapter, the term 'parent' is used to cover a range of people that look after children, including carers, foster parents and grandparents. The school boasts a reputation across the authority and nationally of being an inclusive school. A voiced philosophy is that the 'school never gives up on a child. We often accept and include children that others have given up on' (Arshad and Maclennan, 2008, p. 7).

The school draws from a predominantly white local population. Racism in the community led more than two decades ago to the setting up of a local anti-racist project run by black/minority ethnic community members, which is still in operation. Racism continues to be a 'live' issue, yet the school has in recent years managed to attract a number of black/minority ethnic pupils (home and international pupils and families) from within and outwith its catchment area.

The school had improved literacy and numeracy results and decreased absenteeism. By all accounts, it is a success story, and as researchers we were interested in using the concept of social capital as an analytical lens to study the phenomenon of Fairforall. The proposition that social capital is a key contributor to raising overall achievement in schools is a not a new concept (Sammons et al, 2000). Fairforall appeared to be a school that had achieved substantial improvements and we were interested in how this had happened, and what role social capital had played in the outcomes.

We wanted to explore the nature of networks that existed in the school, particularly networks that the school could draw from to develop an ethos of inclusion and achievement for the pupils as well as the fostering of a cohesive school community. The school also had a local and national reputation for being at the leading edge of many educational initiatives, such as the development of emotional literacy through the curriculum and the promotion of explicit equality and antidiscriminatory practices. Whole-school themes have included antiracism, anti-bullying, and disability and gender awareness, all taught through the domains of sense of self, sense of belonging and sense of personal power. We were intrigued to see if a productive and critical curriculum, combined with strong social capital, were potent ingredients for developing and sustaining a 'socially just school' (Smyth 2004, p 19).

Methodology

The research team consisted of a Principal Investigator (PI) from the School of Education, University of Edinburgh, and a teacher from the school. The teacher was embarking on a Master's course and it was agreed that the research would contribute to one of the module assignments. In order to establish the contribution of social capital to the school achievements, the research team wanted to explore:

• What social networks existed within the school?
• What social networks impacted upon the school?
• Who assisted in building the range of networks and social capital?

The headteacher, however, was keen that the research also provided ideas for further improvements that could be made in the school to promote equality and inclusion. The research design therefore attempted to combine both the interests of the research team and those of the headteacher. The headteacher informed the school and the wider school community of the purpose of the study through the school newsletter at the start of the 2007/08 school session and invited people to become involved in discussions with the researchers. A brief presentation was made to all teaching staff by the researchers as it was felt that this was a vital group from which to gain cooperation for the study. Two categories of participants were identified. The first covered internal participants such as pupils, parents, staff (teaching and support), and the second were those external to the school who made a significant contribution to the school activities, including the local counselling service and the Child and Family Centre.

Data were collected between August and November 2007. Most were small group interviews and began with three questions:

1. What does the school do well in the area of inclusion?
2. What could the school do better?
3. What would prevent the school from becoming better?

It was agreed from the outset that it was important that teachers, pupils and parents were aware that senior school staff were supportive of this study and that any recommendations emerging would be taken seriously. The whole senior management team was interviewed as a group. Identification of staff, pupil groups, parents and external stakeholders to be interviewed was agreed with the senior management team. It was also agreed that the classroom teacher researcher should not interview colleagues, pupils or the senior management team. This would avoid any conflicts of interest and avoid unnecessary sensitivities. The PI therefore conducted these interviews. The classroom teacher, who was respected and trusted by the parents and support staff, undertook these interviews as well as the interviews with external participants.

Interviews took place face to face but were not taped. Pupil interviews were conducted as group conversations with the Pupil Council and as classroom-based activities to seek the views of whole-class groups. With the pupil year groups, pupils were given the three questions mentioned above and were asked to discuss them in small groups. Each group appointed a scribe to write down the answers and to provide feedback to the whole group. The researcher facilitated the session, went around the groups to listen in and prompt discussions and took the feedback. Two class years were selected to take part in the study, Primary 4 (8–9 year olds) and Primary 7 (11–12 year olds). Although most of the interviews with staff were conducted in groups, some were conducted on a one-to-one basis. This was only done with peripatetic staff who could not make the group sessions as they were working in another school at the time of the meeting. Staff who were not present on the day of the interviews because of illness or who worked part time were offered the opportunity to submit written responses, and some did. Some teachers expressed anxiety about the sessions being taped and it was agreed not to tape any of the interviews. The study lost some valuable quotes as a result of this decision. Most of the interviews took place within the school, with a few outside, particularly those with external participants.

Fieldwork was concluded by the end of November as scheduled. By late January the following year, a draft report had been presented to the school senior management team, and the whole report was presented to the school staff in February. There were 33 recommendations in total. The school management team discussed the report with teaching staff in a staff development session and provided their response in May that year. The majority of the recommendations were accepted and some were already being acted upon.

One of the difficulties faced at the outset was that the question framework was very much shaped by the needs of the school and senior management team. It did not consider aspects of social capital, as the headteacher was far more keen to explore issues of inclusion. As researchers of social capital, we had to interrogate the information gained from interviews and group discussion using social capital lenses in order to meet the focus and priorities of the AERS project. This process was assisted by discussion of the emerging themes with colleagues within the AERS network over 18 months. On reflection, this was an example of the usefulness of AERS, as it facilitated the networking of researchers working on similar or connected themes.

Types of social capital in Fairforall

Catts and Ozga (2005) outlined nine school social capital indicators and these were:

- community and family contacts with school;
- attitudes to school among communities and within families;
- school-related social activities among staff and with communities;
- friendship networks among staff, among students, and with communities;
- participation in school governance by staff, students, parents and communities;
- relationships with and among teachers and other school staff members;
- teachers' relationships with other professionals;
- communication and information within schools and with communities;
- responsiveness to particular issues, including diversity.

Fairforall met the above indicators, though particular features stood out. Good and regular communication was seen as important and the headteacher provided time for weekly staff meetings and regular parent evenings and events, as well as a monthly newsletter that was posted on the school website. These news updates were also sent to external partner agencies. The headteacher was particularly conscious that schools are 'structured hierarchies' (Field, 2009, p. 28) and wanted to create an institution that was more democratic. Debate was encouraged as such exchanges were seen to be vital for developing critical thinking and emotional literacy:

> 'What I like about working here is that staff can disagree but within a supportive environment. There is openness and willingness to debate.' (male classroom teacher)

There were clearly strong and bonded networks between teachers in each stage of the school, that is within early years, middle school and senior stages.

Parents were acknowledged as prime educators and it was recognised that parental expectations played a part in their child's academic and social success (or not) and that home norms and values were key shapers. There is a dedicated parents' room within the school, which doubles as a community/meeting room, and observation over the months showed that it was well used by parents and community members. Many of the research interviews for this study took place there. Drawing from the school's own budget, the school employed a home–school liaison teacher (Gemma) whose job was to provide a bridge between staff and parents. What is important to note here is that many schools in Scotland have in the past employed home–school liaison workers, but in Fairforall, this role was given to a qualified teacher so that she had the professional ability to discuss learning and teaching matters with parents, not simply provide a link to the school. This role was viewed by both parents and school staff as being essential and vital to maintaining the bridges the school has with parents and local communities:

> 'Gemma is key. She is pivotal in making this school inclusive. She is hard to replace. She has built up so many relationships with parents and it is the trust. Gemma also nips things in the bud so that things do not escalate to the next stage. For example, to detention.' (female classroom teacher)

Fairforall's parents ranged from those who had lived in the area all their lives to more recent arrivals such as international students and migrant workers; they included those who were vulnerable within society, such as drug addicts, those with moderate learning difficulties and people with a criminal conviction record. The school tried hard not to stigmatise the communities that the children came from. One of the senior teachers in the school had grown up in the area and was viewed by the local community as 'someone who had made good'. This teacher provided a vital link between school and local community. The trust this teacher was able to generate from the credentials of having been 'one of us' was a potential contributory factor to existing social capital. Parents interviewed valued the informality of the relationship with the school:

> 'There is good communication and we are not barred from the school or nursery gates. We are welcomed in, it is informal ... it is a lot more formal in other schools.' (female parent)

This was an achievement, given that many of the parents would have had a negative experience of school when they were growing up and many had tended to avoid education establishments.

The staff prided themselves in being able to work with any child who came to the school to achieve positive outcomes:

> 'We have the confidence to take that last step with children others have given up on. However we succeed, that is still better than nothing. So a child might be consistently late ... but at least they are in. For some of these pupils, the fact they have turned up is itself really positive.' (depute headteacher)

We saw strong collegial networks between staff, particularly within specific school stages, between the home–school teacher, receptionist, janitor and parents, and between the senior management team and the rest of the staff (teaching as well as support staff). However, other strong networks were also evident and these were with particular external agencies. One agency, a child and family centre, indicated that the 'Fairforall model' of working in equitable partnership with external agencies is one that they had taken to other cluster schools as an exemplar of excellent practice. Some of the positive features of this model included systematic forward planning between the school and the external agency, attendance at transition meetings and intake panels, and the setting up of shadowing opportunities for the external agency staff within the school. The high-level involvement of the headteacher and senior management team gave strong signals that external partners were prioritised and valued:

> 'There is a strong community focus in this school, involving parents, staff and children as equal partners across the curriculum and activities. As a result, we all feel committed to the school. Fairforall has an outward vision and looks beyond its geographical area. Diversity and respect for diversity is obvious when you walk in - it is just embedded in the school.' (local community worker)

Another important feature was the refusal of the senior management team or staff to adopt a deficit model of blaming parents, pupils or the local communities for underachievement or absenteeism. Instead, the school took institutional responsibility to set in place mechanisms to improve equality and outcomes. The following were regularly cited as examples of structural processes that assisted the promotion of inclusion and equality:

- The Breakfast Club, which catered for about 100 pupils and was viewed by a substantial number of participants as a great success. The Club and its staff were viewed as an excellent resource for the school in meeting the needs of many pupils.
- An active and 'living' Pupil Council, where young people could have their voices heard.
- An established Buddy System, whereby senior pupils buddy junior pupils, helping them to feel part of the family of the school and providing supportive ties.
- The existence of a dedicated parents' room and a home–school liaison teacher.
- Regular consultation and involvement of staff, pupils and parents when generating or updating school policies and guidelines.

Parents also noted that the school was sensitive to the fact that the majority of the local community lived on the breadline or in severe poverty. At the time of the study, central and local government were pushing a programme called Enterprise in Education. Many schools in the authority were developing business projects and producing goods to sell, and often the 'buyers' were parents and local community members. However, Fairforall, recognising that its catchment consisted of families already economically constrained, channelled the enterprise start-up funds into workshops that helped their pupils consider the type of skills and knowledge that were important to help them improve their life chances.

Pupils as active citizens

The researchers held group discussions with the whole Pupil Council (ranging from ages 5–11 years) and with pupils from two separate year groups (age groups 8–9 years and 10–11 years). There were seven pupils in the Pupil Council, and between the two year groups, approximately forty-five pupils. The pupils echoed what teachers, other staff, parents and partner agencies had stated that the school was welcoming and inclusive.

'This school allows cuddles.' (boy pupil, aged 8)

'When I first came, I had a uniform that was red and black.
Here it is blue. I was different but it was OK. Now I have
a blue uniform.' (girl pupil, aged 10)

Pupils discussed how they were provided with opportunities to develop
awareness of a range of issues, including global issues, and to have
their individual selves celebrated. One of the more animated issues
discussed was the successful 'Bring your pet to school day'. The idea
had been proposed by a pupil and was perceived by members of staff
as impractical. Pupils referred the matter to the Pupil Council, which
endorsed the idea. The Pupil Council proposed to staff that all pupils
should be allowed to bring in a pet, but before doing so, to apply for a
Pet Pass, where conditions were attached to ensure the pet was suitable
to bring in and met health and safety considerations. The pupils also
provided recommendations to the researchers on issues they wished the
school staff to consider, and the most memorable was the reclamation
of the 'Rainbow Bench'. This bench, placed in the playground, was
provided as a safe place in which any pupil feeling sad or lonely, or who
needed help, could go and sit. Sitting on the bench was a signal to other
pupils, teaching and support staff, that that pupil wanted some support.
However in recent months, the bench had been used as a doorstop
propping open the doors from the classroom to the playground.
The pupils missed their bench and used the group discussion as an
opportunity to let senior school staff know that they should not only
reinstate the bench but also refresh it. This was a recommendation that
was readily accepted by school management. The above two examples
provide evidence of the existence of bonding social capital and networks
that enabled pupil voice(s) to emerge.

The majority of the pupils at Fairforall have not had opportunities
to move beyond their immediate geographical area largely due to
poverty. To make the 'think local, act global' slogan real, the school
chose to develop twinning links with a school for refugee children on
the borders of Thailand and Burma. However the links did not follow
the more customary model of raising money for 'poor people in Third
World countries'. Instead, the school engaged in critical thinking with
its pupils. They learnt about the unjust imprisonment of Aung San Suu
Kyi and the plight of refugee and migrant children on the Thai/Burma
border, and reflected on experiences that might be shared despite the
near 8,000 mile distance between the two schools. For example, many
of the children in the refugee school were separated from their parents
due to detention, or parents simply not being around or no longer
alive. This struck a chord with quite a few of the pupils in Fairforall

who were also missing their parents, some being in prison and some just simply not around, while other pupils were in foster care. Pupils in Fairforall are provided with a range of opportunities to move away from the limitations of their geographical or social class by coming into contact with world issues and ideas and do so in line with a solidarity and antidiscriminatory approach.

Field (2009), reflecting on the work of Catts and Ozga (2005), suggests that there is a need to provide further indicators when measuring the level and quality of social capital in schools. He suggests a need to take into account: the levels of trust and mistrust within the school; power relations present; who controls and distributes resources; the quality of relationships between key actors within a school, not simply that these relationships exist; and also openness to others such as the third sector or business. We believe all these indicators were present in Fairforall and that the school had processes in place to enable rather than curtail social capital.

We started out wanting to find out the types of networks that existed, which were potentially productive networks and which were not. Overall, we found many strong networks weaving between individuals and groups within and outwith the school. The school was a hub for local community members and was seen as a safe haven for pupils amidst a social reality of multiple disadvantages. Putnam (2000, p. 19) credits Lyda J. Hanifan for being the first to consider the importance of community involvement in schools by describing 'the school as a community centre'. Parents demonstrated a tangible relationship of trust with the staff, particularly with the home–school liaison teacher, as well as with the school receptionist and janitor. Trust in Fairforall appeared to be both a constituent part of the existing social capital and a necessary ingredient for the development of social capital (Burnheim, 2004).

However, we did detect negative comments and vibes which would suggest that there are individuals and groups who may not see themselves or others as part of networks. For example, white parents (settled communities) and a minority of staff were at best puzzled by, and at worst resentful of specific school initiatives to welcome minority ethnic, international or migrant families (newer communities). There was negativity towards Gypsy/Traveller communities, and some parents, including those who were actively involved in the Parent Councils, clearly felt more 'in partnership' with the school than others. There was also a division, though this was somewhat hidden, between the teachers who took a more politicised approach to social issues and those who engaged in what Causey et al (1999, p. 34) described as 'naïve egalitarianism' based on an unproblematic understanding of what is means to be equal and fair. For example, for the majority of white staff and parents in Fairforall, there was little if any understanding of what Essed (1991, p. 3) has termed 'everyday racism' based on colour, ethnicity or nationality. There was also frustration between staff who were prepared to go the extra mile and those who worked pretty much to their core hours and saw many of the social networking initiatives as going beyond the call of duty.

We were also informed about points in the school life, mainly times of transition, when pupils moved from nursery into school or from primary to secondary, that were testing times which could augment or diminish existing social capital with a resultant impact on inclusivity. We found that Fairforall tried hard to forge productive links with the secondary school to which many of its pupils would transfer. However, this was not always as enthusiastically reciprocated by the secondary school though there were individual staff connections between the two schools that enabled 'transition' activities to be valuable and productive. This was at individual rather than institutional levels and therefore the networks between the primary and secondary schools were weak. As Fairforall pupils moved into secondary schools, it is not known whether the networks and security they had developed from being at Fairforall were retained at secondary school. It is also not known how the strong networks formed by the young people with each other were sustained once they left the primary school. One recommendation from the study was the consideration of 'alumni mentoring', where pupils moving into secondary could return to mentor future pupils as part of a Social Capital Transition Programme. The then headteacher was keen to follow up this recommendation.

The constructive work with parents to build trust and generate an open partnership appeared to cease as parents began a new relationship with the secondary school. What became clear was that the networks and trust that had been formed in Fairforall were not always transferable. Without nurturing and maintenance of established networks and trust, social capital can and does atrophy and eventually die.

Durability of capital and networks within the school

We came away with the view that the existence and maintenance of organic and dynamic social capital was possibly too dependent on the presence of a few key and charismatic individuals (for example headteacher, home–school liaison teacher, receptionist, janitor and one or two classroom teachers) who naturally networked, motivated and enthused others. What would happen if one or more of these key people left?

Fifteen months after the conclusion of the study, the headteacher did leave to work in a school closer to her home. Within months, staff reported that the ethos of the school was changing. While some of the networks were still alive and these helped to retain the range of activities offered in the school such as after-school clubs and parent activities, teachers reported a feeling of despondency as the 'open' culture was being lost. The careful nurturing of networks and lines of communication, held so important by the previous headteacher, were being eroded. For example, the much valued Breakfast Club, while still operating, had its budget reduced. The monthly newsletter was no longer produced. The headteacher appeared much less 'hands on' or accessible to staff, pupils and parents at a time when the school roll had increased. It would appear that literacy attainment rates had dropped by nearly 20% within twelve months. This figure is derived from the annual measurement of test results taken by the Scottish Government, where the percentage of pupils in four year groups who have attained the national standard are recorded. The measure is taken at the end of each school year and does not relate to a particular cohort. As a drop of 20% is a significant figure, on finalising this chapter, we enquired if there was a particularly challenging cohort in one of the four year groups that could have skewed the figures and were advised that this was not the case. One or two charismatic teachers and one depute headteacher who was part of the previous management team tried to keep networks alive. The home–school liaison teacher continued to play a pivotal role and has secured lottery funding for an innovative arts project involving pupils and parents to celebrate diversity in the community. However, the change in Fairforall in a relatively short period (twelve months) brings up questions of the durability and transferability of social capital. The loss of key individuals or their roles would appear to have the capacity to seriously affect the ethos and priorities of the school. For example, the previous emphasis on including marginalised parents and communities, such as refugee, asylum seeker and minority ethnic parents, is likely to diminish unless the new management has similar priorities. To maintain social capital and to ensure durability, greater numbers of the school community need to be involved and committed to the power of networking for the common good, and this must include those at the top of the power chain.

Limitations in the face of multiple deprivation

We found considerable evidence of bonding capital between pupils, staff and parents, but in a school located within an area of multiple deprivation and amidst social issues such as racism, homophobia, sexism and class inequalities, we found the concept of social capital superficial and potentially flimsy in several respects. Firstly, the naïve and somewhat romanticised notion that social cohesion and community capacity could be bolstered from an increase in social capital appears to ignore discussions of power, injustice and structural discrimination that exist in the lives of the pupils, families and communities. Social capital as a concept can be harnessed as a heuristic device for identifying issues of exclusion and inequity, as the headteacher of Fairforall wanted from this study. It can nurture, grow and maintain at a local institutional level quantities of social capital that enable those involved to feel valued, respected and included. Fairforall has therefore been partially successful in transcending the inequalities that face many of its pupils and parents and the communities it serves. For example, despite the racism explicit in the neighbourhood, through persistent efforts by the staff to bring diverse parents together through international evenings and via the extra-curricular activities, sufficient trust was established, albeit thin trust, between the various participants of the school to enable the school to be a community and to be perceived as a resource for surrounding communities. Uslaner (2002) stated that inequality can impact on levels of trust. Poverty and discrimination create divisions, but if openly addressed, what Fairforall demonstrated is that it is possible to partially overcome these inequalities and create a degree of solidarity if a new common purpose can be identified. In the case of Fairforall, the welfare of children was such a purpose and parents and communities were prepared to come together for the good of not just their children but the children of others.

Putnam (2000) and Coleman (1961) have both suggested that those who are able to locate themselves in social and peer groupings have more opportunities to improve and attain. This rationale is problematic for many pupils and families in the Fairforall situation as the social groupings in which these pupils and families are located have few opportunities to move out of the poverty trap and lie within structural inequalities which are beyond the capacity of many individuals to resolve. Garmanikow and Green (1999, p. 5) also question the application of social capital where 'benefits appear to accrue unproblematically to individuals, families, communities or nations by deploying social capital'. In an earlier work, they suggest that the concept 'serves to obscure perceptions of patterns of social inequality' (Garmanikow and Green 1999, p. 60).

The absence of discussions about structural and institutional power led some teachers in Fairforall to remain sceptical about the worth of social capital as a device for promoting inclusion or tackling underachievement.

> 'With budget cuts, excessive risk assessment, lack of support staff ... we can only do our best. But schools like this from poorer areas just cannot afford to send kids to camps. This impacts on the ability to build capital among the young people by providing them with additional activities. We can only do our best but the real issues lie out there and unless those are tackled nothing will change.' (depute headteacher)

The majority of pupils from Fairforall come to school with problems that are often too complex for the school to meet. They include chaotic lifestyles, poor diet, low self-esteem and lack of parental ambition. The teachers wanted to know if developing greater social capital would lift these pupils out of poverty and disadvantage, but if it did not, they felt that it was the latest conceptual fad embraced by politicians and senior managers to mask real issues. None of the staff in Fairforall or partner agencies would dispute that 'relationships matter' (Field 2003, p. 1) and there is a need for self-improvement, mutual improvement and reciprocity, and they accept that 'social renewal lies in being guided by our concern for and empathy with others' (Cruddas and Rutherford, 2010). However, the more astute and politicised staff and parents perceived it as a ruse for policy makers to apportion responsibility for change to those in the least powerful positions. This, combined with the current push in the UK to embrace the concept of the 'Big Society', makes social capital a concept that must be urgently problematised and interrogated. Not doing so could lead to a deficit and blame culture.

Secondly, while we saw strong positive networks and a huge range of partnerships that existed within the school as evidence of bonding and bridging capital, we could not identify much linking capital. As defined by Woolcock, this is capital that 'reaches out to unlike people in dissimilar situations, such as those who are entirely outside of the community, thus enabling members to leverage a far wider range of resources than are available in the community' (Woolcock, 2001, pp. 13–14). Putnam (2000, p. 411) recognised the importance of linking capital and 'venues for social capital creation' such as sports, where people were able to 'transcend our social, political and professional identities to connect with people unlike ourselves'. However it is not simply linking capital that is needed but the type of linking capital available. For example, sporting situations might provide linking capital across class and racial groups, but these are likely to benefit individuals rather than change societal power imbalances. The sporting ability of some people in a lower social class grouping in a team might enable them to become accepted by their more affluent and powerful team mates, or the one black player, as a result of his/her talent or perhaps likeable demeanour, might make it into the majority white social circles. Such individuals might benefit from the linking capital afforded to them by being members of a sports club and enable them to develop new and potentially more powerful social circles. However, the communities and structures from which they come could remain as separate as ever and those with power may remain as elusive. Therefore the type of linking capital and relationships required are ones that would shatter glass ceilings and remove sticky floors, not just benefit the talented or extraordinary individual. For Garmanikow and Green (1999, p. 5) social capital is 'abstracted theory' as it fails to engage with the concrete realities of different social, economic and political contexts.

Can social capital assist greater inclusion?

Putnam (2007, p. 138) suggests that 'in the short to medium run, however, immigration and ethnic diversity challenge social solidarity and inhibit social capital.' Fairforall had begun the process of building bridging capital between individuals and groups who do not naturally coalesce or bond and to assist staff, pupils and parents to become comfortable with diversity. Reducing 'social distance' (Putnam, 2007, p. 159) is one way of engendering trust and cooperation. At the point of the study, Fairforall was grappling with attitudinal issues around difference and diversity. Some of the senior managers were conscious that white parents did not see the point of the school's extra efforts to reach out to minority groups. There were issues of racism and homophobia that reared themselves periodically, sometimes among staff and often among parent groups. The school wanted to continue to provide opportunities for more established groups to engage with those who were seen as 'outsiders' (refugee and migrant families) or at worst, undesirables (Gypsy/Traveller families). 'Bridging' with parents and local communities had not always been easy as the realities of life outside school are often of hardship and survival. Parents and communities, therefore, may not have the time, energy or inclination to 'bridge' with the school beyond the minimum contact required.

When issues of diversity and difference are added to the mix, bridging becomes an even more challenging and complex exercise.

Despite the apparently strong capital in Fairforall, when difference disrupted the 'norm', such differences did become potential dividers. Where there are differences and conflicts and where prejudice and discrimination exist, it would appear that social capital is a somewhat powerless concept until, first and foremost, these hardcore issues are addressed. Perhaps what is more valuable is to reflect on how Fairforall attempted to address these situations. One of the ways was to develop greater understanding among school staff of the dynamics of difference and discrimination and the role of the school in closing the gap and building bridges. In the course of the study, we uncovered a range of understandings about what inclusion meant from those who adopted a simplistic 'no problem here' position to those who wanted to engage with discussions of power inequalities and different forms of prejudice and discrimination. Space was required for people to come together for mutual discussions, learning and engagement. Following the study, Fairforall was considering different ways of achieving this through, for example, bringing diverse groups of parents together over common concerns such as employability prospects for their children and themselves, and the loss of community services. The hope was that as bridging social capital increased between individuals and groups who met in these meetings, barriers would break down and stereotypes and prejudicial beliefs would be replaced with real experiences and shared humanity. However, to achieve the above, the headteacher at the time indicated that it was important for those organising such opportunities to have a robust grasp of the interplay of diversity, difference and discrimination and to be able to interject as necessary so that social capital growth prevailed rather than was fettered.

Implications for policy, practice and research

The study generated discussions across a range of people within the school community and this was in itself positive. When the school management team was seen to actively take on board many of the 33 recommendations that came from the report and to act upon these, this gave the entire process credibility and merit.

One of the significant aspects of the study was the importance of strategic individuals. Two stood out: the first of these, the headteacher, and the second, the home–school liaison teacher, who built bridges (no matter how fragile) between staff and parents, ensuring that contact was ongoing rather than sporadic. However, the liaison teacher was not funded by local authority ring-fenced funding but through the portion of the budget that had been devolved to individual schools. This left the post vulnerable in the face of cuts. The benefits of this post were clear to see yet this is the only school within this authority that has such a post. We assert that the consideration of the importance of a home–school liaison teacher or worker is a clear issue for those who develop and finance education policy. With the correct individual in post, the returns generated by the funding of home-school liaison teachers or workers would appear to be immense as evidenced within the Fairforall case study. In relation to practice, to sustain positive social capital within the school, greater numbers of the school community need to invest in the hard work of sustaining and generating networks. This would leave a school less vulnerable when strategic individuals leave.

At the end of the study, we wondered what was possible for one small primary school to achieve. Smyth suggests that 'while alienation, disengagement and dropping out' have the greatest effect in secondary schools, these 'conditions are incubated in primary schools' (Smyth, 2004, p. 19). The primary school setting has important contributions to make in creating a learning environment that aspires to social justice and challenges discrimination. Although our study concentrated on the value of networks as a resource for promoting inclusion, there are other ways in which a primary school can achieve this in practice. For example, the curriculum can provide pupils with opportunities to look beyond labels and stereotypes, to consider how discrimination manifests itself at a personal, cultural, institutional and structural level. The school experience can build pupil capacity to challenge discrimination against themselves and others. Pupils could be provided with opportunities to stand up for themselves and to explore how people have resisted injustices locally and globally. They could be provided with opportunities to take action against injustices and have a part in decision-making processes in school related to equity and to challenging discrimination. Bridging social capital networks can assist in developing a sense of belonging and in building possibilities for collective action. Strong capital between year groups would enable peer support and mentoring to develop. In this case study, we saw many of the above approaches and initiatives.

Fairforall provided the opportunity through organisational structures, particularly at a personal and group relationship level, and went some way to developing what Field describes as the 'collective quality' (Field 2009, p. 24). However, it struggled to overcome the limited opportunities that disadvantaged pupils and parents faced. This study left Fairforall pondering how it could broker linking opportunities to enable pupils and parents to move on and up.

Two areas emerge from this study that would benefit from further research. The first is a study to consider the possibilities and constraints for primary schools of the development of linking social capital when working with children and families in areas of multiple deprivation in order to assist in closing the gap between the powerful and the powerless. Such a study might also identify concrete examples of how such linking is taking place and to monitor its effectiveness. The second area for further explotation is how the social capital fostered in primary schools assists the capacity for networking and the maintenance of self-esteem as pupils transfer into secondary schools. Does such social capital assist the young person to bridge and bond outwith their familiarity zones and with people who are different, for example, in terms of ethnicity, faith and belief, sexual orientation, social class and abilities?

Too often the focus in discussions between primary and secondary schools about pupil transition revolves around the technical (pupil ability and level of curriculum attained) and bureaucratic aspects of transfer rather than the 'soft' factors such as pupil networks and identities. The findings from this study suggest that secondary schools in particular need to work far more closely with their primary counterparts to nurture the social capital built in primary schools as the process of transition to secondary school occurs.

In terms of research methodology, the partnership of an academic with a classroom teacher working together proved practically useful in many ways. The partnership built bridges between a university teacher education faculty and a local primary school. The teacher was able to open doors in the school for the academic researcher and access was therefore not an issue. The teacher who worked on the research benefitted directly as she wrote the study up as part of her contribution to a Master's-level assignment. This assessed work was informed by discussing the themes and analysis with the academic partner. The partnership also enabled a sharing of labour with the external (the academic) working with pupils and teachers while the classroom teacher interviewed parents as well as external stakeholders. This demarcation of tasks reduced any conflicts of interest, particularly for the classroom teacher. Having two perspectives assisted in the analysis. For example, the academic was able to see areas of tension as well as gaps which the classroom teacher was not always aware of given her closeness to the situation. This opened up different ways of seeing for the classroom teacher. The classroom teacher was able to help the academic to understand the subtleties of relationships within the school which would have been missed by someone merely visiting to conduct interviews, thereby enriching the research process with experiences and insights that could only be gained from an insider perspective. At the end of the research process, and in contributing to the writing of this chapter, the classroom teacher indicated that for her it had been an interesting process to enable her to learn how a piece of research is shaped, carried out, analysed and then peer reviewed: 'it has been really useful to see the research process from beginning to end'. For the academic partner, the valid analysis of the current context of the school was only made possible because of the continued presence of the classroom teacher at Fairforall.

In conclusion, it would be fair to say that from an initial enthusiastic embrace of the concept of social capital, we moved over the course of this small study to a more critical position. Social capital, no matter how strong, cannot address institutional, structural or societal disadvantage. The discourse does not normally question dominant hegemonies. It is not a substitute for economic solutions to social problems and it cannot compensate for poverty or other forms of discrimination and therefore remains a contested and weak concept which may be 'used as a means to maintaining social hierarchies' (Sivasubramaniam, 2008, p. 72). However, we see the possibilities of it being the 'social glue' that Catts and Ozga (2005, p. 1) talk about as being useful to give individuals hope in an increasingly fragmented and uncertain world.

References

Allan, J., Ozga, J and Smyth, G. (2009) *Social capital, professionalism and diversity*, Rotterdam: Sense Publishers.

Arshad, R. and Maclennan, S. (2008) 'Can we possibly be any more inclusive?' paper presented at the *Scottish Educational Research Association Conference*, Perth, 23 – 25 November.

Burnheim, C. (2004) Education and social capital, Monash Centre for Research in International Education Social Capital Seminars, www.education.monash.edu.au/research/seminars/show.php?id=205&archive=true

Catts, R. and Ozga, J (2005) *What is social capital and how might it be used in Scotland's schools*, Briefing paper No 36, Edinburgh: Centre for Education and Sociology, University of Edinburgh, www.ces.ed.ac.uk/PDF%20Files/Brief036.pdf

Causey, V.E., Thomas, C.D. and Armento, B.J. (1999) 'Cultural diversity is basically a foreign term to me: the challenges of diversity for pre-service teacher education', *Teaching and Teacher Education,* vol 16, pp 33–45.

Cruddas, J. and Rutherford, J. (2010) 'The big society: the anatomy of the new politics by Jesse Norman: book review', *New Statesman*, 15 December, www.newstatesman.com/books/2010/12/labour-society-social-norman

Coleman, J (1961) *Adolescent society: the social life of the teenager and its impact on education*, New York: Free Press

Dika, S. and Singh, K. (2002) 'Applications of social capital in educational literature: a critical synthesis', *Review of Educational Research*, vol 72, no 1, pp 31–60.

Essed, P. (1991) *Understanding everyday racism*, London: Sage.

Field, J. (2003) *Social capital*, London: Routledge.

Field, J. (2009) 'A social capital toolkit for schools', in J. Allan, J. Ozga and G. Smyth (eds) *Social capital, professionalism and diversity*, Rotterdam: Sense, https://www.sensepublishers.com/files/9789087908195PR.pdf

Garmanikow, E. and Green, A. (1999) 'Developing social capital: dilemmas, possibilities and limitations in education', in A. Hayton (ed) *Tackling disaffection and social exclusion*, London: Kogan Paul, pp 46–64.

Putnam, R.D. (2000) *Bowling alone: the collapse and revival of American community*, New York: Simon and Schuster.

Putnam, R.D. (2007) '*E pluribus unum:* diversity and community in the twenty-first century: the 2006 Johan Skytte prize lecture', *Scandinavian Political Studies*, vol 30 no 2, pp 137–74, http://www.utoronto.ca/ethnicstudies/Putnam.pdf

Sammons, P., Power S., Robertson, P., Campbell, C., Elliot, K and Whitty, G. (2000) 'Evaluating the new community schools initiative in Scotland', paper presented at the *European Conference on Educational Research*, Edinburgh 20-23 September, http://www.leeds.ac.uk/educol/documents/00001682.htm (Used with permission of S Sammons.

Sivasubramaniam, M. (2008) 'Social capital, civil society and education for all: a gendered lens', in S. Fennell and M. Arnot, (eds) *Gender education and equality in a global context: contextual frameworks and policy perspectives*, Abingdon: Routledge, pp 67–84.

Schuller, T. (1999) 'Social capital: analytical tool or clingfilm wrap?', *Concept*, vol 9, no 1, pp 8–10.

Shucksmith, M. (2000) 'Endogenous development, social capital and social inclusion: perspectives from LEADER in the UK', *Sociologia Ruralis*, vol 40, no 2, pp 208–18.

Smyth, J. (2004) 'Social capital and the "socially just school"', *British Journal of Sociology of Education*, vol 25, no 1, pp 19–33.

Uslaner, E. (2002) *The moral foundations of trust*, Cambridge: Cambridge University Press.

Woolcock, M. (2001) 'The place of social capital in understanding social and economic outcomes', *Isuma: Canadian Journal of Policy Research*, vol 2, no 1, pp 1–17.

NINE

Transitions to secondary schooling: a social capital perspective

Kevin Stelfox and Ralph Catts

Introduction

The transition from primary to secondary school has been identified as of interest, with much research focused on the articulation of the curriculum provision (Galton et al, 2000). Our aim was to explore the experience of transition from the perspective of social capital to see whether this could add to our understanding.

The research was undertaken in two phases over a period of twelve months. The first phase was based in a primary school that was located in an urban area just outside a city centre. The catchment area could best be described as a medium-size working-class estate. Using the National Statistics Socio-economic Classification (ONS, 2004) the majority of the parents had occupations classified as skilled manual or unskilled occupations and some were unemployed. The school was ranked in the second lowest quartile on the Scottish Index of Multiple Deprivation (Scottish Government, 2004). The second phase was undertaken in the secondary school to which the majority of the primary school pupils moved.

Data were collected from students in classroom activities during the final months of primary school and the follow-up occurred near the end of the first year of high school. In both phases, the data included interviews with selected pupils, a class teacher and the head teacher. The views of parents were also sought through a survey in primary school.

Previous research and policy on transition

In published research into the primary to secondary school transition, the major focus has been on the effects of transition on attainment and on the changes in school culture (Galton et al, 1999; Anderson et al,

2000; Demetriou et al, 2000; Galton et al, 2000; Ward, 2000; Topping, 2007). These studies focused on curriculum links and also on links between teachers. An exception was the study reported by Zeedyk et al (2003), which focused on institutional differences between primary and secondary schools which, they argued, risked creating among individual students a sense of helplessness. There are significant differences between primary and secondary school contexts that can be categorised as being to do with structure, philosophy and curriculum focus. These differences may reduce the sense of belonging to both a physical space and a social group (Boyd, 2005). More recently Evangelou et al (2008) concluded that a major concern for young people in the transition to secondary school was developing new friendships and that young people found the experience stressful. However, in all these studies, the responses to these perceived changes focused on addressing issues of continuity of curriculum, rather than on continuity of teachers, peers and place.

Another significant difference between primary and secondary school is the social position of the pupils in a school context. The upper-stage pupils in primary schools are encouraged to participate in decision-making processes and to engage in the discussion of contemporary social issues that interest them both in the classroom and during pupil council meetings. In contrast, in the early stages of secondary education, these young people are seen as 'newcomers'. They are given little opportunity to take an active role in school governance (Deuchar, 2009). Even when social networks and pupil voices are considered, the focus remains on curriculum and attainment (Demetriou et al, 2000).

The current policy context in Scotland and in other regions where a broader cross-curriculum focus on citizenship and participation is encouraged opens up the possibility of focusing more on the social context of schools and in particular, pupil networks and social relationships. Concerns for the social outcomes of education have a long history in some countries, especially in Scandinavia, but are also central to policies in Europe as articulated in the Lisbon Declaration (European Commission, 2005) and in broader international policy forums (OECD, 2006).

Developing broader capacities in young people through the subject-based curriculum requires that these capacities are embedded and achieved through building and sustaining positive relationships. There is an inherent contradiction, however, since the focus of secondary curriculum policies has also been on the development of an individual performance culture within education. This may explain why there has been little research that focuses on the social relationship aspects of education in the school context.

Social capital in schools

Catts et al (2007, p. 51) suggested that social capital is characterised by the 'notion of belonging to and existing within relational bonds'. It is this focus that we used to explore the relational structures and activities within a school and in particular the point of transition as a point of change in space that causes discontinuity in social relationships. With young people who have been together in the same class group for up to seven years, we expected to find some close reciprocal connections, and one of our questions was what would happen to these relationships in the transition to secondary school. Both bonding with some close peers and bridging social capital with the broader school community were expected outcomes of primary schooling (Catts and Ozga, 2005). In addition, linking social capital was seen as enabling connections between people across differences in social status, for example, links between parents of children at a comprehensive school. Links may connect individuals to agencies or services that they would otherwise not access and thus help people to deal with change requiring new sources of information or support. The notion of 'fields' developed by Bourdieu, (1979, 1986) situates individuals and locates their social position. The position of the individuals in the field is determined by their interaction with others, by the rules of the field, and by the individual's economic, cultural and social capital. Applying these concepts of social capital within a school context allowed us to explore the effects of changing the space in which learning occurs from the smaller primary school to a larger high school. This may involve the creation of new social networks, and this provides the potential for individuals to seek to interact with new 'others' and hence to redefine their position within new fields.

Social capital, in the form of relationships and networks, has also been promoted as a means of mediating negative effects of poverty by the development of human capital opportunities through schooling. Coleman (1988) argued that family social capital is a resource that supports the education of children just like financial and human capital. Coleman focused on this mediating role especially for social capital accessed through the family and through peer groups. To the extent that schools reflect middle class norms and values, the social capital in schools can result in the norms and values of the family and immediate neighbourhood being pitted against those promulgated by the school.

In his early work Coleman (1961) noted the potential for adolescents to develop peer cultural and social capital that opposed school goals. We therefore looked for evidence of conflicting values between home and school as a potentially destabilising force in the lives of young people.

Putman (1993, 2000) considered the process through which individuals can bond within groups, bridge within networks and form loose links across networks. These terms have become widely embraced in social capital literature (McGonigal et al, 2007). Because social capital is not fungible (Coleman, 1990), it can be argued that rebuilding social capital needs to be facilitated during the transition to secondary school by addressing the issues around the continuity and discontinuity of relationships and the fostering of institutional and generalised trust within the secondary school environment. However the greater size and diversity of the peer population and the number and diversity of disciplines among secondary school staff mean that there may also be opportunities for linking social capital that will provide adolescents with access to new norms and values which better fit their emerging identity.

Trust and social capital

Putman (2000) considered trust to be a component of social capital along with norms and values, and identified two types of trust. 'Thick trust' occurs within dense networks and is based on personal experience from familiar sources about a person's trustworthiness. This seems consistent with the level of trust in primary schools developed over an extended period. 'Thin trust' is characterised by limited common experience, norms and values between the individual and another. Putman also suggested that thin trust is useful in that it creates the potential for linking and bridging.

Whereas Putnam (2000) considers trust as a component of social capital, Fukuyama (1999) argues that networks and trust are epiphenomenal, arising as a result of social capital, but not constituting social capital itself. Uslaner (2002) agrees that while trust and social capital can operate in tandem, trust is a distinct construct. Uslaner argues that the formation of particularised trust encourages bonded social capital, which emphasises the distinction between social groups, while generalised trust supports the formation of links and bridges to others. Uslaner also argues that within institutional settings trust is especially vulnerable to any breach of either implicit or explicit contracts. We conclude that trust must be considered in relation to the nature of social networks, especially within the institutional school setting.

We explored both the meanings and practices of trust with the young people while they were still in primary school. We did so because the transition to secondary school involves breaking networks established over six or seven years and we wanted to see what impact this had on trust. It is possible that in building new networks in secondary school, those children with an orientation to generalised trust will have better success in circumstances where they need to relate to a new and relatively larger and potentially more diverse school community.

Methodology

The aims of the case study were to explore the transition from primary to secondary school through a social capital perspective; to develop an understanding of strength and density of networks; and to explore issues of cohesion and distance within school and community networks. A case study approach as a form of research has been defined by Yin (2009) as an empirical enquiry that investigates a contemporary phenomenon in depth and within a specific context. This case study followed one class of pupils in their final year of primary school (P7) through the transition to their first year of secondary school (S1). Hence this is a single longitudinal case study undertaken over a period of twelve months. The research questions were:

- What were the social networks that young people shared in the final year of primary school?
- What were the effects of the change from primary to secondary school on the social networks which each participant accessed at school?
- What were the implications for the well-being and learning opportunities of the participants?

Underlying the analysis of social networks is the assumption that individuals act in response to the behaviours of others around them and that their desire for friendship and acceptance by others can influence the sense of security and the behaviour of individuals (Knoke and Yang, 2008). This essentially sociological approach contrasts with the focus of psychology on the behaviour of the individual. While attributes such as gender, race and religion remain unchanged in different social settings, the relationships which exist in school settings are in most cases not utilised beyond the school gate. Hence there are likely to be substantial changes in school-based social networks as a result of the transition to secondary school. Although social networks are necessarily dynamic, the transition to secondary school involves a discontinuity in the networks caused by the change in physical location; the change in the organisation of schooling between primary and secondary schooling necessarily means that not only are links with teachers broken, but many peer links are also disrupted.

In order to analyse the social networks in which the participants operated we defined three types of networks, namely their classroom network, their network based around their family, and their local community beyond school. Our focus, however, was on the networks in which our respondents operated within the school. By asking participants to draw a diagram of their networks and to distinguish between best friends, a wider circle of friends, and people to whom they say hello, we sought to explore the nature of the social networks in which they operated. We elected to define the differences in networks in terms of the number of people they identified (size) and the extent to which their school networks were reciprocal. The concept of reciprocity was defined as links where the other person identified the respondent in their network, as compared to aspirational networks where the person identified people who did not in return identify the respondent as belonging to their network. This concept can be used as a quantitative indicator of strength and depth of networks (Knoke and Yang, 2008). However, for this small case study, our focus was on the change in network size and reciprocity for the individual.

The methods employed to collect data involved network mapping by the young people, interviews with pupils and with their teacher, and a parent survey. The first stage of the data collection was undertaken in the last months of primary schooling, with information collected from the young people, their teacher and parents. First, a classroom discussion explored the concepts of family, friendship, trust and community with the young people. This allowed them to clarify the meanings of these concepts and provided useful insights as to how they viewed these constructs, which were incorporated in the wording of interview questions. The second part of the activity was a mapping exercise which focused on individual young people's perception of their networks in relation to school, family and community. This classroom activity included 27 out of the 29 pupils in the class. Pupils who had completed each section of data collection before the allotted time were asked to write a short paragraph on 'what I like or dislike about living with my family', 'what I like or dislike about living in my community', or 'what I like or dislike about the school', depending on the section that they had just completed. This additional exercise was to address any ethical concerns about any young people who perceived themselves as having sparse networks completing the mapping exercise quickly and sitting waiting for the rest of the class to finish the activity. The data collected in this supplementary exercise were not used in the study because of time constraints.

Interviews formed the second major part of phase one of the data collection process. They were conducted with eleven young people in the class who were selected because they had either extensive or the most sparse networks, or because of a contrast between the size of their self-reported network and the network reported by their teacher. These interviews allowed us to explore in more depth the experiences of those with dense and those with sparse networks, with the distinction defined by counting the number of school friends reported on their network map.

Interviews were also conducted with both the class teacher and the headteacher. The class teacher was asked about her perception of the level of trust she had in pupils in terms of their behaviour in the school, and about the nature of the social networks she had described in her class mapping task. The headteacher was interviewed to gain contextual information about the school, including the extent of community and parental involvement, and to explore her notion of trust in relation to parents and pupils.

Finally, with the permission of parents, a range of school performance data and attitudinal data was collected for the group of young people from school records. This included Performance Indicators for Primary School (PIPs) (CEM, 2006) that provided standardised scores on attitude toward school and attainment in reading, maths and science.

The second phase of the study was conducted in June 2007 and involved mapping pupil networks in S1 and follow-up interviews with young people. Data attrition from the original 27 participants was experienced for a number of reasons, including the dispersion of some pupils to other secondary schools, absence on the day, and in one case withdrawal of consent. Eleven out of the 21 pupils who transferred to the zoned secondary school were available and participated in the follow-up classroom activities of discussions and mapping of networks. We also interviewed six young people, of whom four had previously been interviewed in P7. Two of these had dense networks in P7 and two had previously identified less dense networks. Two other students who had not previously been interviewed at the P7 stage but had completed the mapping activity in P7 were interviewed in S1 because they also had less dense networks in P7.

Results

We asked the pupils in P7 what the word 'trust' meant for them. The key components for the young people were reciprocity and shared norms and values. They described trust as 'gives swaps', and 'keeping promises'. They also explained trust in terms of 'tells you the truth', 'keeps secrets' and will not 'tell' others about things that you have shared with them where this would result either in punishment for breaking school rules, or ridicule by peers. This implied that there were implicit sanctions that maintained their networks, as suggested by Putnam (1993).

This understanding and meaning of trust was confirmed in the interview data we collected from the pupils both in the final year of primary schooling and toward the end of their first year of secondary schooling. The following examples illustrate the generally held views of students about trust:

> 'Somebody that wouldn't say stuff behind your back and that would share secrets with you and wouldn't tell secrets and if I told someone a secret they wouldn't go say it to somebody that I said don't tell, they know you're there and stuff.' (P7)

> 'Someone's loyal and they don't speak about you or tell your secrets and you can tell them anything and they'll maybe help you with it or they'll fix or make sure that you're ok if it's something that's bad then they'll always make sure you're ok and trust them to do anything for you and keep your secrets.' (P7)

> 'Uhm, it's like, you can trust your friends, you can tell them stuff without them telling other people, ehm, like, or, like say I says to Bob "I don't like him," then if he goes away and tells him then I can't trust him any more.' (S1)

We conclude that the meaning of trust for the young people is part of the norms and values inherent in friendship and social networks. They described friends as somebody that 'shares with you', 'has hobbies in common', 'do things together', 'somebody who looks out for you', 'sticks up for you', 'shares secrets' and 'does not speak about you'.

In the year of transition to secondary school, eight out of the eleven pupils followed via the mapping activities displayed a loss in the number of their reported network members at school. In contrast, the three pupils who had the most sparse networks in P7 reported an increase in the numbers in their school network at the end of the first year of secondary education. However, the interpretation of the finding about size of secondary networks needs to be addressed with some caution. It was not possible to explore the degree of reciprocation in the secondary network maps given the number of pupils and the scope of this study. Hence we could not establish whether or not reciprocity was evident in the secondary peer networks.

With a larger pool of peers in the secondary school, and access to more young people due to changes in class composition between subjects, the results may reflect a substantive change in access to social capital; however, they may also reflect a change in aspirations for peer group membership as young people move into early adolescence. Another interpretation could be that some P7 pupils were largely excluded by their primary school peers, but freed from the boundaries of a single class group and the hierarchical structure of peer networks in the relatively closed primary school network, these pupils found new opportunities to establish networks and to connect with other adolescents. Finally, the quality of the networks reported in secondary school was different from those in primary school, if only because new friendships were necessarily of less than one year in duration, whereas some of the primary friendship links had been extant for six years or longer. The reasons for these changes need careful elaboration because they could have implications for practices in the final year of primary school as well as for the transition experience.

In the primary school, most pupils nominated in their school network some friends, older or younger, who were not in their class. These were friends in the community or friends of a sibling. It is important therefore to note that there is an overlap between school and community-based social capital and hence the size of school networks reported may to some extent be influenced by whether or not the young people were from the local community surrounding the school. Another issue is the distinction between aspirational and reciprocal social capital. The data we collected from P7 pupils revealed that some pupils had claimed others as friends, but that this was not reciprocated. We therefore defined aspirational social capital as social links that were claimed by one person but not recognised by the recipient.

All eleven primary school pupils reported a loss of some peer connections at the point of transition. Moving to a different school from your peers was a common reason, which had a significant impact and was in most cases beyond their control. Some reported that this loss was difficult to come to terms with or rationalise:

'I haven't wrote any of their names down, because I've went to a different school to them, I won't see most them. I see Del, I see Del, I go to his house. I used to play football with him, but then we both quit our team. I sometimes see [primary school teacher], I see [primary school teacher] at the community centre with that educational thing, and apart from that … don't really see anybody else except … I've seen Alvin once, at Somerfield, and I've seen Ryan and I've seen Shane or whatever, just once.'

It is particularly noteworthy that in this quote, a primary school teacher is included as a friend. This is a point to which we return shortly. A number of pupils had indicated that they used either email or social networking sites to stay in contact with some friends from their primary school. These electronic networks had been established in primary school and were used in some cases to continue contact outwith the school context. It was interesting to note that one student talked about 'seeing' people via electronic contact:

'Well, Jane and Mel are there. They went, most have went to Mainfield School, Jane went to Pools school, and I don't see them now any more until, like, I'm on the computer.'

There is also a loss of connections among those attending the same secondary school due to the way these schools are structured and organised.

'We're not in the same classes. So, I don't see a lot of … that, so … we're not in any of the same classes. And she hangs about with … different people from me.'

The structure and organisation of the secondary school also resulted in the loss of adults within the pupils' networks. All the primary students included one significant adult in their school network, be it their teacher, a former teacher, a dinner lady or the janitor. In contrast, teachers were absent from all but one of the network maps at secondary school.

'Well, we just stick to like one teacher for, like, the whole day, and then here we've got like seven different teachers in one day, instead of one or two.' (S1)

'I don't really know a lot of my teachers at this school.' (S1)

This could perhaps be explained by the fact that pupils move from class to class, having very little time to develop a social relationship with the teachers. It may also indicate that it takes longer than one year for pupils to build trust in teachers when they see so little of each one, relative to the time spent with their P7 teacher and support staff. Whatever the reason, we think it significant that there is a loss of connection with a significant adult as part of the transition to secondary school.

Attitudes to school and the size of social networks

We used the number of reported friends in primary school as an indicator of the quantity of each pupil's school social capital. To do this we included 'best friends' and 'friends' but excluded the 'just say hello to' category. The number of reported friends is a simplified proxy for school social capital, but to the extent that it reveals possible relationships between the variables of interest, it raises the possibility that social capital is a factor in attitudes to school. Our interest in this link was prompted by findings reported by Veronneau and Vitaro (2007, p. 428), who summarised a range of studies that suggest that close and reciprocated friendships throughout pre- and early adolescent years 'can contribute to psychological and academic adjustment'.

The dependent variables considered which were collected from all P7 pupils were attitudes to school, maths, reading and science. Our hypothesis was that number of friends will be related to feeling safe and secure and hence result in a more positive attitude to school and toward learning. The distributions on all the relevant variables were approximately normal, with no substantial or significant variations in relation to kurtosis or skew. The distributional characteristics of the variables under consideration are summarised in Table 9.1. It will be noted that number of friends is a simple count and that there is a wide range of reported number of friends. The dependent variables are calculated on a continuous scale with a minimum of 1 and maximum of 5. The scales measuring attitudes toward science and toward school have narrower distributions than for either maths or reading.

The data indicate relationships among attitudes to various subjects that are predictable in terms of previous research, and that also seem reasonable in terms of teacher expectations. For instance there is a positive correlation between attitudes toward maths and science ($r = 0.48$) which was statistically significant even with this small number of cases. This result is consistent with the finding by Kumar and Morris

(2005) of a 0.31 correlation between attitudes toward science and mathematics among college students. Likewise the negative correlation between attitudes toward maths and reading ($r = -0.23$) fits with both prior research and widely held stereotypes. These findings support our contention that the results of interest provide exploratory evidence that warrants further investigation.

Table 9. I Descriptive statistics for dependent and independent variables (N=23)

	Minimum	Maximum	Mean	Std. Deviation
No. of friends	2	46	17.87	8.85
Attitude to school	3.14	4.86	3.85	0.48
Attitude to maths	2.17	5.00	3.82	0.69
Attitude to reading	2.29	5.00	3.65	0.92
Attitude to science	3.00	4.43	3.67	0.46

Table 9.2: Correlations between number of friends and attitudes to school and subject areas (N=23)

Variable	Statistics	Number of Friends	Attitude to school	attitude to maths	Attitude to reading	Attitude to science
Number of Friends		1				
Attitude to school	Pearson correlation	0.27	1			
	Sig. (2-tailed)	0.21				
Attitude to maths	Pearson correlation	0.13	0.26	1		
	Sig. (2-tailed)	0.55	0.23			
Attitude to reading	Pearson correlation	0.21	0.31	−0.23	1	
	Sig. (2-tailed)	0.35	0.16	0.30		
Attitude to science	Pearson correlation	0.08	−0.03	0.48(*)	0.36	1
	Sig. (2-tailed)	0.74	0.88	0.02	0.10	

* Correlation is significant at the 0.05 level (2-tailed).

The analysis in Table 9.2 shows that the correlation between number of friends and attitude to school (0.27) is in the predicted direction and is sufficient to warrant further study with a larger group and more sophisticated estimates of social capital. The correlations between numbers of friends and attitude toward maths and science are smaller and may not warrant further study, but the effect size for attitude toward reading (0.21) is sufficient to speculate that the correlation may be significant and of substantial importance in further studies. Of course, further research would need to consider alternative explanations such as that girls may like reading and have more friends. It is also possible that the postulated relationship between social capital and attitudes toward school and learning may be because young people who like school and learning have more friends, but other literature suggests that this is not the case. One argument in favour of the directionality that we have postulated is that not all our dependent variables correlate with the independent variable, number of friends, which suggests that number of friends is important in terms of some attitudes but not others.

Discussion

One way to view transitions in the school context is to view the relational aspects as interdependent constructs being both spaces for social practices and physical places to occupy. Viewing these places through a socio-spatial temporal lens allows us not only to see places in terms of location but also in terms of space and time. The characteristics of these space and time dimensions have been well established and have been identified and summarised as follows:

> It is now widely held that 'the spatial' and 'the social' are reciprocally constructed. Spatiality is primarily to be seen not in terms of a backdrop against which action takes place but rather in terms of activity or practice. In other words, space is enacted or performed: constituted through action, for example, acts of occupancy or appropriation. (Mulcahy, 2006, p. 55)

Linking spatial and social dimensions allows us to explore the places identified by the young people in relation to social interactions and to ask questions not often addressed in the world of schools and education. Although we assume that young people and teachers share space and time within the bounded community of the primary school, there was little evidence of them sharing this in the social context. What space and time there was between the teacher and the young people was seen in formal terms (i.e. the classroom and the curriculum). There is limited room for movement within these formalised spaces that are regulated, governed and controlled. As Gordon et al (2000, p. 164) suggest, the idea that every limitation is at the same time an opportunity for enactment is born out in our analysis of everyday activities in schools. In spatial praxis, students are inscribed into particular subject positions. But they are able to experiment with ways of locating themselves in those positions.

This type of analysis extends understanding of the implications of the differences in the physical organisation of places between primary and secondary schools. Within the primary school, the places and spaces where bonding and bridging take place are well defined by the classroom structure and organisation. Young people had a classroom place for the year and had regular contact with a limited number of teachers and other staff. There were significant differences in relation to place and space for the young people when they moved from primary to secondary school. For most pupils, the places and spaces for developing and practising bonding and bridging with peers were significantly reduced in the secondary school. Places and spaces identified in the primary school included the classroom and the playground, where practices of bonding and bridging were evident. Although these spaces exist in the secondary school, they are seen as more transitory and hence there is less security for bonding and bridging links to be consolidated. The young people confirmed that the loss of places and spaces affected their networks:

> 'I don't see them till like I'm in a subject with them.' (S1)

> 'Well, ... we're not really supposed to speak in class, but we have the occasional conversation.' (S1)

The playground was also redefined in the secondary setting. Instead of the young people self-organising a group football game, they tended in the secondary school to visit the 'chipper' with perhaps one other person. The 'chipper' was a food shop away from the school campus, so they actually lost use of school space as well as peer connections. This redefinition of places and spaces reduced and limited the possibility of bonding and the practice of bridging within their class group for young people. These factors may help to explain why the majority of pupils displayed a reduction in the size of their networks between P7 and S1.

A further notable difference between the P7 and S1 maps was the presence of an adult school staff member (teacher or support staff) in 18 out of 27 primary pupil school friendship maps, and the absence of adults in all but one of the 11 secondary maps. While it might be understandable that in their first year in a new setting, the students had not had time to establish longer term links with adults, it nonetheless highlights how, after one school year, most secondary pupils had not established access to adult mentors whom they felt able to report as friends. This may be significant in relation to the influences on the formation of norms and values by young adolescents.

There were examples of continuity of relationships with peers but also many examples of discontinuity and a sense of loss in many of those whom we interviewed. Significantly, friendships were often not maintained even when young people moved to the same secondary school but were not in the same classes. Those few friendships that continued were those that had neighbourhood or other community-based support. These durable friendships were sustained either through neighbourhood links or a shared cultural or sporting interest outwith the school community and were supported particularly via internet messaging sites.

Young people and parents trusted teachers especially if they shared the same norms and values as them. However, teachers were more reserved in their trust of pupils and parents. For example, teachers held the view that in order to be trusted, parents and pupils needed to hold the 'same values as the school'. The conditionality of 'trust' in young people by school staff is an important issue for further research.

During the transition from primary to secondary school, there is the potential to establish new social networks. These were developed during the initial transition period despite the limiting influences of school organisation. All had established new friendships within the first year of secondary school, but the new networks were mostly at an early stage of development. The durability of these new networks as class groupings change is an area for future research. More durable networks were those existing networks from within their own communities which were accessed beyond the school context.

Reflections on the research process

Prior to the research activity, informed consent was gained from the parents of the young people in the class in question. Two young people failed to return the consent forms and therefore did not participate in the activity. Beyond this formal process, the risks identified were minimised by the observance of confidentiality. In our reporting, we adopted pseudonyms where names were referred to by our respondents.

Undertaking research into friendships raised sensitive issues about the effects on young people who might not be conscious of this aspect within a school context. By placing these issues in the foreground, there was a possibility that we could bring an isolated pupil to the attention of peers and teachers, resulting in their isolation being more visible. A major challenge therefore was the need to be aware of this sensitivity when interviewing 'isolates', the need to consider language when working with young people, and the ethical issues raised when interviewing young people about friendships and their view of trust.

The tools developed in this case study offer potential for refinement and application in a larger study. For instance, the network mapping provided a rich vein of information, but there was evidence that for some young people, it reflected their aspiration to belong to social networks rather than a realisable form of social capital. By asking who helped them in times of difficulty, we located in one instance a fellow student who did not appear on the respondent's network map. Likewise, due to the greater dispersion of pupils across different class groups for different secondary subjects, it was not feasible to identify reciprocal links from the responses of a particular group of students selected because of their primary school affiliation. We think that this may indicate a limitation in the quantitative network mapping approaches that warrants careful consideration. Asking for evidence of utilisation of social networks may not be as easily codified in quantitative form but may generate more important information about the security of the social context for the individual.

The utility of social capital

Social capital allows us to view schools as social places and as providing spaces for relationships. At primary school, over time the relationships with other young people and between young people and school staff can lead to what was originally a bridge becoming more like a bond. Hence, the notion of social capital practices as bonding, linking or bridging may be better explained as fluid network links which can change their form and strength over time, especially among young people who are forming their personal and social identities. When reciprocity develops, links become more permanent within the school setting, but the boundary of many of these links is the physical space of the school.

Trust was central to the concept of friendship for young people, and breaches of trust were a reason why networks were disrupted. However, trust appears to be a distinct construct which may be a prerequisite for the formation of social capital. The one-sided trust in the relationship between teachers and both pupils and parents raised further issues for the role of social networks in schools. The lack of teacher trust in others might explain why the influence of schools in disadvantaged communities is not as pervasive as would be expected because the conditionality of teacher trust is likely to be evident to the families concerned. A specific example of differences in norms was the contrast in parental and teacher attitudes to the response to bullying. Teachers expected to be told of such instances whereas both parents and the young people took the view that this was the responsibility of the young people and the community, to the exclusion of teachers.

Implications for policy, practice and further research

The possibility of schools as social places and spaces seems underappreciated in policy circles. Recognition of relationships and the role that these can play in terms of outcomes for young people should be considered within and beyond the curriculum framework. This notion of schools as social places and spaces may have resonance in many national education systems.

The loss and reforming of social capital in the transition to secondary education presents a challenge to the way policy makers and school leaders think about transitions from primary to secondary schools. As noted earlier, transitional studies have tended to focus on continuity of learning and have defined learning within the school context in the narrow sense of subject-based cognitive gains, rather than social learning. Most studies have failed to take into account pupils' social experience of transition, and especially the impact on their social networks. Viewing schools through a social capital lens provides an additional perspective through which to view the transition. Lucey and Reay (2000) identified the significant role that the stage of school plays in the development of the self. The primary school stage normally provides a home classroom and hence a secure place in which to nurture social capital, whereas in the secondary school places are more transitory.

Social issues around transition in relation to the development of personal identities therefore need to be addressed. Given the evidence for the importance of social identity in the development of personal identity (Kroger, 2004), the formation of social networks in the first year of secondary school raises for us questions about the role of secondary schools. Support for the development of networks among peers and with trusted teachers seems to be important in developing confident individuals, especially among those pupils who are socially excluded. In this study, we did not explore the norms and values shared by friends. It seems likely, as Veronneau and Vitaro (2007) point out, that the networks that young people form may be either supportive or disruptive of positive attitudes to school. Further research may need to link the quantity and quality of social networks to more fully explore the effects on attitudes toward school.

Finally, if there is a substantial relationship between attitudes toward school and the size of the network that individuals access at school, as seems possible from the data presented for the P7 class, then any loss of social capital in the transition to secondary school raises interesting possibilities in relation to the known drop in performance in the first year of secondary schooling, and for potential changes in attitudes toward secondary school among some young people. While this has been thought to be due to adolescent maturation effects or loss of continuity in curriculum (Sainsbury et al, 1998), it may also have to do with a loss of attention by pupils due to a loss of social capital leading to greater uncertainty and less sense of security in commencing secondary school. This possibility warrants further research.

Acknowledgements

Robert Doherty, and Kay Livingston, both from Glasgow University, were involved in the design and early stages of the conduct of this study. Additional funding for this case study was provided by Aberdeen City Council and by the University of Stirling.

References

Anderson, L.W., Jacobs, J., Schramm, S. and Splittgerber, F. (2000) 'School transitions: beginning of the end or a new beginning?' *International Journal of Educational Research*, vol 33, no 4, pp 325–39.

Bourdieu, P. (1979) *Distinction: a social critique of the judgement of taste* (R. Nice, trans.), Melbourne: Routledge and Kegan Paul.

Bourdieu, P. (1986) 'The forms of capital', in I. Richardson (ed.), *Handbook of theory and research for the sociology of education* (R. Nice trans.), Westport, CT: Greenwood Press, pp 241–58.

Boyd, B. (2005) *Primary–secondary transition: an introduction to the issues*, Paisley: Hodder Gibson.

Catts, R., Allan, J. and Smyth, G. (2007) 'Children's voices: how do we address their right to be heard?' *Scottish Educational Review*, vol 39, no 1, pp 51–9.

Catts, R. and Ozga, J. (2005) *What is social capital and how might it be used in Scotland's schools? CES Briefing No. 36*, Edinburgh: Centre for Educational Sociology, University of Edinburgh, *www.ces.ed.ac.uk/ PDF%20Files/Brief036.pdf*

CEM (2006) *PIPS: introduction*, Durham: Durham University, www. cemcentre.org/pips/introduction

Coleman, J. (1961) *Social climates in high schools*, Washington, DC: US Department of Health, Education, and Welfare, Office of Education.

Coleman, J. (1988) 'Social capital in the creation of human capital', *American Journal of Sociology*, 94 (Supplement) pp S95–120.

Coleman, J. (1990) *Foundations of social theory*, Harvard, MA: Harvard University Press.

Demetriou, H. Goalen, P. and Ruddock, J. (2000) 'Academic performance, transfer, transition and friendship: listening to the student voice', *International Journal of Educational Research*, vol 33, no 4, pp 425–41.

Deuchar, R. (2009) 'Seen and heard, and then not heard: Scottish pupils' experience of democratic educational practice during the transition from primary to secondary school', *Oxford Review of Education,* vol 35, no. 1, pp 23-40.

European Commission (2005) *Communication from the Commission on the social agenda*, COM(2005)33 final, Brussels: European Commission.

Evangelou, M. Taggart, B. Sylva, K. Melhuish, E., Sammons, P. and Siraj-Blatchford, I. (2008) *What makes a successful transition from primary to secondary school? Findings from the effective pre-school, primary and secondary education 3–14 (EPPSE) project*, Research Brief DCSF-RB019, London: Department for Children Schools and Families, http://education.gov.uk/publications/standard/publicationDetail/Page1/DCSF-RR019

Fukuyama, F. (1999) *Social capital and civil society*, Washington DC: IMF Institute and the Fiscal Affairs Department.

Galton, M., Gray, J. and Ruddock, J. (1999) *The impact of school transitions and transfers on pupil progress and attainment*, DfES Research Report no. 131, Cambridge: DfES.

Galton, M., Morrison, I. and Pell, T. (2000) Transfer and transition in English schools: reviewing the evidence, *International Journal of Educational Research*, vol 33, no 4, pp 341–61.

Gordon, T. Holland, J. and Lahelma, E. (2000) *Making spaces: citizenship and difference in schools*, London: Macmillan.

Knoke, D. and Yang, S. (2008) *Social network analysis* (2nd edition), Los Angeles, CA: Sage.

Kroger, J. (2004) *Identity in adolescence: the balance between self and other*, London: Routledge.

Kumar, D. and Morris, J. (2005) 'Predicting scientific understanding of prospective elementary teachers: role of gender, education level, courses in science, and attitudes toward science and mathematics', *Journal of Science Education and Technology*, vol 14, no 4, pp 387–91.

Lucey, H. and Reay, D. (2000) 'Identities in transition: anxiety and excitement in the move to secondary school', *Oxford Review of Education*, vol 26, no 2, pp 191–205.

McGonigal, J., Doherty, R., Allan, J., Mills S., Catts, R., Redford, M., McDonald, A., Mott, J. and Buckley, C. (2007) 'Social capital, social inclusion and changing school contexts: a Scottish perspective', *British Journal of Educational Studies*, vol 55, no 1, pp 77–94.

Mulcahy, D. (2006) 'The salience of space for pedagogy and identity in teacher education: problem-based learning as a case in point', *Pedagogy, Culture & Society*, vol 14, no 1, pp 55–69.

OECD (2006) *Measuring the effects of education on health and civic engagement*, Paris: OECD.

ONS (2004) *The National Statistics socio-economic classification*, http://www.ons.gov.uk/ons/guide-method/classifications/archived-standard-classifications/ns-sec/index.html

Putnam, R. (1993) *Making democracy work: civic traditions in modern Italy*, Princeton, NJ: Princeton University Press.

Putman, R. (2000) *Bowling alone: the collapse and revival of American community*, New York: Simon & Schuster.

Sainsbury, M., Whetton, C., Mason, K. and Schagen, I. (1998) 'Fallback in attainment on transfer at age 11: evidence from the summer literacy schools evaluation, *Educational Research*, vol 40, no 1, pp 73–81.

Scottish Government (2004) *Scottish index of multiple deprivation*, www.scotland.gov.uk/Publications/2004/06/19421/38087

Topping, K. (2007) *Group work: transition into secondary: end of award research report*, Swindon: ESRC, http://www.leeds.ac.uk/educol/documents/190603.pdf

Uslaner E. (2002) *The moral foundations of trust*, Cambridge: Cambridge University Press.

Veronneau, M.H. and Vitaro, F. (2007) 'Social experiences with peers and high school graduation: a review of theoretical and empirical research', *Educational Psychology*, vol 27, no 3, pp 419–45.

Ward, R. (2000) 'Transfer from middle to secondary school', *International Journal of Educational Research*, vol 33, no. 4 pp 365–74.

Yin, R. (2009) *Case study research: design and methods* (4th edition), Los Angeles, CA: Sage.

Zeedyk, S., Gallacher, J., Henderson, M., Hope, G., Husband, B. and Lindsay, K. (2003) 'Negotiating the transition from primary to secondary school: perceptions of pupils, parents and teachers', *School Psychology International*, vol 24, pp 67–79.

TEN

Multiple capitals and Scottish independent schools: the (re) production of advantage

Bob Lingard, Joan Forbes, Gaby Weiner and John Horne

Introduction

This chapter reports on findings from the Scottish Independent Schools Project (SISP), a project developed to complement a range of other case studies supported by the Schools and Social Capital Network of the Applied Educational Research Scheme (AERS), which focused largely on 'disadvantaged' groups or communities. SISP, in contrast, sought to explore how social and other capitals work in and through the spatio-temporalities (Sassen, 2001, Gulson and Symes, 2007) of a more privileged setting – that of independent schooling in Scotland. The assumption here was that there is a relationship between the (re) production of advantage and disadvantage and that bonding social capital on a global scale is a feature of contemporary processes of the production of advantage. Succinctly, the research was predicated on the assumption that understanding the production of advantage would also provide insights into the reproduction of disadvantage and the policies and practices required to address it.

Social capital embraces the idea that social networks are valuable assets for individuals and societies, and is one of a number of 'capitals' defined by Lin (2001, p. 3) as 'investment of resources with expected returns in the marketplace'. As outlined below, SISP worked across two theoretical frameworks of social capital: namely that of Putnam (1993, 1995, 2000), Coleman (1988) and Woolcock (1998) on the one hand and that of Bourdieu (1977, 1986, 1991, 2003; and Bourdieu with Wacquant, 1992) on the other, eventually adopting an approach we described as multiple capitals. Bourdieu focuses on multiple capitals and the potential of all forms to be transformed into economic capital linked to the production of advantage, whereas Coleman, Putnam and Woolcock are more sanguine about the ability of social capital to address disadvantage and open up opportunities.

The research sought to understand the differentiated nature of independent schools in Scotland and how different capitals worked in and through them. As such, a preliminary analysis of independent school websites was undertaken. This showed how such schools represent themselves, revealing also the complexity of categorising independent schools in Scotland, given their differentiated nature. Case studies were then carried out in the only three independent schools that agreed to participate, and involved the collection of data by means of interviews, focus groups and questionnaires. It proved impossible to include in the research the highest status, highest profile schools or to explore the capitals held by them.

The overall research question was: 'How do social and other capitals work in and through independent schooling in Scotland?' Subsidiary research questions included:

- How can the range of independent schools in Scotland be categorised, analysed and understood?
- How do schools represent themselves in prospectuses and websites?
- To what extent do current and former students, parents, teachers and headteachers in the case study schools acknowledge the effects of different capitals on their lives?
- How do these capitals work through (case study) school buildings and organisation of space?

Having set the scene, the next section outlines the methodology utilised, with some commentary on the issues that arose. Subsequently, the findings and emergent themes of the research are considered. This is followed by reflections on the concept of social capital and its utility in this study of independent schools in Scotland and on the production of advantage. The study indicates the strength of bonding social capital across the case study schools and the extent of evidence of such capital among independent schools in Scotland more generally, at the same time as identifying an absence of bridging and linking social capital (Woolcock, 1998). Furthermore, the study shows the significance of multiple capitals, as described by Bourdieu, and also demonstrates the global reach of the aspirations of students at the case study schools. The chapter concludes with a summary of the empirical findings and a discussion of the implications of the research and its theoretical significance.

Theoretical framing and methodology

As noted in the introduction, the project worked with two theoretical approaches to the concept of social capital. The first draws on the work of Putnam (1993, 1995, 2000), Coleman (1988) and Woolcock (1998) to analyse bonding, bridging and linking as sub-types of social capital. This position argues for the building up of social capital in or through, for example, commitment to and support for family relations, community organisations and civic participation (Coleman, 1988; Putnam, 2000). The accumulation of these aspects of social capital are seen as leading to a more unified community, enhanced civic society, vibrant democracy, and greater social equality and cooperation generally. The second social capital approach is derived from Bourdieu (1977, 1986, 1991, 2003; and Bourdieu with Wacquant, 1992), and was used in the project to develop the notion of intersecting 'multiple capitals' (for example, economic, social, cultural, and reputational, national, cosmopolitan). Bourdieu views the stock of such capitals as a zero sum game, in the sense that capital is limited and differentially distributed, and is used by elites to reproduce existing relations and practices of power, that is to (re)produce advantage and reaffirm disadvantage. Further, intersecting capitals can potentially be converted into economic capital. Bourdieu (1986) is therefore less confident than Putnam and Coleman about the contribution of social capital to societal development and improvement and increased opportunities for disadvantaged individuals.

Bourdieu across his sociological oeuvre focuses more on the seemingly effortless production and legitimation of inequality across generations, with schooling as central to such reproduction. SISP confirmed the centrality of a meritocratic framing for such reproduction and also the extent to which, underpinned by liberal feminism, young advantaged women had similar educational and professional aspirations to young men.

Other capitals were also taken up in the research, including: cultural capital, developed by Bourdieu (1986) to refer to embodied dispositions and dispositions towards and possession of cultural artefacts, and identified by Lin (2001, p. 43) as that involved in mutual 'social identification' and 'reciprocal recognition' among different social and class groups; and national capital developed from Bourdieu in relation to the Scottish nation by McCrone (2005; see also Bourdieu, 2003). A further interest was the impact of globalisation, and the extent to which the case study schools were constructed as Scottish, British or cosmopolitan. We were interested also in the space of aspiration, seeing aspirations as culturally and collectively framed practices (Appadurai,

2004). Sport (interpreted as containing physical and embodied capital) also took on greater salience due to its evident importance in the case study schools. It was noted that these schools made a greater investment in sport as a form of physical capital compared with state schools (see Shilling, 2004). Gender also featured in the analysis, due, among other things, to the single-sex character of two of the case study schools and the different gender regimes visible in the different research settings. Finally, a framework concerning the dimensions of power (Bishop and Glynn, 1999) helped illuminate the processes of legitimation, representation, benefits and so forth both within and outside the schools.

Contact with the independent school sector proved difficult initially and raised doubts about whether research access to the sector as a whole was feasible. The difficulties of access confirmed, in a methodological sense, the ways in which power operates, and the need for researchers' reflexivity regarding sensitivity to potentially intrusive investigation. Refusal to participate (by several schools) thus resonated with the constraints experienced by other projects seeking to research the powerful (e.g. Fitz, 1994). In a sense, these schools were able to utilise a powerful mix of various capitals (social, cultural and reputational) to block research access. After extended negotiation, three schools agreed to participate: an all-girls, an all-boys and a co-educational school. The three schools were given pseudonyms: Augusta (girls), Balfour (boys) and Charteris (co-educational).

Access operated differently for each school, and was least difficult at Augusta, probably reflecting the profile and research orientation of the school's leadership and its self-perceived strong positioning as a leader of Scottish schooling. Access to the co-educational school involved lengthier negotiations, concerning the potential impact on the school's reputation of any perceived unfavourable findings and thus a more overt wish to constrain the research team's independence. This possibly reflected a less certain market position than those of the other two schools. Additionally, Augusta's ready agreement to participate in the research appeared to influence Balfour's agreement to participate. These two schools appeared less concerned about publicity or publications emanating from the research than Charteris. Augusta was the only case study school to request, during access negotiations, a presentation to staff of the research findings at the end of the project.

In a methodological sense, the access issue taught us much about the dependence of these schools on market positioning and the centrality of reputational capital to their maintenance of status. Augusta, with outstanding academic outcomes and Balfour, with a particular positioning in the spectrum of Scottish independent schools in relation to, for example, its facilities, science education and culture of care, were more confident about research access. Thus, the ease of access offered by Augusta reflected the confidence of the school's leadership and its academic orientation. And the capitals valued at Augusta, together with its underpinning of liberal feminism, were conducive to participation in the research. This was indicated in the request from the headteacher for the research team to address a full school assembly about the nature of social capital and the purposes of the research.

The research team developed a range of instruments for the collection of data: interview schedules, focus group schedules, questionnaires for pupils and observational schedules. For each case study, data collection involved the following:

- examination of school documentation, including prospectus, promotional materials, websites, yearbooks etc;
- interviews with heads and/or senior members of the school management team;
- interviews with five teachers in each school, including the head of sport/ physical education;
- tour of the school and observations of the use of space;
- observations of daily routines such as assemblies, refectory-use, beginning and end of the school day;
  questionnaire completed by all Year 8/S2 students (aged 13–14);
- focus groups with two groups of Year 8/S2 students.

Initially, the websites of all schools in the Scottish independent sector were analysed with the aim of distinguishing the different orientations of the schools (see Forbes and Weiner, 2008). Following this, the website texts of the case study schools were further analysed using a critical discourse-based approach (Mills, 1997; MacLure, 2003) which focused on the schools' self-positionings, identifications and aspirations in the discourses and language used. Discourses invoked and used by the school were analysed to show how schools discursively construct themselves and their 'assumptive worlds' (Nisbet and Broadfoot, 1980). The interview, questionnaire and focus group data from the three case study sites were initially sorted and a preliminary analysis undertaken using a commercially available qualitative data analysis (QDA) computer software package. Additionally, the questionnaire responses to the question 'School is like a ...' were examined and classified into seven categories (A–G), ranging from unambiguously positive to unambiguously negative and according to gender as well as emergent themes such as accessibility, territoriality, social inclusion and participation. Responses were read closely and analysed to uncover how the school was imagined as a unique place and space (de Certeau, 1984; Lefebvre, 1991). Observational data and field-note data also underwent analysis as to the significance of space and school routines in relation to the schools' narratives and use of capitals.

Findings

Initially, the research team developed and examined data sets to categorise independent schools in Scotland according to characteristics such as location, structure and fees (see Forbes and Weiner, 2008). The details of this categorisation are not reported here but suggest that the independent sector in Scotland is differentiated, with each school developing a distinctive set of norms linked to an institutionally based emphasis, for example, concerning particular philosophies and ideas on liberal feminism, new or softer forms of masculinity, provision of English or Scottish curricula and examinations, and so on. Differentiation was also associated with the fraction of the English and Scottish middle classes that each school served.

Findings from the website analyses of the three case study schools indicated that their profile of activities was targeted at supporting pupils' wider potential achievement beyond the specifically academic (see Forbes and Weiner, 2008). Thus, the websites suggested particular values and a menu of practices that produced particular forms of capital that in the view of the school were of particular benefit to 'their' young people. Individual expression and fulfilment, creativity, endurance and teamwork, character formation and the provision of comfortable surroundings were all exemplars of discursive elements which were interwoven with the central promise of exacting high academic standards from students. Discourses were thus invoked both of excellence in academic attainment and of a broad-based curriculum made up of aesthetic, cultural, linguistic, sporting, travel and other experiences. Characteristics specific to individual schools included a more traditional gender regime at Charteris, indicated, if with irony, by an 'infomercial' on the school website showing a schoolteacher and mother extolling the benefits of a product for cleaning sportswear, especially rugby shirts.

Scottish independent schools are differentiated in the sense that each case study school demonstrated a distinctive set of norms that its pupils were expected to understand and identify with, connected to its particular positioning in the field of independent schooling and

Scottish and British education more broadly. Working with social capital was a strong feature of all the case study schools, in particular utilisation of intra-school (and its community) bonding norms, networks and connections. This might be seen as form of social class closure or solidarity (van Zanten, 2010). Other expressions of social capital, such as bridging and linking, were evident across like schools within the independent sector, involving shared sport, and academic and extra-curricular activities. In teacher interviews, talk of 'other schools' in Scotland tended to mean other independent schools; state schools were treated as invisible.

The websites invoked specific and differentiated interpretations of school group networks, norms, values and identity positions, all of which served to enhance reputation; in social capital terms, this meant the trust and regard in which particular schools were held by distinctive fractions of Scottish society. The websites also provided the schools with the opportunity to construct specific educational narratives, contained, for example, in discourses of 'value-addedness' in relation to the provision of a range of activities and curricular opportunities, as well as wider experiences and achievements beyond the academic.

As already noted, there were noticeable 'gender regimes' (Connell, 1987, p. 99) in each of the three schools, although the single-sex schools demonstrated something of gender convergence among their (middle-class) girls and boys in terms of subject choice and career aspirations (Walby, 1997). The liberal feminism underpinning school practices and the academic focus of Augusta aimed to ensure access to university and professional careers for its female students, in competition with male contemporaries on the basis of a class-based meritocracy (compare the situation in French independent schools – see van Zanten, 2010). In contrast, the Balfour case study illustrated the differentiation of the category 'boys' and how social class intersects with the construction of masculinities. It also indicated that recuperative masculinity politics continues to impact on schools, and that the construction of elite masculinities has been affected by the economic, cultural and labour market impacts of globalisation. Balfour showed how school leaders have worked to remake masculinities to meet the perceived demands of the global market and to construct cosmopolitan masculinities. The co-educational school, Charteris, had a more traditional gender regime in which boys constituted the 'normal' subject of the schools' dominant cultural values in relation to the foregrounding and privileging of traditionally masculine sports, academic subjects and extra-curricular activities (informal curriculum pursuits), and the senior management team was predominantly male, with little apparent awareness or interest in gender relations in the school. All three case study schools were cosmopolitan in outlook, directing their activities and the schooling of young people toward participation in a globalising economy. In so doing, school discourses employed terms such as 'Scottish' and 'international' in specific and strategic ways.

Emergent themes

A number of generic themes emerged from the research, in the sense that they apply to the three case studies, examples of which include utilisation of social capital (which is discussed separately and more fully below), social reproduction and the respective roles of tradition and gender.

Tradition

Emphasised by senior management at Charteris, but also evident in the other case study schools, tradition was characterised by the swift induction of new staff and pupils into the particular school networks, norms and ways of doing things. Central importance was given to intra-school norms relating to rituals, for example prize giving, assemblies, church services, sponsored walks and runs and sports weekends. Also included in the traditional were 'bridging and bonding' inter-school sporting matches and intra-school and intra-house team building events and competitions. School architecture was designed (in both senses of the word) to evoke, signify and project a traditional 'public' school ethos – although in terms of their symbolic capital, the buildings of the girls' school differed somewhat from those of the boys' and mixed schools. Augusta's buildings could be seen as feminised in the sense that they were folded *into* a city suburb in a more 'liveable, human-scale neighbourhood' (Jarvis, et al 2009, p. 190). This offers a contrast to the more masculinised self-imposition *on to* the cityscapes and landscapes of the privatised gated and walled communities of Balfour and Charteris.

Relationships to the state

Autonomy is exercised in general decision making and in understanding the specific needs of the fraction of the social class to which the school aspires – that is the Scottish parents who share the dominant narrative(s) of individual schools. However, the schools are reliant on the legitimation/legitimising functions of the state regarding, for example, inspections of care, boarding accommodation and examinations. Good inspection reports from the state were thus seen as essential to the maintenance and preservation of each school's reputational capital.

Privilege as normalised

Both staff and pupils in the case study schools position students in state schools (96% of the Scottish school population) as 'the silent other', exemplified in the statement from a Charteris teacher, about 'most of the schools in Scotland' (meaning Scottish independent schools). Solidarity with other schools in the sector was further indicated by the resistance from staff to comparing/ranking their own and other independent schools (whether in Scotland or England).

Social class reproduction

Social class reproduction is a strong, though varying feature of the case study schools. For Augusta, it was linked to outstanding academic achievements, responses in curricula to global changes (such as teaching Chinese), the development of a cosmopolitan disposition, and a 'girls can achieve anything' ethos, accompanied by an awareness of the privileged position of the school, particularly among staff. For Balfour, social class reproduction focused on producing young men with a range of skills, including 'soft' skills for national and global labour markets in the professions and business. For Charteris, its main task was to educate the professional social classes, including lawyers, engineers and doctors, with the emphasis on 'good' discipline and socio-cultural conformity, rather than elitism or privilege. In Charteris too, however, as in the other schools, a wide menu of European and global travel was available to pupils, as well as the opportunity of developing sporting, musical and cultural links.

Gender: socio-cultural identifications and aspirations

The range of opportunities, roles and relationships, in other words 'what is expected, allowed and valued' (UN OSAGI, 2001) for girls and boys, women and men in the schools, were significant in shaping the specific socio-cultural contexts through which capitals worked in the case study schools. As already noted, Charteris exhibited a traditional gender regime, exemplified in its privileging of boys' sports, boys' greater overall confidence, and apparent lack of awareness of gender issues among the school staff. Augusta and Balfour exhibited a sharper awareness of gender. For example, at Augusta, liberal feminism produced an explicit discourse of girls' high academic achievements and professional career aspirations. At Balfour, traditional practices of masculinity, for example, as performed on the rugby pitch, were negotiated alongside newer, more urbane, cosmopolitan and sensitive forms of middle-class masculinities (see Lingard et al, in press), suitable for the work demands of a new privileged globalised masculinity.

Space was also found to be gendered. For example at Balfour and Charteris there was a dominant narrative of boys as necessarily active and needing space – a narrative used to justify their extensive playing fields. This narrative was also articulated by the Balfour boys themselves in focus groups, and offered a contrast to the feminised crowded space of Augusta, where girls clustered together to talk and socialise. At Augusta, the community building rather than extensive playing fields was central to girls' interactions with each other and to the life of the school. During the lunch break, the girls at Augusta crowded together, in contrast to the boys at Balfour who spread themselves out across the extensive playing fields. Thus at Augusta's heart was the new and architecturally distinctive community centre, whereas it was the playing fields which defined Balfour as connected to an essentialising discourse about boys and masculinities. We speculate that all these aspects are gendered, reflecting a complex interplay between masculinities, femininities and psych-geographies, as well as gendered aspects of social capital.

Schools' discursive positioning

It was observed that the staff and management of the case study schools consciously employed a selection of preferred discourses, for example, relating to high standards of pupil care, exacting standards and excellence in academic attainment, and pupil achievement in activities beyond the required formal academic curriculum. Student discourses were often utopian and nostalgic, for example, Charteris was frequently portrayed as a rural idyll composed of sunny, summer afternoons spent on the grass amidst breathtaking scenery with the quiet noise of sporting activities going on in the background. Staff and students self-monitored their school's positioning in terms of their talk: for example, there was frequent discussion among students of how they were perceived by others as 'snobs' for instance. Countering the idealisation and realisation of school discourses as above, students also articulated criticisms, for example, about cold and uncomfortable spaces, lack of freedom, crowdedness in corridors, lack of places to congregate, and over-strict rules of access.

The differentiated discourses and 'locally constituted cultural practices' (Jarvis, et al, 2009) of the case study schools was evident in their specific spatial social arrangements of gender relations and inequalities, as already mentioned. The co-educational Charteris had a gender regime in which boys' interests predominated, for example, in relation to the rugby fields fronting the main school building, in an emphasis on the 'power' subjects of science and engineering and in the privileging of rugby and pipe-band-related activities and success. The two single-sex schools appeared more critically reflective and conscious of the social relations within, perhaps because of their need to justify their single-sex status. However, as we have seen, there was an essentialising masculinity discourse at Balfour in relation to its buildings, the extensive playing fields that surround the school and the new masculinity that the school was seeking to cultivate. Thus the headteacher noted:

> 'So I think that space is absolutely critical. I mean I don't think you can measure in pounds, shillings and pence ... the impact of space on young people and adults. But I like to describe this school as having a calm sense of purpose ... Some of my staff criticise me because they want bells and I say absolutely not, we're not having bells. I don't want bells, they interrupt time and space with their shrill sound ... We're at the moment going through a massive tree planting programme. I believe that trees ... the joy that these trees have actually given Balfour over the years is incredible. I think that the sense of quietness here and peacefulness is incredible ... I personally think that sense of calmness is why the boys are as they are. It's not frenetic ... they are busy, I mean they never stop at this school, but they have a huge variety of activity every day ... I like buildings to be soft buildings and hence, whether it's replanting roses at the front of the school ... because I want colour, you know, I don't want this slightly austere looking building.'

Further, a sense was conveyed that young people live in the school space, but also in a broader global space and time of almost limitless possibilities. The three schools displayed a cosmopolitanism and internationalism of outlook, as well as much skill in creating and developing the full range of capitals, the all-embracing nature of which was much in evidence. Regarding this reach beyond Scotland, the headteacher of Balfour described the school as 'Scottish plus' to pick up on its British and global orientations and its focus on the remaking of masculinities. Balfour students are expected to follow the English rather than the Scottish curriculum. Thus, the Head observed, "So I'd describe Balfour as a Scottish school with a difference." He expressed strong opposition to the strengthening of Scottish nationalism and indicated that he thought that most parents, including Scottish ones, saw this as a 'dead end'. They wanted instead a more global reach, given the likely futures of many boys in global finance. Balfour at that time drew 15% of its students from outside the UK, mainly from Hong Kong and Eastern Europe, and therefore the boys and the school saw their futures as potentially spanning the globe. Indeed, the headteacher noted:

> 'Inevitably, it's interesting. We have 70 percent of our boys go to universities outside Scotland. Again I think that is a good sign 'cause – it's people going outwards ... Then we've got boys at the moment at Harvard and MIT and again I approve of that.'

It could thus be deduced that, taken together, the range of capitals accumulated by the schools serves to produce advantage for their students in labour markets and in future careers, and moreover that these labour markets and future careers are global in reach. Indeed, the almost effortless ease of boys at Balfour and girls at Augusta, when talking about their aspirations for the future, confirmed the collaborative and culturally framed nature of different class-based aspirations. Regarding social capital, these students demonstrated that in terms of their futures, the globe was the stage upon which they would work and live. The presence of international students at Balfour furthermore served to emphasise such globalised aspirations.

This demonstrates the need for researchers and others to consider the space and place of the social networks that constitute social capital, and to seek to understand how such networks span the globe for the most privileged, in contrast to the most disadvantaged, whose networks are located in the minutiae of the very local (Appadurai, 2004).

Reflections on social capital as a construct: its durability and transferability

Working with social capital proved to be a strong feature of the case study schools as already noted. Outward bridges and links tended to be with other independent schools in Scotland (for social, sporting, debating and other activities) and globally oriented (involving student and staff exchanges). Evident also was a specific relation to trust; a member of staff at Charteris commented that trust is initially afforded to all pupils and that it is the norm until a pupil should break that relation of trust: 'it is given rather than earned'.

There was, however, little evidence of utilisation of social capital on the schools' websites, although other capitals were much in evidence, including cosmopolitan, cultural, physical and reputational capitals. Each school appeared in particular to understand and utilise national (and cosmopolitan) capital in its positioning and representation in the Scottish (and international) independent school market, with for example, Balfour appearing overtly more global in orientation than Charteris.

The concept of 'capitals' proved useful for the analysis, for example, in showing the extent to which the schools (and the parents who pay for their children to attend) invested their resources and the expectations they had of the returns to be gained. Thus, each of the schools 'worked' with its cultural legacy of grounds, playing fields and architecture, and the artefacts contained therein. Highly visible portraits of the headteacher and former headteachers provided an object reminder of the schools' eminent histories and legacies. Furthermore, institutionalised cultural capital was memorialised in the schools' celebration of academic achievement, and particularly, their credentialised success relative to other schools in the state and independent sectors. At Augusta, for example, particular pride was taken in the wide choice of subject options available at public examination level. Career breakfasts with former Augusta students who were by then successful professionals provided a telling example of how social and cultural capital was employed in the interests of class reproduction. Other capitals were similarly used to illustrate particular areas of each school's profile, and the benefits it offered for the students.

Our analysis suggests that independent schools in Scotland are adept at trading in a range of different capitals, yet also recognise the importance of local social relations. It is only rarely that one is reminded that this social capital nexus excludes those who lack economic capital resources and that the educational experiences offered are not for all. One such occasion, on the Augusta website, is that bursary support might be available for those parents who cannot afford the full fee. Each school, rather, aims to create a distinctive market position reflected in its representations concerning, for example, building international citizenship, developing softer versions of masculinity, producing liberal feminist/career oriented young women and providing education for professional careers.

Applying a social and multiple capitals analytic enabled us to discern that there is little sense of discourses of change, except in terms of improvements to school buildings, facilities and the overall school environment. Augusta alone mentioned an aim of increasing diversity in its student population. Balfour articulated a commitment to producing 'new men', though conservation rather than change seemed most important. Nonetheless, opportunities for world travel, learning languages of the new emerging economies, internationalism and diversity ran alongside this static stance, with the websites indicating that the school managements, at least, had some cognisance of recent global economic shifts. Thus, the schools used various research studies to show, for example, the benefits of single-sex schooling (Augusta and Balfour) or particular pedagogical approaches (Charteris). In such ways, the schools strove subtly to reposition themselves vis-à-vis new potential pools of parents in Scotland and other countries and also in relation to local parents who appreciate that their children will need to live and work in a larger, more globalised world.

The process of researching social capital: experiences of collaboration and capacity building

The concept of a collaborative research network was integral to SISP. Aimed at research capacity building (Humes, 2007), SISP membership offered mentoring in all aspects of research through innovative inter-institutional collaborative knowledge production and exchange. SISP connected people who occupied different knowledge, power and status positions in relation to prior research learning and capacity. Thus, SISP members each contributed a range of research interests and other skills to the different aspects of the work of the research team. SISP aimed also to be non-hierarchical, non-bureaucratic, democratic, inclusive and collaborative, welcoming active and flexible participation and collegiality. Thus, the collaborative activities, empirical research, report and paper writing and presentation, and other activities across the life of SISP offered a variety of opportunities for building members' research capacity and reciprocal benefits in the form of enhanced interpersonal and inter-institutional bridging and linking social capital. For some members, initial loose affiliation to networks was strengthened in and through the intensive and sustained programme of SISP research. For others, the opposite occurred. Non-hierarchal and non-directive practices allowed them to slip away. Perhaps they required more direction from the senior academics in SISP. Nevertheless, for most members, the SISP network fostered high levels of reciprocal trust and confidence which were sustained beyond the life of the project. Research collaborations have continued into new research and knowledge exchange projects, including empirical research, proposal development and writing, and co-authoring of papers and chapters.

Implications for policy, practice and research: learning from SISP

Various kinds of learning and confirmations came out of SISP. In terms of methodological insights, we note two in particular. The first relates to researching the powerful. The difficulty of access to independent schools for the purposes of the research demonstrated the ways in which the powerful use their acquisition of multiple capitals to restrict access and avoid the research gaze, both because they can and because of the potential risk to their reputation (and income) arising from negative research findings. The second methodological insight relates to how critical incidents in the research, such as the response of one school to unwelcome data concerning its 'gender regime', are important in exposing and slicing through the taken-for-granted perceptions and school constructed narratives and discourses.

The examination of the other side of 'disadvantage' in SISP reveals schools that, although different in some ways, have a number of commonalities, and that our learning concerning them may have important messages for policy and practice in schools more widely. For example, the case study schools appear committed, through their curricular, extra-curricular and 'caring' activities, to developing in their students the habits and dispositions necessary for 'successful' futures. Habits of hard work and hard play are cultivated in the long school day at Charteris, for example, which often includes extra-curricular activities and considerable travel before and after the school day. Similarly, at Balfour, boys are active from eight in the morning until eight or nine o'clock at night, with opportunities to develop prowess in a wide range of sports and cultural activities. Teachers model hard-working dispositions through their accessibility at afternoon and evening preparation sessions and often at weekends and during school holiday periods. SISP publications to date (see Forbes et al, 2008; Forbes and Weiner, 2008; Lingard et al, in press) provide descriptions and interpretations of the case study schools' use of capitals, and their ability to understand and interpret a changing agenda to their (and their students') benefit.

But how this might be useful to those on the other side of 'advantage' has yet to be more fully explored and is a significant issue which should inform a future agenda of research. Potentially though, it would seem that a comparison of what we have called the 'spatio-temporalities' (Sassen, 2001, Gulson and Symes, 2007), in which the young people in the three case study schools live and develop aspirations for their futures, might be very usefully contrasted with those of less advantaged young people who have a far less 'intensive' educational experience and in much less auspicious surroundings. What we saw with the case study schools was that those young people who began with the most capitals also had a huge amount of capitals invested in them through their experiences of independent schooling.

SISP demonstrated the huge amount and range of capitals invested in independent schools and in the young people who attend them. Indeed, when members of the research team reported back on the research findings to a full staff meeting at Augusta, the headteacher agreed that the silent unspoken foundation of the good education provided at the school was the money (and other capitals) underpinning and invested in all that the school did and achieved in conjunction with supportive parents, who were also well endowed with capitals of all kinds. This was the elephant in the room, she said, in terms of creating greater equality of educational opportunity. At the same time, she argued that what was provided to the girls at Augusta should be provided to all, if society was genuinely committed to widening equity and social justice in and through schooling. Thus, SISP clearly demonstrated the extent required of the redistribution of multiple capitals in schools and communities to ensure greater equality of opportunity and the consequent im/possibility of a meritocratic reality.

Also important to recognise in terms of public policy is that issues of equality and inequality are today played out at a global level and that global as opposed to local dispositions are a further distinguishing feature of the production of advantage (and disadvantage). The policy implications for schooling for the disadvantaged are indeed profound. Nonetheless, the study has confirmed our beginning assumption that understanding the production of advantage would provide insights into the reproduction of disadvantage in and through schooling. Thus, in theoretical terms, SISP has demonstrated the need to consider social capital not only as an entity in its own right, but in conjunction with the multiple capitals approach of Bourdieu, its potential conversion to economic capital, and their implications for the production and reproduction of advantage and disadvantage in and through schooling. A comparative study of schools located in poor communities would also assist in furthering our understanding of the production and reproduction of disadvantage and advantage through schooling.

References

Appadurai, A. (2004) 'The capacity to aspire', in R. Vijayendra and M. Walton (eds), *Culture and public action*, Stanford: Stanford Social Sciences, pp 59–84.

Bishop, R. and Glynn, T. (1999) *Culture counts: changing power relations in education*, Palmerston North, New Zealand: Dunmore Press.

Bourdieu, P. (1977) 'Cultural reproduction and social reproduction', in J. Karabel and A.H. Halsey (eds), *Power and ideology in education*, New York: Oxford University Press, pp 487–511.

Bourdieu, P. (1986) 'The forms of capital', in J.G. Richardson (ed), *Handbook of theory and research for the sociology of education*, New York: Greenwood, pp 241-258.

Bourdieu, P. (1991) *Language and symbolic power*, Cambridge: Polity Press.

Bourdieu, P. (2003) *Firing back against the tyranny of the market*, London: Verso.

Bourdieu, P. and Passeron, J.-C. (1977 [1970]) *Reproduction in education, society and culture*, London: Sage.

Bourdieu, P. and Wacquant, L. (1992) *An invitation to reflexive sociology*, Chicago, IL: University of Chicago Press.

Coleman, J. (1988) 'Social capital in the creation of human capital', *American Journal of Sociology*, 94 (Suppl.), pp S95–S120.

Connell, R.W. (1987) *Gender and power: society, the person and sexual politics*, Cambridge: Polity Press.

de Certeau, M. (1984) *The practice of everyday life*, Berkeley, CA: University of California Press.

Fitz, J. (1994) 'Brief encounters: researching education policy making in elite settings', paper presented at the *Annual Meeting of the American Educational Research Association*, New Orleans, April 4–8.

Forbes, J., Stelfox, K., Lingard, B., Weiner, G., Benjamin, S., Horne, J. and Baird, A. (2008) *The Scottish independent schools* project, AERS Research Briefing Paper 5, Edinburgh: AERS.

Forbes, J. and Weiner, G. (2008) 'Understated powerhouses: Scottish independent schools, their characteristics and their capitals', *Discourse: Studies in the Cultural Politics of Education*, vol 29, no 4, pp 509–25.

Gulson, K.N. and Symes, C. (2007) *Spatial theories of education: policy and geography matters*, London: Routledge.

Humes, W. (2007) 'The infrastructure of educational research in Scotland', *European Educational Research Journal*, vol 6, no 1, pp 71–86.

Jarvis, H., Kantor, P. and Cloke, J. (2009) *Cities and gender: critical introductions to urbanism in the city*, London: Routledge.

Lefebvre, H. (1991) *The production of space*, Oxford: Blackwell.

Lin, N. (2001) *Social capital: a theory of social structure and action*, Cambridge: Cambridge University Press.

Lingard, B., Mills, M. and Weaver-Hightower, M. (in press) 'Interrogating recuperative masculinity politics in schooling', *International Journal of Inclusive Education*.

MacLure, M. (2003). *Discourse in educational and social research*, Buckingham: Open University Press.

McCrone, D. (2005) 'Cultural capital in an understated nation: the case of Scotland', *British Journal of Sociology*, vol 56, no 1, pp 65–82.

Mills, S. (1997) *Discourse*, London: Routledge.

Nisbet, J. and Broadfoot, P. (1980) *The impact of research in policy and practice in Education*, Aberdeen: Aberdeen University Press.

Putnam, R.D. (1993) 'The prosperous community: social capital and public life', *The American Prospect*, vol 13 (spring), pp 35–42.

Putnam, R.D. (1995) 'Tuning in, tuning out: the strange disappearance of social capital in America', *Political Science and Politics*, vol 28, pp 1–20.

Putnam, R.D. (2000). *Bowling alone: the collapse and revival of American community*, New York: Simon and Schuster.

Sassen, S. (2001) 'Spatialities and temporalities of the global: elements for a theorization', in A. Appadurai (ed) *Globalization*, Durham, NC, Duke University Press, pp.260-278.

Schools and Social Capital Network (2006) 'Capturing social capital: Project 2 report', paper presented at the *SSCN Review and Planning Workshop*, University of Stirling, Stirling, UK, Dec 4.

Shilling, C. (2004) 'Physical capital and situated action: a new direction for corporeal sociology', *British Journal of Sociology of Education*, vol 25, no 4, pp 473–87.

United Nations Office of the Special Adviser on Gender Issues and Advancement of Women (UN OSAGI) (2001) *Important concepts underlying gender mainstreaming*, http://www.un.org/womenwatch/osagi/pdf/factsheet2.pdf

van Zanten, A. (2010) 'The sociology of elite education', in M. Apple, S. Ball and L.A. Gandin (eds) *The Routledge international handbook of the sociology of education*, London: Routledge, pp 329–39.

Walby, S. (1997) *Gender transformations*, London: Routledge.

Woolcock, M. (1998) 'Social capital and economic development: towards a theoretical synthesis and policy framework', *Theory and Society*, vol 27, pp 151–208.

ELEVEN

Commentary: schools and social capital: implications for practice

Rowena Arshad

All four contributions in this section recognised the potential gains for young people of being part of social networks as well as the contribution schools and learning environments have made to identity formation. This chapter reflects on some common themes but also discusses distinct aspects of each contribution and implications for practice from a social capital perspective. Readers may pick up on different points and may indeed reflect differently on the same points that I have addressed.

Chapter Ten, by Lingard et al, with its focus on privileged settings, stands out from the other three and makes an interesting contribution to discussions about school and social capital. Lingard et al hoped that in exploring the nature of capitals in advantaged contexts, they would provide insights and learning points about the role of social capital from that of people who worked in disadvantaged and less powerful settings. However, the setting of those with privilege is so starkly different to those from very low income and marginalised communities that the primary impression is to reinforce how poverty and social class reduce life opportunities and chances. A feature that stands out is the way in which independent schools appeared to afford and inculcate into their pupils a belief that it was their right to succeed.

Relationships matter

The independent schools set out to nurture in their pupils a sense of self-belief. This they did by according the pupils membership of an institution rich in history, norms and traditions of which pupils could be proud. There appeared to be an embedded ethos of achievement that all pupils could aspire to and tap into, with the assurance that opportunities for academic achievement and employment both in Scotland and across the world were limitless. This was the 'habitus' created for these pupils. Money and privilege enabled much of this to happen and it could be said that it was not pupil social capital as such that was the catalyst for generating such cultural capital but the fact that these schools could draw from bridging social and other capitals that parents and the wider supporters of such schools could provide for the pupils. A phrase that Lingard et al used, 'the cultural legacy of grounds, playing fields and architecture, and the artefacts contained therein', aptly captured the wealth available not just of space but also of history. This is the type of capital that Bourdieu stated enabled social reproduction and the maintenance of elites (Bourdieu and Passeron, 1990).

How then can public schools, particularly those working in areas of multiple deprivations and without the financial and cultural capital, achieve that sense of confidence for their young people? Here lies the challenge, and Arshad and Maclennan (Chapter Eight) tell the story of one primary school, Fairforall, where the majority of the pupils lived in poverty and faced a myriad of difficult circumstances. The contrast between Fairforall and the schools that Lingard et al looked at is sizeable. While it would be inaccurate to suggest that Fairforall Primary can mirror what the independent schools offered their pupils, the efforts of the staff in providing their pupils with a safe place to be and to learn amidst the difficulties that surround the pupils is also evidence that relationships matter. If, as Field (2003, p. 1) suggests, the central theses to social capital can be summed up in two words, 'relationships matter', then this is one area that Fairforall had invested in heavily. The school invested from a limited budget in the salary of a home–school liaison teacher, who was able to discuss learning and teaching matters with parents. This teacher also ensured good two way communication between school and parents, and spent a great deal of time at the school gates, talking with parents and forming a specific picture of the individual children and their networks. Fairforall was the only school in the whole education authority to take this initiative. Time spent building relationships with parents, whom they acknowledged as the prime educators saw attainment rates rise and absenteeism rates reduced. Investing time to consider how relationships can be built, nurtured and sustained as part of a social justice and social responsibility discourse should be a priority for schools working with those who are marginalised and in poverty.

The lessons coming out of the work of Stelfox and Catts (Chapter Nine) lend support to this conclusion. Their work explored the nature of social networks for pupils moving from primary into secondary school. They suggested that transitions between education stages have focused on continuity of learning and not necessarily the 'places and spaces that incorporate social learning including practices of bonding, bridging and linking'. Consequently, institutional responses have largely coalesced around improving organisational and physical structures, such as ensuring smooth transition at a pedagogical level by providing continuity of curriculum and helping young people learn the new school rules. For Stelfox and Catts, most studies about transition have largely failed to take into account the value of social networks and the social experience of transitions or to make the connection between learning and identity. They conclude that drops in performance for primary pupils moving into secondary schools may be attributed at least in part to a loss of security provided through strong bonding and bridging social capital in primary schools. They suggest that identity-related issues such as a loss of a sense of self (from being a 'senior' in the primary school to being 'the youngest' in a secondary school), an erosion of security as a result of changes in peer and friendship groups, and a diminished sense of belonging were likely to affect motivation and performance. Arshad and Maclennan (Chapter Eight) agreed and found that discussions around transition also revolved around the technical and bureaucratic aspects of moving a young person from A to B rather than consideration for the 'soft' factors that may have assisted transition to be less daunting through nurturing networks between young people, and helping to build their self-esteem and identities. They also concluded that the maintenance of social capital in the transition to secondary school was problematic.

The impact of the lack of networks and relationships is clearly exemplified in the Muldoon and Catts study (Chapter Seven). The unemployed young people in their chapter struggled to forge and maintain relationships and hints of 'formality' or formalising relationships, became a barrier to engagement. School was largely a negative experience for most. Muldoon and Catts stated that the most important finding about the young people in their study was the 'paucity or even complete absence of people in their lives whom they would call friends'. The social capital that existed was largely drawn from home and family contacts. The importance of home and the influence of parents, no matter how negative, is an important factor of which schools and educators need to be mindful. Partnership with parents is a well-trodden educational policy and practice path, and governments, schools and teachers acknowledge the importance of working with parents (Halpern, 2005). However this is an area that is clearly worth revisiting to explore not just the partnership but also the nature of those partnerships. How are parents genuinely brought in as partners, and does this include all parents or only those most vocal or with children most in need? Do schools see themselves as part of the community and therefore engaged in work with third-sector and community organisations or are these external organisations viewed as a bolt-on and only useful for particular circumstances such as for fundraising events and providing placement opportunities for pupils, with little evidence of reciprocity?

Most chapters did not just examine social networks present but also the types of networks that young people needed in order to move on. Some young people had smaller but worthwhile networks, while others had wider but shallower networks. The type of networks that the study by Lingard et al (Chapter Ten) identified, which the other studies appeared to have lacked, are those that drew on linking social capital. This is the type of capital that Woolcock (1998) described as capital that allows individuals to link beyond their immediate circles with the outcome of being able to move outwards and upwards. For three case studies, the focus of networks was largely about surviving through bonding and bridging while in the study on independent schools, strong linking networks were provided by the schools for pupils. These were largely focused on how to link with others who were more powerful, thereby providing the steps to climb the academic, social and economic ladders.

The importance of linking capital

The contrast between the abundance of linking social capital in the independent schools and the lack of linking capital in the other settings had an immediate impact on learning and teaching opportunities. For example, on the topic of global citizens, in the independent schools, there was a clear sense of educating pupils to consider themselves as global citizens and to view employment opportunities around the world as real possibilities. The young people in Fairforall Primary in the Arshad and Maclennan study were also taught to see themselves as global citizens, as teachers tried to connect young people in a deprived area in Scotland with young people living in refugee camps in Thailand. This, however, was a contrast in experiences of poverty and deprivation. For the independent school pupils, the presence of international students in their school meant that the notion that the local is global was a lived reality, and the prospects of being able to finance fieldtrips and visits abroad meant that what they learnt could be experienced at first hand. For the young people in Fairforall, the school was working hard to ensure that the horizons of the young people were opened up, but with financial constraints and a lack of networks to sponsor international trips, what was learnt was in situ and conceptual rather than a practical experience.

Lingard et al had difficulties gaining access into the world of the privileged and powerful. It took them several attempts and plenty of negotiation and persuasion before three schools agreed to take part. Access to schools for others appeared to be far less problematic if at all. If access to the rich and powerful proved difficult to a group of highly educated and articulate academics, it begs the question of how workable the concept of 'linking' capital might be for schools working with pupils living with broken families and communities. How possible is it for schools to develop effective and sustainable linking capital? Can those at the bottom end of a power imbalance really expect help to move upwards?

Nevertheless, the role schools and individual educators can play is in being the 'broker in relationships between people otherwise disconnected in the social structure' (Schuller et al, 2000, p. 21), and this should not be discounted. The role of the key worker identified by Muldoon and Catts (Chapter Seven) and the role of the home–school liaison teacher identified by Arshad and Maclennan (Chapter Eight) provided examples of this, which might suggest that there needs to be a specific allocation of resources in order for schools to develop links of benefit for their pupils. Some might argue that this is an unrealistic expectation of schools, particularly primary schools, as the main purpose of schools is to educate and to enable pupils to succeed in examinations rather than pursue networks that might enhance life and career opportunities. Nevertheless, it is difficult to separate the importance of context and opportunities. If pupils were to be assisted to meet the four key tenets of the Scottish Government's Curriculum for Excellence, which are to produce successful learners, responsible citizens, effective contributors and confident individuals, then schools would need to move beyond developing bonding and bridging capital to include linking social capital. Schools and individual educators may need then to become far more savvy and engaged with how their pupils are being personally, culturally and structurally excluded or disadvantaged. When these aspects are discussed and understood, the types of gaps in linking capital can be identified and hopefully addressed. The description of social capital as the 'social glue' with schools being the site for that glue to start working (Catts and Ozga, 2005, p. 1) is a start, but it must be the type of glue that sticks to other places and institutions, thus creating ladders of opportunities as opposed to a type of glue that creates sticky floors resulting in new forms of 'stuckness' and limited opportunities. Lingard et al, in Chapter Ten, comment on the 'institutionalised cultural capital' that independent schools bequeath to their pupils and alumni. State schools need to consider what such capital might mean for their pupils so as to maximise their opportunities beyond the school years. This might mean that schools and individual educators need to extend their own social networks beyond those in the education community.

Of the four chapters, only Lingard et al's explores capitals in the context of Scotland as a nation state within a global framework. For them, independent schools have harnessed Scotland's reputation as a small nation that punches above its weight in terms of providing a first-class education, with its history as a marketing tool. They have also injected a cosmopolitan aspect through offering both Scottish and English curricula and examinations. These schools are globally oriented for marketing (international student fees) and export purposes as well as providing international employment and entrepreneurial opportunities for their students. Lingard et al acknowledge that for many state schools, particularly those that meet the needs of the most disadvantaged, the focus tends to be on what they called 'the minutiae of the very local'. State schools might argue that this is somewhat unfair given their increasing international approach, particularly in educating young people for their responsibility in supporting global humanity and environmental awareness. However, it is fair to remind teachers to focus outwards in terms of aspirations as well as social responsibility, even while dealing with everyday stresses locally.

Social capital, difference and diversity

The concepts of difference and diversity were addressed in most chapters, but with different emphases and responses. Arshad and Maclennan (Chapter Eight) explored whether schools could harness the concept of social capital to promote inclusion. They concluded that despite what would appear to be strong bonding and bridging capital among pupils, parents and staff, where difference disrupted whatever was perceived to be the norm, particularly within the adult population, these differences became potential dividers. For example, action from the school staff to act to positively include black and minority ethnic parents met with some backlash from white parents who perceived such action as being unfair. In their chapter, they questioned whether social capital was strong enough to break down causes of exclusion such as racism, patriarchy and class inequalities.

Lingard et al (Chapter Ten) discussed the inter-sectionality of gender and class as key characteristics in and through which different capitals worked. In the all-girl school, pupils were educated to believe in their potential and worth and to aspire for the best by entering university or professional career pathways. They described the approach in that school as one that was predicated on classic 'liberal feminism', which believed intrinsically that men and women are equal and should be afforded equal opportunities. In the boys' school, while traditional male and female roles were visible, boys were taught to consider new forms of masculinities, displaying sensitive and caring qualities which are perceived as more acceptable from the contemporary male by middle classes across the world. The final school organised itself in patriarchal lines, unapologetically privileging boys over girls.

Stelfox and Catts (Chapter Nine) did not really engage with issues of diversity in their study of transitions from primary to secondary, which may either reflect a monocultural community or blindness to difference common among majority community members. Though Muldoon and Catts (Chapter Seven) described incidents affecting the young people they studied in terms of class, gender and age, they did not address the implications of such diversities. For example, they described one girl's fear of going out at night and how the boys in the study had no male peers outwith their course members, but there was then no gendered analysis nor comment about the impact of this on social capital formation.

There is a greater need for educators and schools to consider how difference and diversity factors affect peer networks and friendship groups and to consider how these assist or constrain the growth of different types of social capital. The failure to engage with these factors would be to see only part and not the whole picture, as characteristics such as social class, ethnicity, colour, gender/gender identity, sexual orientation, age, faith and belief as well as geography affect life opportunities. Social capital analysis that does not consider the social relations of power alongside diversity characteristics runs the risk of maintaining the status quo rather than providing possibilities for more equity between groups and within institutions. Dwyer et al (2006) suggest that Bourdieu's theoretical framework linking wider social structure, power and ideology provides opportunities for those interested in disrupting norms and dismantling power hierarchies. Psychologist Gordon Allport (1958) argued that as diverse peoples came into contact with each other, inhibitions, prejudices and ignorance would reduce as people learnt more about each other and debunked suspicions and fear. Schools have picked up on this and now play a greater role in promoting intercultural and diversity education and in acting as a broker between individuals and groups that do not normally engage with each other. However, Allport (1958) also warned that prejudices between different groups could only be reduced if the inequalities that exist between groups are also reduced. Therefore, if schools wish to develop bonding and bridging capital between pupils and parents, they would also need to enable such groups to discuss the possibilities and tensions that arise from such differences. Many have written about the positives of social capital where reciprocity, bounded solidarity and trust are key aspects that help bind groups together, but equally such capital can have the adverse effect of keeping those perceived as 'others' apart (Portes and Sensenbrenner, 1993), preferring instead to retain homogeneity (Boslego, 2006; Putnam, 2007).

Implications for practice

There is a need for schools and educators to pay greater regard to the relationships and social networks that pupils and young people have. Arshad and Maclennan, as well as Muldoon and Catts, suggested that the use of specific individuals such as key workers and home–school liaison teachers might allow certain individuals within a school or learning centre to gain greater knowledge of individual circumstances. The bridging roles from school to home and with other community agencies can become more meaningful and relevant when links are facilitated. In the past, schools have appointed guidance staff to take on such roles, but over the years, many of these positions have been eroded as schools rationalised their staffing numbers and responsibilities. However, it is not just the presence of such staff but their skill set and awareness of social and political matters that are important. Such an individual needs to be able to engage with young people in an informal and non-authoritarian way and most importantly to perceive young people as individuals with possibilities rather than as individuals with problems or as disrespecters of the system. Schools could seek to work far more closely with professional groups that are skilled at working with young people such as youth and community education staff. This working relationship needs to be equitable in order to avoid a 'them' and 'us' approach. Some schools in Scotland already have this arrangement but in the wake of budget cuts and the economic recession, these posts are vulnerable at a time when they are probably most needed.

Key staff, as mentioned above, could provide a useful bridging role in times of transition, whether that is from primary to secondary, or on to the world of work or to college and university. Such key staff are particularly vital for young people who are most at risk of being marginalised or overlooked by the system. Such staff would assist the transference of capital from one site to another, thereby reducing the need for the young person to completely start again, or they could help the young person develop new social capital and a more positive identity if previous experiences were negative. Stelfox and Catts' final points in Chapter Nine are worth bearing in mind here, that too much is placed at the door of adolescent maturation as a cause for drops in performance when it might be as much due to a loss of security and identity.

Arshad and Maclennan, in Chapter Eight, remind us that key staff connecting school with home are important as part of improving opportunities for attainment and achievement. However, their study demonstrates the fragility of relying on certain individuals and that for that 'social glue' to work, the majority of people in a school would need to invest in building bridges and valuing relationships and networks outwith their immediate social or professional circles.

More thought needs to be given by individual educators as well as schools and learning centres, to explore how it might be possible for them to develop greater linking capital for the young people with whom they work. This is important especially if those young people are from disenfranchised backgrounds and communities. Linking capital on its own can be negative, as it could lead to individualism and unhealthy practices, such as only choosing to provide linking capital to pupils who are perceived as 'the deserving', or linking for individual gain. We need to know why we are seeking linking capital and how such capital will be sought. The 'why' is about finding route maps for those with fewer opportunities to connect with those who can provide different opportunities; the 'how' needs to engage with principles of ethics, rights and justice, so that schools are wise and careful in deciding from whom they seek support.

There is also a need for educators and schools to engage with diversity as an analytical tool. How do certain characteristics affect the life chances of young people? When two or more of these characteristics interact, what are the implications of this inter-sectionality on the development of relationships and networks?

What is in no doubt from the four cases is that the school is a significant site of influence on the life of a young person. It can be, as Smyth suggests, a stabilising influence and a resource, particularly for young people in hardship who 'cannot find these forms of social capital elsewhere in their lives' (Smyth 2004, p. 32). I started out citing two words that Field used to describe social capital, namely 'relationships matter' and my conclusion from the four cases is that social capital is also about the 'quality of the relationships and the impact on the lives of their participants' (Boeck and Fleming 2005, p. 262).

References

Allport, G.W. (1958) *The Nature of Prejudice,* New York: DoubleDay Anchor Books

Boeck,T. and Fleming, J. (2005) 'Social policy: a help or a hindrance to social capital?' *Social Policy and Society*, vol 4, no 3, pp 259–70.

Boslego, J. (2006) 'Engineering social trust: what can communities and institutions do?', *Harvard International Review*, vol 27, no 1, 6 May, http://hir.harvard.edu/international-health/engineering-social-trust

Boudieu, P an. Passeron. J-C. (1990) *Reproduction in Education, Society and Culture,* London: Sage Publications Ltd

Catts, R. and Ozga, J. (2005) *What is social capital and how might it be used in Scotland's schools?* Briefing paper No 36, Centre for Education and Sociology, University of Edinburgh, ww.ces.ed.ac.uk/PDF%20 Files/Brief036.pdf

Dwyer, C., Modood, T., Sanghera, G., Shah, B. and Thapar-Bjokert, S. (2006) 'Ethnicity as social capital? Explaining the differential educational achievements of young British Pakistani men and women', paper presented at the *Leverhulme Programme Conference on Ethnicity, Mobility and Society*, University of Bristol, 16–17 March, http://www.bristol.ac.uk/sociology/leverhulme/conference/conferencepapers/dwyer.pdf

Field, J. (2003) *Social capital*, London: Routledge.

Halpern, D. (2005) *Social capital*, Cambridge: Polity Press.

Portes, A. and Sensenbrenner, J. (1993) 'Embeddedness and immigration: notes on the social determinants of economic action', *American Journal of Sociology*, vol 98, pp 1320–50.

Putnam, R (2007) '*E pluribus unum*: diversity and community in the twenty-first century: the 2006 Johan Skytte prize lecture', *Scandinavian Political Studies*, vol 30 (2) 137–74, http://www.utoronto.ca/ethnicstudies/Putnam.pdf

Schuller, T., Baron, S. and Field, J. (2000) 'Social capital: a review and critique', in S. Baron, J. Field and T. Schuller (eds) *Social capital: critical perspectives*, Oxford: Oxford University Press, pp 1–38.

Smyth, J. (2004) 'Social capital and the "socially just school"', *British Journal of Sociology of Education*, vol 25, no 1, pp 19–33.

Woolcock, M. (1998) 'Social capital and economic development: toward a theoretical synthesis and policy framework', *Theory and Society*, vol 27, no 1, pp 151–208.

TWELVE

Social capital for young people in educational and social policy, practice and research

Ralph Catts and Julie Allan

As was explained in the introductory chapter, the contributors to this publication were members of the Schools and Social Capital Network, within the Scottish Applied Education Research Scheme, which was supported with research grants from the Scottish Government and the Scottish Funding Council. Through the course of this research, they developed a shared understanding of what social capital meant in the context of schools and their communities, and this is evident in the consistency with which social capital is described in the various chapters of this book. We began with Fukuyama's definition of social capital (1995), which underlined the centrality of trust. We problematised the notion of trust and, along with Uslaner (2002), recognised it as a separate construct, but concluded that it is an essential ingredient for social capital to contribute to well-being and attainment in schools, and is also essential to enable research into the effects of social capital.

The contributors have taken a critical view of the notion of social capital, both in relation to its utility as a construct and in terms of the extent to which it could address the multiple causes of deprivation and disadvantage in society. Both Arshad and Maclennan (Chapter Eight) and MacBride in his commentary (Chapter Six) argue that while enhanced and enriched networks could provide opportunities for young people, such networks could not overcome a lack of economic resources and infrastructure. The pervasive influence of poverty on individuals and upon school communities (Battistich et al, 1995) remains a fundamental barrier to inclusion in educational practices and equity in the outcomes of education. Further, to enhance existing networks and to enrich them with new sources of information requires funding to enable opportunities for youth workers, teachers and community workers to engage with community networks. This is important because from the perspective of young people, the multiple networks within schools were not the only, or necessarily the most important of, their social networks. For instance, Barry noted in Chapter Four that for young carers, the family social capital, the network of young carers and the peer group at school were largely mutually exclusive, meaning that they participated in at least three distinct networks. In some cases, there were two 'home' networks where parents were separated. Allison and Catts (Chapter Five) found that at least in terms of the formation of aspirations among young adolescents, the extended family and immediate neighbourhood were the networks that were most influential in both forming and informing their goals. The utility of social capital appeared to depend upon the ability of individuals to utilise the links they could access. It seems that individual characteristics can make available connections more or less useful to different individuals within the same networks.

The case studies illuminated the perceptions and experience of social capital described by the young people, parents and teachers, and one aspect of particular significance is the impermanence of their school social capital. Arshad and Maclennan (Chapter Eight) identified that the transition to secondary school can lead to a loss of school-related social capital for parents as well as young people. They also identified the disruption of social capital during transitions within the primary school and pointed to the loss of social capital when key people departed. The disruption of social capital for young people at the point of transition to secondary school was of particular interest to Stelfox and Catts (Chapter Nine), who noted how friendships at primary school were vulnerable to disruption even when the young people went to the same secondary school because they tended not to share the same classes, and because the school playground was no longer a territory in which social networks were active. Cross et al (Chapter Two) contrasted the sustainable benefits from new social capital for teachers, with the transience of parent–teacher networks, and highlighted the need for parents to constantly form new school connections as their children changed class and as teachers changed schools. Social capital depends on place, as well as the constancy of that place, and on significant individuals who provide the social norms and values of reciprocity in which a community can access social networks.

Social capital for young people is identifiable at several levels. For all the young people we observed, there were some family bonds that endured which might enhance or restrict opportunities to engage with their community and beyond, and might also aid or inhibit access to opportunities for further education and employment. For most young people we found that bridging social capital accessed through their family was significant in forming aspirations, both for young people from disadvantaged backgrounds, and for those with social advantages reinforced through independent school networks. Beyond the family connections, adolescence is a period of fluid movement in and away from peer and community networks, with frequent changes in membership of networks that afford bridging social capital. For some, semi-permanent peer bonds may form, and there is commonly a reliance on a few significant adults who act as role models and provide sources of information and access to new opportunities. Finally, although we observed linking social capital infrequently, we conclude that this form of social capital could offer young people access to experiences which, for some, may be influential in their decisions about career and in their well-being.

Implications for policy

Inclusion and exclusion and the intergenerational transmission of advantage

In the study of the inclusive network programme for parents and teachers of young disabled people, Cross et al (Chapter Two) refer to what they called 'suspended' social capital. By this they mean a temporary increment in connection to powerful people, but which is easily disrupted by staff movements or transitions in the lives of the children between classes or schools. They suggest that renewing this type of opportunity is resource intensive for people with limited 'social and economic manoeuvrability'. Likewise in the Get Ready for Work programme, Muldoon and Catts (Chapter Seven) note that the social capital established during the twelve week course was in the main not maintained beyond the conclusion of the programme. In contrast, the social and cultural capital fostered in the independent secondary schools was maintained and renewed throughout the school programme over five or six years, and was reinforced by the intergenerational nature of the school experience, with many young people attending the school that had been attended by a parent.

If bridging and linking social capital are recognised as mechanisms by which advantage is transmitted between generations, as Bourdieu (1984) claims, then the challenge for policy makers is immense. How can access to powerful networks be extended to all and utilised to promote equitable access to opportunities for employment and education? The independent schools study indicates that their pupils accessed networks from which others were largely excluded. Attempts to disrupt this preservation of privilege will be met with a strong defence, as Raffo et al (2009) outline.

Short-term funding for marginalised groups

In several case studies, the precarious or short-term nature of funding is identified as a threat to the maintenance of social capital and to the progress of the participants. For instance, in the Fairforall primary school, the important role played by the home–school liaison teacher was dependent upon a decision by the headteacher to prioritise this activity over competing demands for limited funds. For instance, national policies encourage language teaching in primary schools, physical education, and environmental studies, all of which would be advanced by the recruitment of specialist teachers. In addition, school budgets have been squeezed to the point where funds for basic resources such as textbooks and photocopy paper are under pressure. This means that even though there is evidence of benefit from the home–school liaison initiative, the school leaders will face difficult choices.

At least in the case of the Fairforall School, the choice was in the hands of the managers of the school. In the case of the Get Ready for Work Programme (Chapter Seven), the interregnum that arose after the young people completed the 12-week course was entirely avoidable, had the funding providers elected to enable seamless transfers to other activities. When young people who have been out of education and employment for an extended period meet expectations by attending a programme on a regular basis and actively participate, there should be a guarantee of immediate options for follow-on activities. Funding might reasonably be tied to negotiated outcomes as each step is achieved, but with this proviso, the funding and support should be forthcoming. It does not require detailed economic analysis to work out that sustained support for a young person making progress toward achieving post-school qualifications and employment outcomes is money well spent. Another example where funding was dependent on regular grant bids for funds was the young carers' projects (Chapter Four). Again, while there needs to be accountability for funding, there also needs to be greater security in the provision of funds for successful initiatives.

Social capital and institutional transformation

Several authors have commented on the impact on organisations of initiatives to foster social capital. The question we seek to explore here is whether there is evidence from the case studies to suggest that deliberate development of social capital can lead to lasting institutional change. In discussing the Inclusive Learning Network, Cross et al (Chapter Two) conclude with the metaphor of a sandcastle and imply that there is no lasting change to the landscape once the funded initiative has ceased. Likewise, Arshad and Maclennan (Chapter Eight) observe that the inclusive approach to diversity adopted in a school rapidly eroded after the headteacher left, and suggest that there were consequential negative changes that affected attainment and links with the community. However, where deliberate efforts were made to transmit findings, there were some cases in which policies were changed as a result of the experience of linking social capital. For instance Allison and Catts noted (in Chapter Five) that in a youth club, linking social capital provided by the participant researchers led to changes in the way school clusters approached community networks, and that this led to a response in the approach of the school inspectorate to the monitoring of community networks. However, further proposed transformations involving the introduction of volunteers from larger local companies who could bring new education and employment contacts did not eventuate due to funding cuts.

The role of teachers and the school

While several studies note that the respondents recognised that the main purpose of the school was to facilitate learning and achieve qualifications, nonetheless the school seems to play an important role in the development of social capital for adolescents. This was perhaps most noteworthy in the evidence of the absence of bridging social capital in the lives of the 16- and 17-year-old early school leavers observed by Muldoon and Catts (Chapter Seven). This observation raises issues for both policy and practice. In Scotland, there is a policy of following up young people who disconnect from school or who are expelled, and as Allison and Catts note in Chapter Five, there are alternative community learning provisions for young people under the age of sixteen. However, it appears that in too many cases, early school leavers are hard to trace, especially when disruption in their home lives means they have moved address. Perhaps the role of guidance staff in secondary schools would be facilitated if youth at risk of dropping out were assigned a key worker earlier in the process of alienation from school, and if there was a proactive approach to locating young people who leave school without engagement with the careers support that is provided. It seems that there is a gap at the school gate into which some vulnerable young people disappear when their departure from school is associated with disruption in their home and community social capital.

Implications for practice

The role of the school and the community in the development of young people

Although there were different views expressed about the capacity of the school to provide opportunities for youth development, there was agreement that closer links between schools and community organisations could benefit young people. Arshad and Maclennan (Chapter Eight) observed that where a primary school leadership team sought to embrace a multicultural perspective, this had, in the main, positive effects within the school, and because in this case community groups were invited to engage with the school, it led to engagement of the school with the community. Smyth et al noted in Chapter Three that in a primary school, there was success in building bridging social capital between young people from divergent backgrounds within the context of the school community. This was as a result of deliberate practices that were adopted by the school. However, they concluded that because the school did not actively seek to link with the wider community, it seemed that the bridges were restricted to the school location.

In the case observed by Allison and Catts (Chapter Five), there appeared to be little engagement by the secondary school with the experiences of young people in the community. In Scotland, the school inspectorate has placed emphasis on engagement with the local community as a way in which to ensure effective delivery of services to children, so this could well change. In contrast, in the independent schools study (Chapter Ten), Lingard et al concluded that the *raison d'être* of each school was to develop social capital within and between independent schools and among the families of the young people attending each school.

Social capital in secondary schools

Observations within several case studies conducted in state-funded schools suggested that social capital shared with teachers and between peers was slower to develop and less stable in secondary schools. Stelfox and Catts (Chapter Nine), for example noted that at lunch time pupils tended not to use the playground to form social groups, as had been the case in their primary school. In retrospect, however, it is noted that the reports of loss of social spaces came from boys, and that evidence of girls' experience was not obtained. Likewise, Smyth et al (Chapter Three) found that the secondary school provided a less stable environment for bridging social capital and reported that attempts at buddying systems to support marginalised pupils had been abandoned. In contrast, Lingard et al reported in Chapter Ten that the playing fields in two independent schools were a space for male-dominated networks to form, but also reported that girls tended to cluster together in social groups. This suggests that either intentionally, or as a result of the relatively isolated location of the independent schools, there were more opportunities for social capital to form among secondary school peers. This was reinforced by the policy of requiring teachers in independent schools to participate in the leadership of extra-curricular activities, leading to opportunities for young people to bond with teachers, which seemed less evident in the secondary school observed by Stelfox and Catts.

It might be argued that the approach of allowing students to leave the grounds at lunch time, adopted in many state-funded schools, encourages more independence and greater engagement in community activities beyond the school, but within a defined geographic region. This may bring other benefits, especially if systematically supported by school and community links. Connections with the local community may be less easily established in an independent school that draws its students from a wide geographical area, especially in schools with boarders. However, these schools seem to define community in a broader sense and hence maintain an engagement with the exclusive community of parents of pupils. In this sense, independent secondary schools may be more insular and excluding.

The role of significant adults

In several of the case studies, significant adults were identified as playing an important role in the lives of young people. In the youth club case study (Chapter Five), Allison and Catts noted that the community-based volunteers were able to use social sanctions to maintain a positive and drug-free environment for the participants and were also a significant source of information. Respondents reported to Barry (Chapter Four) that the people providing the young carer support centres were there for them in times of need and understood their situation. In the Get Ready for Work context (Chapter Seven), Muldoon and Catts also identified the key worker as the necessary agent who created the links to multiple services for young people with multiple causes of disadvantage.

Teachers can also be significant adults in the lives of young people. Arshad and Maclennan noted in Chapter Eight that key staff were identified as central to the success of the school in achieving inclusion. The home–school liaison teacher was described as making an essential contribution to connecting community groups and the school. It was also notable that a teacher who was known to have come from the local area was considered a role model for pupils. Stelfox and Catts noted in Chapter Nine that 18 out of 27 young people identified a member of the primary school staff as a friend. Barry reported in Chapter Four that young carers found some teachers understanding and supportive, but that others were perceived as aggressive and authoritarian. Allison and Catts noted in Chapter Five that young people who were successfully participating in the youth club setting reported that they were not always successful at school, and said that they would like their teachers to know of their achievements in the community setting. Our studies therefore support the widely acknowledged view that while peer group influences play an increasingly important role during adolescence (Coleman, 1988), significant adults within the school and the community are also necessary to support young people in their personal and social development.

School and community social capital

There is evidence from the case studies that demonstrates the importance of community networks in the achievement of outcomes from schooling, and that there can be differences in norms and values between teachers and parents and community members. The notion of the reconstruction of knowledge in different settings, described by Evans (2008), indicates that for learning to be utilised beyond the specific context in which it is attained, active steps are needed to enable the capacities to be applied across contexts. This is where the notion of networks that involve engagement between schools and communities are vital to the realisation of the social goals of schools in enhancing inclusion and citizenship. Arshad and Maclennan identify in Chapter Eight how a school can facilitate this engagement with a staff member having a particular responsibility for connecting community agencies and schools to achieve shared objectives. Community networks also have the potential for community learning to contribute to the goals of schooling, as illustrated by Allison and Catts (Chapter Five). However, it seems that the hierarchical power claimed by schools makes it necessary for them to initiate opportunities in order for others to contribute, and, as Cross et al observed in Chapter Two, social capital networks accessed by parents can be transitory.

However, as Bourdieu (1984) has argued, schools can reinforce the aspirations and expectations of the home where the norms and values of the school are congruent with those of home. This was observed to be the case in the study of independent schools (Chapter Ten), where Lingard et al found that the pupils' aspirations from home were 'confirmed' by the school. They quote one headteacher as identifying the goal for pupils as being to move beyond Scotland for higher education and career opportunities, claiming that this was consistent with, and reinforced, the destinations advocated by parents.

The role of linking social capital within schools

In most of the case studies, bonding or bridging social capital was observed. As linking social capital is often the most productive (Woolcock, 2001), the question arises as to whether this can be accessed and utilised in schools. The relative absence of reports of linking social capital may be as a result of the hierarchical structure of schools, resulting in norms and values that exclude groups from power and influence, or it could be that linking social capital is accessible but is hard to observe because it is the most transitory form. The alternative explanation, that schools tend not to foster linking social capital, would fit with the notion (Bourdieu, 1984) that social capital in schools is the mechanism by which advantage is transmitted between generations. In this context, the study by Lingard et al (Chapter Ten) provides an interesting foil to other case studies. They conclude that independent schools seek to foster bridging social capital with other independent schools but ignore the possibility of links with state-funded schools. This approach has the consequence that pupils and staff from state schools are excluded from access to privileged networks.

Implications for research

We now turn to issues that emerge about the relevance of social capital for research into how young people achieve access to employment, further education and well-being. Among the issues raised in the case studies, the following seem to be salient.

Observing linking social capital in schools

If linking social capital occurs in a transitory manner in schools, then critical incidence interviewing (Gonczi et al, 1990) is more likely to identify instances than would be the case with observation. Muldoon and Catts (Chapter Seven) have provided an illustration of the potential of such an approach by seeking to document the life history of early school leavers. However, the advantage of the critical incidence technique is that it focuses upon transient but defining events. While the integrity of the experiences of schooling reported by the young people they interviewed has saliency in its own right, it may be necessary to seek confirming evidence such as may be found either in school records or from interviewing school personnel if the purpose is to guide policy.

Situatedness of social capital and transferable capitals

Social capital is about networks shared by individuals and hence is an asset shared between people. In most of the chapters, the authors have commented upon the impermanence of much of the bridging social capital that young people access. They agree with Coleman's argument (1988) that social capital is not fungible. Unlike economic capital, one cannot cash in social capital in one community and use the assets to purchase new social capital in another society. Nor is social capital like human capital which can be recognised by different institutions or employers to the advantage of an individual. The fluidity of adolescent bridging social capital suggests that the processes by which young people access and renew social capital are important, and studies that rely upon a snapshot of youth social capital either at one time, or in one context, may be of limited benefit in understanding the opportunities accessed through various social networks.

Access to social capital for research

In several case studies, access in order to observe social capital and to estimate the effects of social capital proved a challenge and depended upon the development of trust between researchers and participants. This was true in both the case study in the most advantaged setting (independent schools) and in the case study that accessed young people with multiple causes of educational disadvantage (Get Ready for Work). In each of these studies, access was achieved through building links with gatekeepers whose position enabled the researchers to approach the sites of interest. However, in both these sites, the findings caused some disquiet. In the case of the independent schools, the disclosure of the conclusion that there was a gender bias in one school was contested by the headteacher, while in the community centre, the suggestion that some aspects of the programme could be refined also met with an initially hostile reception from the programme managers.

While findings from any evaluation that raises questions about the assumptions of those responsible for delivery of services are likely to be unwelcome, the risk of such reactions seems high in studies that explore the role of social capital, because it is an agent for enabling economic opportunities. We conclude that the ethics of conducting social capital research, which require disclosure of the purpose of the study, may lead to researchers being excluded from not only sites of privilege, but also potentially from other sites where the practitioners may feel threatened by the identification of the limits of their interventions. Therefore, researching social capital requires the expenditure of resources in building networks with the stakeholders and especially building trust and mutual understanding and respect, and also an agreed process to negotiate how the findings from a study may be reported and utilised. Lingard et al (Chapter Ten) have suggested that a comparative case study that explores the role of space and networks in privileged and disadvantaged contexts may prove to be a useful further study, but such a study would need to be negotiated carefully.

The relationship between social capital and opportunities for individuals

Notwithstanding the broad curriculum goals espoused in national education policy documents in many developed countries, the focus in school policies on individual attainment is still pervasive, especially in secondary schools. This means that for educational research, how social capital may affect outcomes for individuals needs attention. Putnam (1993) argued that lateral social capital in the north of Italy led to better economic outcomes than was the case in the south, where hierarchical forms of social capital operated through both the church and the mafia. However, the case studies in this collection indicate that lateral social capital is not strictly egalitarian in nature. Stelfox and Catts noted in Chapter Nine that some people have many more connections than others, and Allison and Catts reported in Chapter Five that access to the youth club depended upon not only whom you knew, but also on how well connected you were to others in the group. A related issue is how individual characteristics influence whether or not people activate the links they have for their personal benefit. Therefore, questions for further research are whether individuals can all benefit equally from the networks to which they belong and whether there is a place for teaching people how to utilise their social capital networks to access opportunities for employment, well-being and education.

Cross et al (Chapter Two) point out the potential benefit from transient social capital acquired but then lost by people in relatively powerless positions. They suggest that skills and understandings can be acquired from such transient links that enable them to be more effective in subsequent dealings with people who have the power to affect their lives and the lives of their children. Further research might establish whether there is a case for deliberately developing the capacity for people to access recontextualised learning about social capital skills in different settings.

Differentiating the role of social capital from other factors to explain change

The complexity of the home, school and community environments makes the identification of the singular effects of various forms of social capital difficult to discern. It is important that the effects of social networks be considered in terms of the benefits for young people so that these links may add to the effectiveness of services provided by schools. In the youth club case study, access to information was noted as of importance to forming and reinforcing aspirations. For instance, the opportunity afforded to one participant to try out for a second football club was only available because one of the volunteers offered the information and used his bridging social capital to create a link for the young person to a network which otherwise he could not have accessed. One way to differentiate the effects of social capital may be the use of multivariate statistics to control for alternative explanations of effects.

Do we need to quantify social capital?

One of the objectives of the Schools and Social Capital Network was to explore ways in which to measure social capital. Although models for quantifying social capital were considered (Catts, 2007) we found that the notion of quantification was somewhat problematic because we came to recognise that social capitals did not constitute either a univariate construct, nor a stable variable in the way that both economic and human capital can be measured. While winning a lottery can enrich one, or a social trauma or environmental disaster can alter material well-being in specific cases, in the main parents or carers tend to remain relatively rich or poor throughout the developmental stage of a child's life. Likewise, one's parents normally retain the same degree of human capital. If anything, differences in economic and human capital tend to be magnified across the adult life course as those who have an abundance benefit more from the investment of their economic and human capital, while those who lack resources are more vulnerable to economic downturns. For instance, research into adult education confirms that those with higher qualifications are more likely to undertake further education and training (Healy and Slowey, 2006).

Case studies suffer from limitations in relation to reporting quantitative data. The first is that the sites are not chosen at random and hence the observed effects are not amenable normally to inferential statistics. The small scale of the studies means that descriptive differences will not normally lead to the identification of statistical significance. The small numbers in each case also normally rule out the use of covariates as a means to control for alternative explanations for observed effects.

While noting these limitations, several of the case studies have identified some quantitative evidence in support of claimed effects. Arshad and Maclennan report in Chapter Eight that a decline in social capital led to a 20% drop in literacy and numeracy attainment rates within 18 months. This was related to a change in leadership of the school, and of course there are other variables that may help to explain this change. The evidence for a decline in certain networks within the school needs to be linked in a causal manner to the change in attainment levels for the case to be substantiated. Stelfox and Catts (Chapter Nine) also identify a potential relationship between the reported number of friends in the final year of primary school and attitudes toward reading. However, again in a single case study, other possible explanations could not be eliminated. Muldoon and Catts (Chapter Seven) used comparative scores on well-established measures of health and well-being to support qualitative evidence.

The claimed relationship between social capital and well-being, school attainment and health are of importance for policy and practice. Research that includes quantification of these benefits can inform policy makers of the return on investment in initiatives that support the development of social capital. It may be desirable, therefore, to investigate specific relationships using quantitative methods where the outcomes are of particular importance. The above examples are areas where such an enquiry could be undertaken using multilevel statistical analysis to explore the evidence across a local authority or at a national level, but the costs of such studies mean that the issues to be subjected to systematic inferential analysis would need to be ones that policy makers identify as a priority. There would need to be agreement that the findings would not only be of importance, but that the outcomes would be supported with funding.

Mapping youth social capital

A further issue that concerns quantitative methods is the use of network mapping. There are well-established descriptive models for this (Hanneman and Riddle, 2005) which have been used to contrast the quantity of connections individuals claim, and there is some evidence that the quantity of networks is correlated with outcomes of schooling. Stelfox and Catts (Chapter Nine) make a small contribution to this thinking in their study of school transitions. However they also note that there appears to be a difference between the networks that young people report that they aspire to and the networks that are actually reciprocated. It is both the reciprocity of connections and the quality of the support that is shared that provide people with a basis for feeling secure and hence able to concentrate on learning. We conclude, therefore, that network analysis, while offering possibilities for exploring social capital effects, needs to be undertaken with a sound underpinning of evidence of the validity of the networks reported.

Conclusions

Our various enquiries have demonstrated that the role of social capital should be considered in the formation and implementation of policies that address the needs of young people. Service delivery to young people can be enhanced by taking into account the contributions social capital can make to their security and well-being, to the formation of their aspirations, and to the creation of opportunities for them to access information, education and employment. However, as has been pointed out by several contributors, social capital cannot overcome the multiple causes of deprivation, and the pernicious influence of intergenerational poverty will not be resolved by building social capital. We conclude, therefore, that fostering social capital is a necessary component of good policy and of effective practice, but not sufficient for resolving social inequalities.

Social capital differs from economic capital in three important ways. Firstly, social capital has to be utilised and constantly renewed. This is of particular importance at points of transition in young people's lives. Secondly, it cannot be transported from one society or community to another, so people cannot cash in their social capital in a community living in deprivation and reinvest the assets in a community with advantages. This means that for opportunities to be made available to people from disadvantaged backgrounds, the information and opportunities for access have to be brought to the community, rather than the individual or community relocated to the site where the resources reside. In the case of socially disadvantaged young people, whose lives are disrupted in ways that cause them to change schools, or to be absent from school, there needs to be an active intervention when the young people present at a new school or other agency. Early engagement with them is necessary to help them to establish a sense of security and inclusion. Passively waiting until the young person makes trouble through frustration or fear will compound any existing problems. Thirdly, the case studies suggest that it is not necessarily the quantity of social capital that an individual can access, but rather the quality of the social capital that is important. This presents challenges for research and especially for methods that are based on quantity of connections or networks.

Bonding social capital, especially within the family, may provide young people with a stable platform from which to launch themselves into peer and community networks in order to explore their opportunities and develop their identity. Bridging social capital seems the most in need of constant renewal, and this is something that teachers and others should strive to maintain both within the school and with community agencies. Linking social capital may be the hardest to identify, but though often transient, may be significant in enabling young people to access opportunities for further education and employment. Access to linking social capital requires initiatives by policy makers and providers of services to engage with local community leaders, through whom the resources can be made available to individuals and to community members. This, however, takes time and effort by the providers. It seems that developing an appreciation of the challenges and the positive dimensions of a community and respect for existing community networks are essential prerequisites. This can lead to the development of mutual trust and respect between practitioners and the community leaders and through them a basis of respect can be established with young people and other adults in the community of interest.

Social capital has been seen as a mechanism through which to challenge the dominance of intergenerational advantage, but as Lingard et al illustrate in Chapter Ten, those who are most advantaged have, through independent schools, insulated themselves from the risk to their privileged state implied by widening access for others to influential networks. This means that enhancing opportunities for people living in deprivation could be at the cost of what has been referred to in political circles as the squeezed middle. An approach that effectively enables young people from poor backgrounds to gain access to information and to networks through which they can better advance their needs may well be interpreted as unfair by those who have some limited advantages in the present system. It matters, therefore, how policy is presented and how practice is implemented.

People can make the difference, and not only in the one-to-one stories of inspiration with which many teachers and others in children's services can identify. Beyond these stories of individual success, there is a separate need to create access to social networks and to information for all. There is a need also to be sensitive to difference in terms of gender, race, beliefs, sexuality and disability, so ways of accessing resources have to be grounded in the cultural capital of diverse groups of people.

Finally, the process of enhancing opportunities through access to social capital requires a continuing commitment to renewing and extending networks. People can acquire the capacity to access and utilise networks through practice. Hence it seems to us that it is also through learning how to engage in the constant process of forming and renewing social capital that young people can gain benefits.

References

Battistich, V., Solomon, D., Kim, D.-I., Watson, M. and Schaps, E. (1995) 'Schools as communities, poverty levels of student populations, and students' attitudes, motives, and performance: a multilevel analysis', *American Educational Research Journal*, vol 32, no 3, pp 627–58.

Bourdieu, P. (1984 [1979]) *Distinction: a social critique of the judgement of taste* (trans. R Nice), London: Routledge, pp 241–58.

Catts, R. (2007) 'Quantitative indicators of social capital', in M. Osborne, K. Shankey and B. Wilson (eds) *Social capital, lifelong learning and the management of place*, London, Routledge.

Coleman, J. (1988) 'Social capital in the creation of human capital', *American Journal of Sociology*, vol 94 (Suppl.), pp S95–121.

Evans, K. (2008) *Putting knowledge to work*, TLRP Research Briefing 60, www.tlrp.org/pub/documents/EvansRB60.pdf

Fukuyama, F. (1995) *Trust: the social virtues and the creation of prosperity*, London: Hamish Hamilton.

Gonczi, A., Hager, P. and Oliver, L. (1990) *Establishing competency-based standards in the professions*, Canberra: AGPS.

Hanneman, R.A. and Riddle, M. (2005) *Introduction to social network methods*, Riverside, CA: University of California, http://faculty.ucr.edu/~hanneman/

Healy, T. and Slowey, M. (2006) 'Social exclusion and adult engagement in lifelong learning: some comparative implications for European states based on Ireland's Celtic Tiger experience', *Compare: A Journal of Comparative and International Education*, vol 36, no 3, pp 359–78.

Putnam, R. (1993) *Making democracy work: civic traditions in modern Italy*, Princeton, NJ: Princeton University Press.

Raffo, C., Dyson, A., Gunter, H., Hall, D. and Kalambouka, A. (2009) 'Education and poverty: mapping the terrain and making the links to educational policy', *International Journal of Inclusive Education*, vol 13, no 4, pp 341–58.

Uslaner E. (2002) *The moral foundations of trust*, Cambridge: Cambridge University Press.

Woolcock, M. (2001) 'The place of social capital in understanding social and economic outcomes', *Canadian Journal of Policy Research*, vol 2, no 1, pp 1–17.

Index

Note: the following abbreviations have been used: f = figure, t = table